Authority and Interpretation

Authority and Interpretation
A Baptist Perspective

Edited by
Duane A. Garrett
and
Richard R. Melick, Jr.

BAKER BOOK HOUSE
Grand Rapids, Michigan 49516

Copyright 1987 by
Baker Book House Company

ISBN: 0-8010-3817-0

Library of Congress
Catalog Card Number: 87–70876

Printed in the United States of America

Contents

Introduction

Southern Baptists are, above everything else, a "people of the Book." We do not, like Roman Catholics, assert the authority of the institutional church with its popes and councils over doctrinal questions. We have many founding fathers but no single, towering figure—a Luther, Calvin, or Wesley—to whose writings we look to help establish the bounds of our tradition and orthodoxy. Indeed, apart from the Bible itself, it is doubtful whether there is any single book of doctrine, devotion, prayer, or hymnody that we could all agree to be of major importance for the church and the Christian life.

One should not be surprised, therefore, that the current debate over the nature and meaning of biblical authority has become a major battle and decisive moment in the life of the Southern Baptist Convention. Apart from the Bible we have no other document or source of authority whereby we can define the faith we hold and proclaim. It is the sole basis for our teaching, evangelism, missions, and ethics. Apart from it we, above all other Christians, have no Christianity.

Keeping all this in mind (and it is a great deal to keep in mind), we offer to Southern Baptists the contributions of this small book about the reliability and truthfulness of Scripture.

The articles of this book have one common purpose: to investigate various aspects of biblical authority. In keeping with this purpose, we have tried both to define the nature of biblical authority and to describe how that authority is interpreted in the life and ministry of the church. Perhaps it is in the latter area that this work is distinctively Southern Baptist. Volumes have been written about the nature of biblical authority. Being Baptists, however, we cannot deal with these academic issues without drawing the practical concerns of preaching, missions, and social ethics into the discussion. We include essays in these areas without apology since we believe them to be the essence of the discussion. This book focuses on both the authority of the Bible and how that authority is doctrinally and practically interpreted, explicitly from a Baptist perspective.

We have no illusion that every Baptist will agree with this work, so we have not, therefore, called it "*the* Baptist perspective." Nevertheless, we assert the position taken here to be in agreement with the historic position of the Baptist church and urge our fellow Baptists (and all Christians) to consider it seriously. This position, simply put, is that the Bible is completely true and authoritative in all areas of faith and practice.

In keeping with this thesis, the reader should understand that the purpose of the book is doctrinal, not polemic. We desire the reader to understand that our position, generally called the inerrancy of the Bible, is not only academically defensible but also proper and necessary for the Christian faith. To explain this position, we have cited those scholars (Baptist and otherwise) who reject it. This has been done to clarify issues, not to embarrass any Baptist theologian who disagrees with our position. Rather, we have tried to demonstrate that belief in inerrancy can exist in a climate of genuine theological reflection and to assert that objections to inerrancy are not, in fact, insuperable. We believe the positions described here are natural and necessary correlatives to the other doctrines of the Christian faith. This book is therefore a call to faith, not a call to political action.

This book is divided into two parts: doctrinal foundation and practical implications. David S. Dockery begins our study with an examination of the meaning of inspiration and defines the nature of biblical authority. Duane A. Garrett follows with the assertion that the interpreter must position himself under the authority of the Bible as its pupil and not stand over it as its judge. L. Russ Bush continues with an explanation of what is and what is not meant by the assertion that the Bible is to be understood literally. Richard R. Melick then examines the hermeneutical question of how this ancient Book, arising out of a past age and from cultures unlike our own, can speak to us. Thomas J. Nettles concludes the academic discussion with a chapter asserting that the fundamental challenges to inerrancy are not new to the church, except that now, for the first time, they arise from within the church as well as from its enemies.

The practical implications for these ideas are developed in the latter part of the book. David Allen and Jerry Vines affirm that the preaching ministry of the church is dependent on a strong doctrine of biblical authority. William Wagner shows that the traditional understanding of world missions is lost and missions is in retreat wherever the truth of the Bible is compromised. Finally, Carl F. H. Henry, the dean of Baptist theologians, describes how a meaningful social ethic must stand upon a Bible that is wholly true and gives guidelines for developing that social ethic.

Finally, a word about the intended audience of this book. We have struggled with the task of writing essays that would be comprehensible to a seminary student, a pastor, or an informed layman without being disdained by professional theologians. To some, the language of these articles may at times seem obscure, while to others we may seem to go to unnecessary lengths to explain things that need no explanation. We have tried, however, to find a balance between the two extremes.

Duane A. Garrett
Richard R. Melick, Jr.

Contributors

David Allen is pastor of Audelia Road Baptist Church, Dallas, Texas, and is adjunct professor of New Testament at Criswell College.

L. Russ Bush is associate professor of philosophy of religion at Southwestern Baptist Theological Seminary.

David S. Dockery is professor of systematic theology and New Testament at Criswell College.

Duane A. Garrett is assistant professor of Old Testament at Mid-America Baptist Theological Seminary.

Carl F. H. Henry is lecturer-at-large with World Vision International.

Richard R. Melick, Jr., is professor of New Testament and Greek at Mid-America Baptist Theological Seminary.

Thomas J. Nettles is associate professor of church history at Mid-America Baptist Theological Seminary.

Jerry Vines is pastor of the First Baptist Church, Jacksonville, Florida.

William Wagner is regional consultant for evangelism and church growth in Europe and the Middle East with the Foreign Mission Board of the Southern Baptist Convention.

PART 1

A Doctrinal Foundation

1

The Divine-Human Authorship of Inspired Scripture
David S. Dockery

Every Lord's Day, Christians around the world gather in churches of various denominations to hear the Bible read and expounded. What is true in these congregations is characteristic of many Baptist churches as well.[1] It is common in these churches to hear such phrases as "Let us stand together as we read the Word of God." What is assumed by many faithful believers—that indeed the Bible is the Word of God—has become a major problem

---

1. Baptists, by self-designation, are "people of the Book." What can be said about the masses in Baptist life is also typical of Christianity at large. While the contributors to the symposium are all Baptists and the articles are directed primarily to a Baptist audience, the issues under discussion are broader and cross all denominational lines. Two very helpful sources on Baptist approaches to the Bible and biblical authority are L. Russ Bush and Thomas J. Nettles, *Baptists and the Bible* (Chicago: Moody, 1980) and J. Leo Garrett, "Sources of Authority in Baptist Thought," *Baptist History and Heritage* 13 (July 1978): 47–49.

for many who struggle with what it means that the Bible is the Word of God.[2]

In Baptist life there are a great number of people who have been taught in their homes and churches to believe that the Bible is a divinely inspired book written by godly men. The Bible, as it stands, is believed to be God's revelation to men and women, and since it is God's revelation, it is to be studied and obeyed. An often heard response among these faithful believers is "The Bible says it; I believe it; that settles it." Such people gladly accept the biblical report that Jonah was swallowed by a fish, that an axhead floated on the water, that Jesus walked on water, and that he was raised from the dead on the third day.

Conversely, others who have been influenced by Enlightenment philosophy and liberal theology have great difficulty accepting these biblical accounts as miraculous without reinter-

---

2. The literature on the subject over the past fifteen years is massive. Some of the more significant books that have wrestled with the issues historically, theologically, or exegetically include Clark Pinnock, *Biblical Revelation* (Chicago: Moody, 1971); Meredith G. Kline, *The Structure of Biblical Authority* (Grand Rapids: Eerdmans, 1972); Dewey M. Beegle, *Scripture, Tradition and Infallibility* (Grand Rapids: Eerdmans, 1973); G. C. Berkouwer, *Holy Scripture,* trans. and ed. Jack B. Rogers (Grand Rapids: Eerdmans, 1975); David H. Kelsey, *The Uses of Scripture in Recent Theology* (Philadelphia: Fortress, 1975); Jack B. Rogers, ed., *Biblical Authority* (Waco: Word, 1977); Carl F. H. Henry, *God, Revelation, and Authority,* 6 vols. (Waco: Word, 1976–83); Jack B. Rogers and Donald K. McKim, *The Authority and Interpretation of the Bible: An Historical Approach* (New York: Harper and Row, 1979); Roger Nicole and J. Ramsey Michaels, eds., *Inerrancy and Common Sense* (Grand Rapids: Baker, 1980); Paul Achtemeier, *The Inspiration of Scripture: Problems and Proposals* (Philadephia: Westminster, 1980); William J. Abraham, *The Divine Inspiration of Holy Scripture* (Oxford: Oxford University Press, 1981); I. Howard Marshall, *Biblical Inspiration* (Grand Rapids: Eerdmans, 1982); William Countryman, *Biblical Authority or Biblical Tyranny?* (Philadelphia: Fortress, 1982); John D. Woodbridge, *Biblical Authority* (Grand Rapids: Zondervan, 1983); Donald K. McKim, ed., *The Authoritative Word* (Grand Rapids: Eerdmans, 1983); Clark Pinnock, *The Scripture Principle* (San Francisco: Harper and Row, 1984); Gordon R. Lewis and Bruce Demarest, eds., *Challenges to Inerrancy* (Chicago: Moody, 1984); D. A. Carson and John D. Woodbridge, eds., *Scripture and Truth* (Grand Rapids: Zondervan, 1984); idem, *Hermeneutics, Authority, and Canon* (Grand Rapids: Zondervan, 1986). This list is certainly not exhaustive but is representative of different approaches and conclusions regarding biblical inspiration and authority. Of course, the classic works by James Orr, B. B. Warfield, and Louis Gaussen are still valuable and are foundational for many of the references cited above.

preting or demythologizing them.[3] While many have difficulty believing the miraculous accounts, they nevertheless confess that the Bible is an important book. Although for them it is essentially a human book, it is important because it is a record of humanity's quest of, and experience with, God. Most Christians, including most Baptists, would want to confess more than this limited affirmation. It is believed that in some way God reveals himself through the collection of human books. Even though the books may be contradictory, the reader can still hear God's truth through the writings.[4]

In between these positions are numerous opinions that attempt to explain carefully and fairly the two-sided character of the Bible as a divine-human book. The Bible is a book written by numerous authors over a period of hundreds of years, and yet at the same time it is the Word of God. The variety of views, which will be surveyed later in this chapter, have attempted to do justice to the mystery of Scripture's divine inspiration and still maintain its human authorship. Clark Pinnock, who followed a survey of several approaches to this subject, acknowledged, "The prime theological issue which became evident in our survey of options on biblical authority is the need to maintain with equal force both the humanity and divinity of the Word of Scripture."[5] The precise relationship between divine revelation and the human writings that comprise the canonical Scripture has been and continues to be a subject of contention.[6]

It is our belief that the divine-human tension is the most crucial issue in contemporary discussions concerning Scripture. The purpose of this chapter is to examine the meaning of the divine inspiration of Scripture including the relation of its divine and human aspects. First, we will investigate the divine author-

3. This position is rarely defended in Southern Baptist life. It was, however, widely confessed in American Baptist life early in the twentieth century. The works of Shailer Matthews are exemplary. Contemporary statements include James Barr, *The Bible in the Modern World* (London: SCM, 1973); D. E. Nineham, *The Use and Abuse of the Bible* (London: SCM, 1976).

4. Cf. Dale Moody, *The Word of Truth* (Grand Rapids: Eerdmans, 1981), 38–77.

5. Clark Pinnock, "Three Views of the Bible in Contemporary Theology," in *Biblical Authority*, ed. Jack B. Rogers, 71.

6. Cf. Donald G. Bloesch, *Essentials of Evangelical Theology,* 2 vols. (San Francisco: Harper and Row, 1978–79), 1:51–56.

ship of the Bible and then the human authorship. We will attempt to explain how the writings of the human authors are truly human words and truly God's. We will then survey the numerous attempts to explain the mystery of the Bible's inspiration. Our concluding section will focus on the result of inspiration, including the questions relating to an inerrant and normative Scripture.

Scripture cannot rightly be understood unless we take into consideration that it has a dual-sided authorship. It is not enough to affirm that the Bible is a human witness to divine revelation because the Bible is also God's witness to himself. An affirmation that Scripture is partly the Word of God and partly the words of humans is inadequate. What must be affirmed is that the Bible is entirely and completely the Word of God and the words of the human authors (Acts 4:25).

It is not entirely appropriate to make a direct correspondence between Scripture and Jesus Christ, but nevertheless there is an observable analogy.[7] Just as the conception of Jesus came by the miraculous overshadowing of the Holy Spirit (Luke 1:35), so Scripture is the product of the Spirit's inspiration (2 Tim. 3:16). Likewise, as Jesus took on human form through a human mother, so the Bible has come to us in human language through human authors. The result is that Jesus is the living Word of God, the God-man, and the Bible is the written Word of God, the divine-human Scripture.

An affirmation that Scripture is completely the Word of God

---

7. We recognize that diverse conclusions have been drawn from the analogy between the divine and human in Jesus and in Scripture by scholars with differing theological positions. It is not absolutely clear whether the analogy can be applied to the human authors through whom God was active in the composition of Scripture or to the actual result of inspiration. The doctrine of the incarnation does account for the true activity of God in the human dimension, thus allowing for at least the possibility that God could work in human beings to communicate his Word in human words. While we have noted parallels, there are enough differences and complexities so as not to build the entire theology of Scripture on the analogy. More important to the theology of Scripture than the analogy described above is Jesus Christ's own view of Scripture. It is outside the scope of this chapter to deal with the subject, but cf. John W. Wenham, *Christ and the Bible* (London: Tyndale, 1972) and R. T. France, *Jesus and the Old Testament* (London: Tyndale, 1971).

and the very words of humans also points to its dual-sided nature. Because it is the Word of the infinite, all-knowing, eternal God, it speaks eternal truth that is applicable to readers of all time beyond the original recipients. Yet, at the same time, it is the word from godly men to specific communities addressing problems and situations within certain contexts and cultures.

Some have contended that the Bible is primarily, if not entirely, a human product of an illumined religious consciousness.[8] Such a view maintains the possibility that the Bible could possibly lead its readers to divine truth but would deny that the Bible is a revelation of divine truth. By comparison with the heretical views in the early christological statements, we could classify this position as ebionitic, a view that stresses the humanity while losing sight of the essential deity.[9] On the other hand, the divine aspect of Scripture has been emphasized so predominantly by many that the human element is only an outward appearance of the divine. Such an approach denies the Bible's genuine humanity as well as its historicity. Again, parallel to the unorthodox views of the person of Christ, the latter view has tendencies toward a docetic view of Scripture.[10]

We can see the importance of affirming a balanced view of Scripture. But how does the Christian community maintain such a balance? How can it be affirmed that Scripture is the inspired Word of God when it is a collection of books by human authors? Can the words of the Bible be identified with the Word of God? Is some of the Bible God's Word or can this be affirmed for all of the Bible? How is it possible that the Bible can simulta-

8. Gene M. Tucker and Douglas A. Knight, eds., *Humanizing America's Iconoclastic Book* (Chico, Calif.: Scholars, 1980).

9. For further discussion of the Ebionites, cf. Bloesch, *Evangelical Theology* 1:134.

10. For an analysis of a docetic Christology that does not give full weight to the humanity of Christ but emphasizes his deity, cf. Bloesch, *Evangelical Theology* 1:134–35. Cf. the discussion of the docetic view of Scripture in John Gerstner, "The Church's Doctrine of Biblical Inspiration," in *The Foundation of Biblical Authority*, ed. James Montgomery Boice (Grand Rapids: Zondervan, 1978), 12; Klaas Runia, *Karl Barth's Doctrine of Holy Scripture* (Grand Rapids: Eerdmans, 1962); James Tunstead Burtchaell, *Catholic Theories of Biblical Inspiration Since 1810: A Review and Critique* (London: Cambridge University Press, 1969), 290–91.

neously be the Word of God and a human composition? It is to these questions that our discussion is addressed.

The Divine Authorship of Inspired Scripture

In the history of the church, the divine character of Scripture has been the great presupposition for the whole of Christian preaching and theology. This is readily apparent in the way the New Testament speaks about the Old Testament. That which appears in the Old Testament is cited in the New Testament with formulas like "God says" and "the Holy Spirit says" (Acts 4:24, 25; 13:47; 2 Cor. 6:16). Scripture and God are so closely joined together in the minds of the New Testament authors that they naturally could speak of Scripture doing what it records God as doing (Gal. 3:8; Rom. 9:17). The introductory phrase "It is [stands] written" *(gegraptai)* is also used of New Testament writings (John 20:31). The New Testament concept of faith is in accord with the divine character of the apostolic word (Rom. 1:5; 10:3; 16:26). The reference to the divine character of the apostolic word in its written and oral form deserves unconditional faith and obedience.

Because of the apostolic word's divine origin and content, Scripture can be described as "sure" (2 Pet. 1:19), "trustworthy" (1 Tim. 1:15; 3:1; 4:9; 2 Tim. 2:11; Titus 3:8), "confirmed" (Heb. 2:3), and "eternal" (1 Pet. 1:24, 25). As a result those who build their lives on Scripture "will not be disappointed" (Rom. 9:33; 1 Pet. 2:6). The Word was written for "instruction and encouragement" (Rom. 15:4), to lead to saving faith (2 Tim. 3:15), to guide people toward godliness (2 Tim. 3:16b), and to equip believers for good works (2 Tim. 3:17).

The purpose of Scripture is to place men and women in a right standing before God and to enable believers to seek God's glory in all of life's activities and efforts. But Scripture is not concerned only with a person's religious needs. On the contrary, the divine character, origin, and content of Scripture teaches us to understand everything *sub specie Dei*—"humanity, the world, nature, history, their origin and their destination, their past and their future."[11] The Bible is not only a book of conversion but also

---

11. Herman Ridderbos, *Studies in Scripture and Its Authority* (St. Catherines, Ontario: Paideia, 1978), 24.

a book of creation and history. It is a book of redemptive history, and it is this perspective that best represents and defines the divine character of Scripture.

We must recognize that central to Scripture is the unifying history of God's redeeming words and acts, of which the advent and work of Christ is the ultimate focus. Jesus Christ is the center to which everything in Scripture is united and bound together—beginning and end, creation and redemption, humanity, the world, the fall, history and the future.[12] If this overriding unity is ignored, Scripture is denatured and can lose its "theological-christological definition" and become "abstracted from the peculiar nature and content of Scripture."[13]

As we have noted, we cannot construct dualistic operations of Scripture that stress only its religious or pietistic sense.[14] This possibly leads to distinctions between what is and what is not inspired Scripture, what is and what is not from God. We must resist relating divine inspiration merely to content and not to form, to the Bible's purpose and not to its essence, or to its thoughts and not to its words. The entirety of Scripture is divinely inspired and is God's light upon our path and God's lamp for our feet. We now turn our attention to the nature of inspiration and the Bible's witness to itself.

The Bible's Self-Witness

There are many passages, in addition to those mentioned in our previous section, that address the divine aspect of Scripture (e.g., Ps. 119; Luke 24:25–27; John 10:34–35; Heb. 1:1–2; 2 Pet. 3:16), but the primary witness of the Bible to its own inspiration[15] is found in 2 Timothy 3:16–17, "All Scripture is God-breathed

12. Numerous possible solutions to explain the unity of Scripture are found in D. L. Baker, *Two Testaments: One Bible* (Downers Grove: InterVarsity, 1976).

13. Ridderbos, *Studies in Scripture,* 25.

14. Cf. Roger Nicole, "The Biblical Concept of Truth," in *Scripture and Truth,* ed. D. A. Carson and John D. Woodbridge, 287–98; a different perspective can be found in Frank Stagg, "What is Truth?" in *Science, Faith and Revelation,* ed. Robert E. Patterson (Nashville: Broadman, 1979), 239–60. There are hints of this dualism in E. Y. Mullins, *The Christian Religion in Its Doctrinal Expression* (Philadelphia: Judson, 1917), although his purpose was to affirm the religious and soteriological nature and purpose of Scripture.

15. On the Bible's witness to itself, cf. Wayne A. Grudem, "Scripture's Self-Attestation and the Problem of Formulating a Doctrine of Scripture," in *Scripture and Truth,* ed. D. A. Carson and John D. Woodbridge, 19–59, where he lists

and is useful for teaching, rebuking, correcting and training in righteousness, so that the man of God may be thoroughly equipped for every good work" (NIV).

The term *inspiration (theopneustos)* has a long heritage in the theological literature, but it is always used with further explanation and disclaimers. This is because *theopneustos* means "God-breathed."[16] In contemporary usage the term *inspiration* suggests the idea of "breathing into." Secular emphasis is generally synonymous with illumination or human genius. But the New Testament emphasis is that God "breathed out" what the sacred writers convey in the biblical writings. A preferable term might be *spiration* rather than *inspiration* in order to emphasize the divine source and initiative rather than human genius or creativity. "In short, the Bible's life-breath as a literary deposit is divine."[17] Recognizing these shortcomings with the term *inspiration,* we shall continue to use the word primarily because of its long-term standing in theological literature. The point that must be stressed when using this term is that it points to God as the source of Scripture.

It has been suggested that 2 Timothy 3:16 does not refer to all of Scripture because of the possible translation "every Scripture

---

over fifty passages that address Scripture's self-witness; also James M. Grier, "The Self-Witness of the Bible," *Grace Theological Journal* 1 (1979): 71–76; John Murray, "The Attestation of Scripture," in *The Infallible Word: A Symposium,* ed. Ned B. Stonehouse and Paul Wooley (1946; reprint, Phillipsburg, N.J.: Presbyterian and Reformed, 1978), 1–54; Edwin A. Blum, "The Apostle's View of Scripture," in *Inerrancy,* ed. Norman L. Geisler (Grand Rapids: Zondervan, 1979), 39–53. The approach of self-attestation is sometimes rejected on the grounds of circular reasoning. But the dilemma involved in this approach is apparent— either the Bible has its starting point upon itself or upon some other foundation, in which case it would be guilty of inconsistency. We can allow for additional testimony, but surely the Scripture's own claim must be given prior consideration. As with all points of theology, a consistent method would call for a theological statement in Scripture about itself to be considered prior to an examination of the phenomena in Scripture. Yet Beegle (*Scripture, Tradition and Infallibility,* 175–97) seeks to develop a theology of inspiration based upon the phenomena of Scripture. His approach and conclusions differ from those in this volume.

16. Carl F. H. Henry, "The Authority and Inspiration of the Bible," in *The Expositor's Bible Commentary,* ed. Frank E. Gaebelein, 12 vols. (Grand Rapids: Zondervan, 1979), 1:13.

17. Ibid. Cf. J. N. D. Kelley, *A Commentary on the Pastoral Epistles* (New York: Harper and Row, 1963), 203.

inspired of God is also useful" (NEB).[18] I. Howard Marshall has noted that this suggestion can be confidently rejected, since no New Testament author would have conceived of the possibility of a book being classified as Scripture and yet not being inspired of God.[19] We realize that some disagree with Marshall and affirm a limited inspiration for the so-called salvific parts. The problem with this approach is its difficulty in distinguishing the salvific parts from the nonsalvific. Thus one cannot tell precisely what parts of the Bible are inspired.

It must be acknowledged that 2 Timothy 3:16 refers primarily to the Old Testament writings *(graphē)*. There are fifty occurrences of *graphē* ("Scripture") in the New Testament, all of which primarily refer to the Old Testament, though the entirety of canonical Scripture is not ruled out. Furthermore, it is not too much to affirm that the construction used in verse 16 has a broader meaning that allows for the inclusion of the New Testament writings as well. The anarthrous construction, *pas graphē* ("all Scripture"), can have a characteristic idea, so that the phrase can mean "all that has characteristics of canonical Scripture."[20] In addition, it needs to be observed that *graphē* includes

18. For an example of this approach, cf. Martin Dibelius and Hans Conzelmann, *The Pastoral Epistles*, trans. Philip Buttolph and Adela Yarbro (Philadelphia: Fortress, 1962), 120. However, such a translation is highly unlikely because it makes the *kai* ("also") quite awkward. It is doubtful that the apostle would affirm that Scripture has a second characteristic ("also") before affirming its initial characteristic. The passage evidences a predicate construction and calls for the more straightforward translation: "The whole of Scripture is inspired . . ." (e.g., KJV, NASB, NIV). Cf. C. F. D. Moule, *An Idiom Book of New Testament Greek* (Cambridge: University Press, 1953), 95. Also Gottlob Schrenk, *"graphō"* in *Theological Dictionary of the New Testament,* ed. Gerhard Kittel and trans. Geoffrey W. Bromiley (Grand Rapids: Eerdmans, 1964), 1:759, who comments, "This obviously means every passage of Scripture." The extent of inspiration is discussed adequately by Millard J. Erickson, *Christian Theology* (Grand Rapids: Baker, 1986), 210–12. Ridderbos *(Studies in Scripture,* 27) says that "the predicative significance of *theopneustos* is not in my opinion disputable."

19. Marshall, *Biblical Inspiration,* 25.

20. It is highly probable that the author is not making a distinction in his mind between the LXX and the MT in making this assertion. If that is the case, then all translations that take on the characteristics of canonical Scripture could be described as inspired or at least virtually inspired. Cf. Homer A. Kent, Jr., *The Pastoral Epistles* (Chicago: Moody, 1982), 281; also Nigel Turner, *Syntax,* vol. 3 of *A Grammar of New Testament Greek* (Edinburgh: T and T Clark, 1963), 199.

references to New Testament writings in 1 Timothy 5:18 and
2 Peter 3:18.

The Inclusiveness of Inspiration

The passage in 2 Timothy 3 focuses primarily upon the product of inspiration, while it includes the secondary aspects of purpose and process. What is being asserted is the activity of God
throughout the entire process, so that the completed, final product ultimately comes from him. It is a mistake, however, to think
of inspiration only in terms of the time when the Spirit moves the
human author to write. The biblical concept of inspiration allows
for the activity in special ways within the process without requiring that we understand all of the Spirit's working in one and
the same way. Just as in the processes of creation and preservation of the universe God providentially intervened in special
ways for specific purposes, so too we can say that, alongside and
within this superintending action of the Spirit to inspire human
writings in the biblical books, we can posit a special work of the
Spirit in bringing God's revelation to the apostles and prophets.[21]

God's Spirit is involved both in revealing specific messages to
the prophets (Jer. 1:1–9) and in guiding the authors of the historical sections in their research (Luke 1:1–4). It is not outside the
view of inspiration, then, to include the literary processes that
take place on the human level behind Scripture. Summarizing
the inclusiveness of inspiration, we can say that it encompasses
". . . the collection of information from witnesses, the use of written sources, the writing up and editing of such information, the
composition of spontaneous letters, the committing to writing of
prophetic messages, the collecting of the various documents together, and so on. At the same time, however, on the divine level
we can assert that the Spirit, who moved on the face of the waters
at creation (Gen. 1:2), was active in the whole process, so that
the Bible can be regarded as both the words of men and the Word
of God."[22]

Turner's comments are ambiguous. It is best to take *pas* in an inclusive fashion.
We could translate it as "Everything that takes on the character of Scripture,"
and thus the New Testament is inferred. The Old Testament is what is primarily
in view as the term *graphē* indicates. Note the reference to the Holy Scriptures in
verse 15.

21. Marshall, *Biblical Inspiration*, 43.
22. Ibid., 42.

Concursive Inspiration

This approach to inspiration attempts to take seriously the human factors in the composition of the Bible. Theologians have described the activity of the Spirit with the activities of the human writers through which the Bible was written as a concursive work. While this perspective of inspiration is consistent with a plenary view of inspiration (see p. 35), it avoids any hint that God mechanically dictated the words of Scripture to the human authors so that they had no real part in the Scripture's composition.[23] Our approach to inspiration attempts to take seriously the circumstances of the human authors.

This concursive approach allows for a viewpoint that gladly confesses that God's purpose is accomplished through the writer, but the emphasis of the Spirit's work is on the product of inspiration (the inscripturated Word). We can assert that inspiration extends to the choice of words based upon a comprehensive, encompassing approach.[24] This is accomplished by the Spirit's leading the human author in points of research, reflection, and subsequent writing. It is possible that revelation and inspiration happen simultaneously at certain points in Scripture, such as the Ten Commandments and perhaps apocalyptic works like Daniel and Revelation.[25]

---

23. Even though John R. Rice, *Our God-Breathed Book* (Murfreesboro, Tenn: Sword of the Lord, 1969), 192–287, accepts the term *dictation,* he denies the idea of mechanical dictation. Non-inerrantists wrongly characterize inerrantists as advocates of mechanical dictation (so Moody, *Thy Word Is Truth,* 46–47), but this is not the case. Rice is perhaps one of the few fundamentalists who uses the term *dictation,* but he denies mechanical dictation (p. 287). Cf. the discussion of the fundamentalist approach to Scripture in Donald K. McKim, *What Christians Believe about the Bible* (Nashville: Nelson, 1985), 56–57. Harold Lindsell, in *The Battle for the Bible* (Grand Rapids: Zondervan, 1976), 33, says he does "not know any scholar who believes in biblical inerrancy who holds that the Scriptures were received by dictation." Many wrongly trace the dictation approach to John Calvin. Calvin used the word *dictation* in the *Second Epistle of Paul to the Corinthians* and the *Epistles to Timothy, Titus and Philemon,* trans. T. A. Small and ed. D. W. Torrance and T. F. Torrance (Grand Rapids: Eerdmans, 1964), 329–31. While he uses the word *dictation,* numerous Calvin scholars, such as John Gerstner, W. Robert Godfrey, Kenneth Kantzer, and J. I. Packer have shown that Calvin did not have a developed doctrine of dictation. His view of inspiration was a "plenary" approach; cf. J. I. Packer, "Calvin's View of Scripture," in *God's Inerrant Word,* ed. John W. Montgomery (Minneapolis: Bethany, 1974), 102 ff.

24. Bloesch, *Evangelical Theology* 1:55–56.

25. We grant that at these points and perhaps at some points where the

The Scope of Inspiration

It might be contended that we have contradicted ourselves by allowing for such direct inspiration at certain points or by asserting that inspiration extends even to the very words of Scripture, while simultaneously allowing for the genuine human authorship. We think not. We believe the answer is found in the spiritual characteristics of the biblical writers. These men of God had known God, learned from him, and walked with him in their spiritual pilgrimage for many years. God had prepared them through their familial, social, educational, and spiritual backgrounds for the task of inscripturating his Word. The experiences of Moses, David, Jeremiah, Paul, Luke, and Peter differ, yet throughout their lives God was working to prepare and shape them (even their vocabulary) to pen the Scriptures. Beyond this, we dare not say much regarding the *how* of inspiration, except to affirm God's providential oversight in the entire process of inspiration.[26] We think it quite plausible to suggest that just as revelation came in various ways (Heb. 1:1–2), so the process of inspiration differed with each author.

The quality of inspiration may differ within passages and genres, but the nature of inspiration is the same throughout—God is the source of Scripture and his purposes are accomplished efficaciously.[27] This affirms that the Sermon on the Mount or the Epistle to the Romans may be more readily recognized as inspired Scripture than the historical accounts in Kings or Chronicles. Yet, this is due in part to the subject matter. The inspiration in such historical passages assures the general characteristic of reliability that is brought to these records. Even if inspiration differs and is somehow less recognizable to the reader in some

---

prophets utter "Thus says the Lord . . ." that dictation may be possible, though not probable. However, the Ten Commandments are quite likely dictation material, but we cannot know for sure about other portions of Scripture.

26. Erickson, *Christian Theology,* 215–20. This subject has been addressed in B. B. Warfield's classic work, *The Inspiration and Authority of the Bible* (Philadelphia: Presbyterian and Reformed, 1948), 155–56.

27. Cf. Pinnock, *Scripture Principle,* 1–82. This is not to affirm that some parts are more inspired than others, but that the nature of inspiration is different between Luke's Gospel, the Proverbs, the Apocalypse, and the Ten Commandments. The biblical writers themselves either acknowledge or give indication of such differences.

places, the entire Bible (*pas graphē,* i.e., "all canonical Scripture") can be characterized as inspired *(theopneustos)*.

The previous section, which focused on the Bible's teaching about itself, provided us with a framework in which to operate. Now, our focus must shift to the vantage point of the phenomena of Scripture, that is, to its humanness and historicity.[28]

The Human Authorship of Inspired Scripture

The biblical writers employed the linguistic resources available to them as they wrote to specific people with particular needs at particular times. The human authors were not lifted out of their culture or removed from their contexts. They were not autonomous, but functioning members in communities of faith, aware of God's presence and leadership in their lives. Whether or not they were fully aware that they were writing inspired Scripture, they did demonstrate a God-consciousness.[29] Obviously, the writers were not unbiased historical observers; they were men committed to faith. Thus the concursive action of Spirit and human authorship is informed by the spiritual commitments of the writers.

Image of God and Cultural-Temporal Distance

It is quite true that the biblical writers were limited to their own contexts, yet they share similarities that span beyond times and places. The primary similarity is one the writers share with all human beings, since all men and women have been created in God's image (Gen. 1:26–27), and as a result, share certain common characteristics.[30] As theologians since the time of Augustine have observed, human beings created in the image of God

28. For a full treatment of the human dimension, cf. Pinnock, *Scripture Principle,* 106–29; Gordon R. Lewis, "The Human Authorship of Inspired Scripture," in *Inerrancy,* ed. Norman L. Geisler, 229–64. If we take the human and historical situation seriously, it shows how important it is to study Scripture not only theologically and devotionally but also grammatically, historically, contextually, and critically. Cf. George E. Ladd, *The New Testament and Criticism* (Grand Rapids: Eerdmans, 1967) and I. Howard Marshall, ed., *New Testament Interpretation* (Grand Rapids: Eerdmans, 1977).

29. Erickson, *Christian Theology,* 204–6.

30. Cf. Anthony A. Hoekema, *Created in God's Image* (Grand Rapids: Eerdmans, 1986).

can have memories of the past, considerations of the present, and expectations of the future. To the extent that these potential capacities are employed, persons—contrary to objects—are neither temporally nor culturally bound. The writers are certainly time-related but not necessarily time-bound. Moses and Paul, among others, demonstrated cross-cultural influences and experiences. The writers were certainly not entirely culturally or behaviorally conditioned. Even though they were obviously influenced by the time and culture in which they wrote, nevertheless, it can be observed that the writers freely rejected some concepts of their culture and freely endorsed others.[31]

Eugene Nida has observed that humans created in God's image can develop ability to think and communicate in linguistic symbols. Because of this, communication is a possibility among the diverse linguistic cultures of the world for three reasons:

1. The processes of human reasoning are essentially the same, irrespective of cultural diversity.
2. All people have a common range of experience.
3. All peoples possess the capacity for at least some adjustment of the symbolic "grids" of others.[32]

We do not want to press these assertions beyond their limits. Nevertheless, it can be granted that a revelation written through a human author in a particular language (Hebrew, Aramaic, or Greek) can be intelligible to those who know other languages. God can communicate with humanity, who have been created in his image. Likewise, humans can communicate with other humans cross-culturally and cross-temporally. By maintaining these observations about humanity, we can affirm the genuine humanness of Scripture without denying that God can speak through a divine-human Scripture. D. E. Nineham draws attention to the cultural and temporal distance that exists between the biblical writers and our world and has concluded that the Bible is basically unusable today.[33] Because of the common-

31. Lewis, "The Human Authorship of Inspired Scripture," in *Inerrancy*, ed. Norman L. Geisler, 244–46.

32. Eugene Nida, *Message and Mission* (New York: Harper, 1960), 90.

33. Cf. Nineham, *Use and Abuse of the Bible*, who has presented useful insights regarding cultural and temporal distance. Yet his work is basically negative in its approach, although he does not deny entirely the possibility that God

ality discussed above, however, we affirm that God's revelation can be communicated through human authors who lived two thousand years ago in various cultures. The biblical text is indeed the words of human authors in temporal-cultural contexts, but this does not limit the plausibility that God's eternal revelation can be communicated through their writings to contemporary men and women. We fully recognize the humanness and historicity of the text but simultaneously acknowledge that God's revelation can be communicated through this situation. The fact that the biblical authors were men of faith informs the issue of concursive inspiration; in the same way, recognition that every person bears the image of God has implications for the possibility of communication across cultures and ages.

Variety in the Biblical Message

The stress upon human authorship in contemporary theological literature reveals the diversity of beliefs and theologies among the biblical writers.[34] The concept of overall unity, characteristic of evangelical theology in the past and perhaps to lesser degrees in the present, emerges from a full-orbed concept of biblical inspiration. As we have observed, the overriding themes of redemptive history and the Bible's inspiration form the basis for recognizing the theological unity in the Bible. Yet, this theological unity must be carefully examined in light of the genuine variety brought about by unique theological emphases of the different authors and the diverse human and historical situations in the writings.

It is readily obvious that the Bible is composed of different types of literature.[35] Likewise, the form in which the teaching is

---

can speak through the Bible. We agree with Pinnock *(Scripture Principle)* that "we must resist a misuse of cultural relatedness as a cloak to evade what the Scriptures really want to teach" (p. 110). "God's Word comes to us in human language, it is true, and there are features in it incidental to its teaching purposes. But 'in all things necessary' that the Bible wishes to teach us it is true and coherent and possesses the wisdom of God" (p. 115).

34. Walter Bauer, *Orthodoxy and Heresy in Earliest Christianity,* trans. and ed. Robert A. Kraft and Gerhard Krodel (Philadelphia: Fortress, 1971); James D. G. Dunn, *Unity and Diversity in the New Testament* (Philadelphia: Fortress, 1971); D. A. Carson, "Unity and Diversity in the New Testament," in *Scripture and Truth,* ed. D. A. Carson and John D. Woodbridge, 65–95.

35. Ralph P. Martin, "Approaches to New Testament Exegesis," in *New Testament Interpretation,* ed. I. Howard Marshall, 226–47.

expressed is influenced by the literary genre. Each genre (legal, prophetic, lyric, gospel, epistolary, apocalyptic) has distinctive characteristics. It is from the various collection of writings that the basic prophetic-apostolic message is discovered.

Not only is there variety of genres, but there is often variety within a particular genre. For instance, the different theological emphases among the synoptic writers demonstrate the variety even within the genre of gospel. Matthew's kingdom theology differs from Mark's servant theology, and they are each different from Luke's stress upon Jesus as Savior of the world.[36] Yet the central unity of Jesus Christ and the developing history of redemption cannot be ignored.

Beyond this matter is the possibility of theological development within the Old and New Testaments and even within the individual authors.[37] Donald Guthrie's succinct comments on this difficult issue are extremely appropriate:

> The idea of progressive revelation is familiar in Old Testament interpretation and also in the area of the relation of the Old Testament to the New Testament. . . . With Christ the Old Testament ritual system became obsolete, as the epistle to the Hebrews makes clear. . . . One obvious area where this is undeniable [development in the New Testament] is the difference between the gospels and the rest of the New Testament. Before the death and resurrection of Christ the revelation given to the disciples was limited. In the nature of the case, Jesus could not give a full explanation of his own death to his disciples until they had grasped the fact of it. But after the resurrection the apostolic preachers were guided into an understanding of it, although again not in any stereotyped way, but with rich variety.[38]

We can see that the differences between the writers themselves and the development (progressive revelation) occurring

36. George E. Ladd, *A Theology of the New Testament* (Grand Rapids: Eerdmans, 1974), 13–210; Leon Morris, *New Testament Theology* (Grand Rapids: Zondervan, 1986), 91–221. These different emphases point to the possible and helpful use of redaction criticism as a tool for theological interpretation of the Gospels.

37. Peter Toon, *Development of Doctrine in the Church* (Grand Rapids: Eerdmans, 1979); Richard N. Longenecker, "On the Concept of Development in Pauline Thought," in *Perspectives in Evangelical Theology,* ed. Kenneth Kantzer and Stanley N. Gundry (Grand Rapids: Baker, 1979), 195–200.

38. Donald Guthrie, *New Testament Theology* (Downers Grove: InterVarsity, 1981), 51.

within the Testaments and even some of the writers themselves (e.g., Isaiah, Paul) point to the genuine humanness of the biblical text. There is diversity, or variety in the sense of variations, in the expression of the central message of the gospel. The basis of unity is located in the oneness of the gospel. Therefore, diversity works within the limits of the gospel.[39]

Diversity does not imply contradiction. The different writers, with their own emphases, varied their expression according to their unique purposes and settings. But within this very real and rich variety that evidences the humanness of Scripture, there is a genuine unity that is the result of the divine superintending work of inspiration.

Various Explanations of the Divine-Human Authorship of Inspired Scripture

Divine inspiration does not necessarily mean that the men who spoke and wrote inspired Scripture were temporarily stripped of their limitations in knowledge, memory, language, and ability to express themselves in specific contexts during certain periods of history. We would not naively maintain that the Bible fell from heaven on a parachute, inscribed with a peculiar heavenly language that uniquely suited it as an instrument for divine revelation, or that the Bible was dictated directly and immediately by God without reference to any local style or perspective. The presence of a multiplicity of historical, contextual, linguistic, and cultural factors must be maintained and accounted for.[40]

A number of views have arisen in recent years attempting to account for the divine-human character of Scripture.[41] A brief survey of these attempts will prove helpful for our discussion.

39. Ibid., 59.

40. R. C. Sproul, "Controversy at Culture Gap," *Eternity* 27 (May 1975): 13.

41. A classic work that presents different approaches to Scripture and revelation is H. D. McDonald, *Theories of Revelation: An Historical Study 1700–1960* (1959, 1963; reprint, Grand Rapids: Baker, 1979). Recent updates include J. I. Packer, "Encountering Present-Day Views of Scripture," in *Foundation of Biblical Authority,* ed. James Montgomery Boice (Grand Rapids: Zondervan, 1978); Robert K. Johnstone, ed., *The Use of the Bible in Theology: Evangelical Options* (Atlanta: John Knox, 1985); McKim, *What Christians Believe about the Bible;*

Many of the contemporary theories are attempts to deal seriously with the two-sided character of Scripture and also to explain how a book penned two thousand years ago should be understood in a post-Enlightenment era.

The Enlightenment era was a watershed in the history of Western civilization. It was then that the Christian consensus was broken by a radical, secular spirit. The Enlightenment philosophy stressed the primacy of nature, a high view of reason and a low view of sin, and an antisupernatural bias, and it encouraged revolt against the traditional understanding of authority. This philosophy was foundational for much of the liberal theology that dominated nineteenth-century European and early twentieth-century American thought. It was initiated by Friedrich Schleiermacher's *On Religion: Speeches to Its Cultured Despisers* at the turn of the nineteenth century. The contemporary assaults upon classic formulations of scriptural inspiration and authority can be traced to pre-Enlightenment attacks upon the Bible.[42] The positive element that has resulted from the questions raised by post-Enlightenment scholars has been a more careful consideration of the human authorship and historical context of Scripture.[43] In the following survey, the dictation view has basically ignored the Enlightenment, the illumination view has surrendered to the Enlightenment, and in assorted ways, the encounter, dynamic, and plenary views have attempted to respond to the Enlightenment and still maintain the church's confession that the Bible is the Word of God.

D. A. Carson, "Recent Developments in the Doctrine of Scripture," in *Hermeneutics, Authority, and Canon,* ed. D. A. Carson and John D. Woodbridge, 10–48.

42. Bruce Demarest, "The Bible in the Enlightenment Era," in *Challenges to Inerrancy,* ed. Gordon Lewis and Bruce Demarest, 11–47. A very fine discussion can be found in Colin Gunton, *Enlightenment and Alienation* (Grand Rapids: Eerdmans, 1985), 111–52; also cf. Helmut Thielicke, *The Evangelical Faith,* trans. and ed. Geoffrey W. Bromiley (Grand Rapids: Eerdmans, 1974), 38–63. Bernard Ramm, *After Fundamentalism* (San Francisco: Harper and Row, 1983), has attempted to articulate a post-Enlightenment/evangelical doctrine of Scripture. The response to his proposal has not been entirely favorable.

43. Cf. Ronald Nash, *The Word of God and the Mind of Man* (Grand Rapids: Zondervan, 1982); idem, *Christian Faith and Historical Understanding* (Grand Rapids: Zondervan, 1984), in which he deals with the impact of Enlightenment thought upon Scripture and history. Also cf. Morris A. Inch and C. Hassell Bullock, eds., *The Literature and Meaning of Scripture* (Grand Rapids: Baker, 1981).

Dictation View

The dictation theory places the emphasis upon God's actual dictation of his Word to the human writers. The theory is developed from the passages, primarily found in the Old Testament prophets, where the Spirit is pictured as telling the writer what to communicate. What is a proper assessment of particular aspects of Scripture ("Thus says the Lord . . .") is applied to the whole Bible. This approach fails to consider seriously the distinctive styles of the different authors or the particular contexts to which they were addressed.

While it is right that the prophets claimed to hear God addressing them and then proclaimed his Word, this is not always parallel with the way the other writers depict themselves. For example, Luke tells his readers that other people before him had attempted to write the story of Jesus and that he consulted these works and did additional research before compiling his Gospel (Luke 1:1–4). Thus, it can be seen that the dictation theory cannot account for all aspects of Scripture. The dictation approach is without doubt confessed (perhaps unconsciously) by numerous faithful believers. Because of this it is often assumed that advocates of a plenary view hold to the dictation view, but adherents of the plenary view take great pains to disassociate themselves from the dictation theorists.[44] It is right to judge the dictation theory as docetic and, therefore, less than orthodox.

Illumination View

The view that maintains little more than the Spirit's working within the human authors to raise their religious insight and express themselves with eloquent language can be called the illumination approach. In this view inspiration is the illumination of the authors beyond their normal abilities to express themselves creatively as men of human genius. Inspiration is very limited when understood in this manner, not only in relation to the nature of inspiration but also to the extent of inspiration. Portions of Scripture such as poetry, proverbs, and parables best exemplify this type of literary or religious insight. Thus, it is eas-

44. Cf. footnote 23. It is proper to assign the charge of docetism to the dictation view alone. The other views take seriously the human authorship of Scripture (in varying degrees).

ily seen that this approach fails to explain the inspiration of the entire Bible.

The illumination view emphasizes the freedom and creativity of the human author but fails to account for the Spirit's guidance of the writers in the communication of divine truth; there is only a mere increase in sensitivity regarding spiritual matters. This view of inspiration characterizes the ebionite error we noted earlier and is a failure as far as accounting for the divine character of Scripture.[45] Nevertheless, it needs to be observed that this view is more akin to the English term *inspiring* than the biblical concepts of a God-breathed Scripture *(theopneustos)*. Fortunately, there are better options than these first two extreme positions, neither of which accounts for the two-sided character of Scripture.

Encounter View

A more complex approach developed by Karl Barth can be classified as an encounter view of inspiration.[46] This view states that in regard to its composition, the Bible differs little from other books. Yet, the Bible is unique because of the Spirit's ability to use it as a means of revelation to specific individuals or communities. Through the *ongoing work of inspiration,* the Bible becomes revelation. The Bible is correlated as a witness to God's original act of revelation.

Inspiration brings the Bible to the contemporary human situation as a source of God's revelation. It is in this way that Barth

45. Lotan Harold DeWolf, *A Theology of the Living Church,* rev. ed. (New York: Harper and Brothers, 1960), 48–75. Cf. the discussion in McKim, *What Christians Believe about the Bible,* 38–48.

46. In some ways Karl Barth shares this view with Emil Brunner, Reinhold Niebuhr, and, to a much lesser extent, Rudolf Bultmann. We focus on Barth because he was not only the first but also, in many ways, the greatest and most brilliant of neoorthodox theologians. J. I. Packer ("Present-Day Views," in *Foundations of Biblical Authority,* ed. James Montgomery Boice) comments that Barth " is likely to have more long-term influence than other theologians of this type; also because neoorthodoxy appears at its strongest intellectually and noblest spiritually in the writings of Barth, and his weaknesses, however great, are comparatively less than the corresponding defect of others on the same trail. It should, however, be realized that Barth stands at the extreme right of the neoorthodox spectrum." Cf. Colin Brown, *Karl Barth and the Christian Message* (London: InterVarsity, 1967), 99–140; and Karl Barth, *Church Dogmatics,* trans. Geoffrey W. Bromiley and ed. T. F. Torrance, 2 vols. (Edinburgh: T and T Clark, 1956), 1:1, 51–335.

seeks to take seriously the human authorship of Scripture and the Bible as the Word of God. He attempts to avoid a concept of inspiration that in some way confines the Holy Spirit in the Bible. It is a misunderstanding on his part, however, to assume that those who hold that the Bible was Spirit-inspired in its original composition ignore the Spirit's illumination of the text, thereby bringing it to life for present-day readers. Barth's stress upon ongoing inspiration seems to ignore inspiration at the time of the Bible's composition.

Barth, however, seeks to make it possible for God's Word to be encountered through Scripture.[47] In evaluating Barth's contention, I. Howard Marshall states that "it is doubtful whether Barth's view does justice to that very character of the Bible as inspired Scripture which makes it possible for the Spirit to continue to witness through its words to the Word of God which it embodies."[48]

This view is inadequate to account for the human and divine aspects of inscripturation. In comparison to the illumination theory, there are many strengths and much to admire, yet it does not fully explain why we should trust the text as Barth himself does. Barth preached the errancy of the text; however, as Clark Pinnock has observed, he "treated it with reverence and practiced its inerrancy."[49] However, Colin Brown's note is an appropriate concluding evaluation: "It is impossible to maintain high doctrines of revelation and inspiration without at the same time being willing to defend in detail the veracity and historicity of the biblical writings."[50]

Dynamic View

This widely held approach endeavors to be a *via media,* in contradistinction to the liberal and fundamentalist camps, which seek to emphasize the combination of divine and human elements in the process of inspiration. A. H. Strong, E. Y. Mullins, and W. T. Conner are Baptist representatives of this view.[51] More

47. Cf. Runia, *Karl Barth's Doctrine of Scripture.*

48. Marshall, *Biblical Inspiration,* 36.

49. Pinnock, "Three Views of the Bible," in *Biblical Authority,* ed. Jack B. Rogers, 37.

50. Brown, *Karl Barth and the Christian Message,* 146.

51. Augustus H. Strong, *Systematic Theology* (Westwood, N.J.: Revell, 1907), 211. Cf. also the discussion by J. Leo Garrett in *Are Southern Baptists "Evangelicals"?* ed. J. Leo Barrett et al (Macon: Mercer University Press, 1983), 87–127.

contemporary advocates with nuanced approaches include G. C. Berkouwer (1975), Paul J. Achtemeier (1980), and William J. Abraham (1981).[52]

In many ways this approach originated as a reaction to the dictation theory. It sees the work of the Spirit in directing the writer to the concepts he should have and then allowing great freedom for the human author to express this idea in his own style through his own personality in a way consistent with and characteristic of his own situation and context.

More contemporary approaches have expanded the view beyond the human author to see the place of the community in the Scripture's composition. The complexity of this position sees the Bible arising out of several traditions that confess what God has done within the situation of the community, recognizing the respondents or authors who take up the traditions and reformulate them in specific situations. The result is Scripture. Inspiration is generally limited to God's initiating impulse, and thus the stress of inspiration falls not upon the product, but upon the purpose and process.

The dynamic view's strength is in its attempt to maintain the two-sided character of Scripture. Its stress upon the creativity of the human author and his community is quite commendable. Inspiration, however, refers to the entire process, not just the momentary event of initiation. In some ways, similar to Barth, inspiration and illumination are confused. The theory properly stresses the relation of inspiration to concepts, but it fails to account for the relationship between ideas and words. In emphasizing the process of inspiration, it does not place the emphasis where Scripture itself places it—on the product of inspiration. The real shortcoming of this approach, with its various nuances, is its imbalanced stress upon God's initiating impulse rather than his superintending work over the entire process and product. Finally, it must be seen that in this approach the emphasis is more upon the biblical writers (who, granted, are referred to in 2 Pet. 1:19–21) than upon the writings (which are referred to in 2 Tim. 3:16).

52. Achtemeier, *The Inspiration of Scripture;* Abraham, *The Divine Inspiration of Holy Scripture;* Berkouwer, *Holy Scripture.* Cf. the discussion in Marshall, *Biblical Inspiration,* 37–40; and the response to older views similar to the illumination view (and also the dynamic view) in B. B. Warfield's *Limited Inspiration* (Philadelphia: Presbyterian and Reformed, 1974).

Plenary View

The last theory that we shall examine is careful to see the Spirit's influence both upon the writers and (primarily) the writings. It also seeks to view inspiration as extending to all (thus the adjective *plenary*) portions of Holy Scripture, even beyond the direction of thoughts to the selection of words. Even though the words are those that God wants communicated, the human writer expresses this message in a way that evidences the situation of the writing and the author's unique style, background, and personality.[53] We must recognize the element of mystery involved in this process, which does not fully explain the *how* of inspiration.[54]

The approach, as described, seeks to do justice to the human factors in the Bible's composition and avoids any attempt to suggest that entire books of the Bible were dictated. We believe that this view, that of the contributors to this volume in agreement with others of evangelical faith, best accounts for the divine character of Scripture and the human circumstances of the Bible's composition.[55]

The Result of Inspiration

The Possibility of a Normative Scripture

In what sense can we confess that Scripture, which evidences genuine human authorship written in time-related contexts, is normative? Or must we conclude that Scripture is wholly descriptive and the student of Scripture is little more than a his-

53. Henry, "Authority and Inspiration," in *The Expositor's Bible Commentary*, ed. Frank E. Gaebelein, 1:13–35; idem, "Bible, Inspiration of," in *Evangelical Dictionary of Theology*, ed. Walter A. Elwell (Grand Rapids: Baker, 1984), 145–49; idem, *God, Revelation, and Authority*, vol. 4; and Erickson, *Christian Theology*, 199–220.

54. In a previous article in *Southern Baptist Convention Today*, May 1986, we attempted to explain the nuances represented within the position of plenary inspiration. This includes the "absolute inerrancy" of Harold Lindsell, the "limited inerrancy" of Daniel P. Fuller and I. Howard Marshall, the "qualified inerrancy" of Donald G. Bloesch, the carefully "nuanced inerrancy" of Clark Pinnock, and the "critical inerrancy" of D. A. Carson.

55. J. Ramsey Michaels, "Inerrancy or Verbal Inspiration? An Evangelical Dilemma," in *Inerrancy and Common Sense*, ed. Roger Nicole and J. Ramsey Michaels, 49–70; Clark Pinnock, "The Inspiration of the New Testament," in *The Bible: The Living Word of Revelation*, ed. Merrill C. Tenney (Grand Rapids: Zondervan, 1968), 143–64.

torian or an antique keeper, who displays the exhibits in the best possible way? We think a wholly descriptive approach is unacceptable and lacks all the dynamic of the experience of the biblical authors and their communities of faith.[56]

Perhaps we should rephrase the question. Does any Bible student accept a descriptive approach completely? Is not the real issue to what extent is the Bible normative for the contemporary church? Even Rudolf Bultmann, while maintaining that first-century cultural patterns cannot be considered normative, nevertheless, sought to reinterpret these patterns for the contemporary church.

Although the cultural background and environment have changed since the biblical writings were penned, the human condition has not changed. It is to the human condition, men and women created in the image of God, yet fallen, that the unity of the biblical message speaks in a normative character that can be confessed for the following reasons:

1. They are the result of divine inspiration.
2. They proclaim the saving acts of God.
3. They are historically proximate to the saving acts of God.
4. They are based on the prophet-apostolic authority.[57]

Even with cultural advancements and scientific progress, the need of men and women for a right standing and a right relationship with God remains unchanged. The reason is that even the advancing wisdom and knowledge of the world cannot help humanity in the ultimate aspects of life (cf. 1 Cor. 1–4). The basic problem of how sinful humans are to approach a holy God and how these persons are to live in relationship to the life-giving Spirit of God is the same for all ages.

It is our belief, therefore, that the purpose of divinely inspired teaching concerning God and matters relating to God and his creation *(sub specie Dei)* is normative for the contemporary church. When such matters are proclaimed and confessed in the

56. Guthrie, *New Testament Theology,* 953–82.
57. Cf. R. P. C. Hanson, *The Bible as a Norm of Faith* (Durham: University Press, 1963), 7; idem, *Tradition in the Early Church* (London: SCM, 1962), 213–24; H. E. W. Turner, *The Pattern of Christian Truth* (London: Maybrays, 1954); and Edward J. Carnell, *The Case for Orthodox Theology* (Philadelphia: Fortress, 1959).

twentieth century, however, mere repetition of early Christian beliefs may not be sufficient; a restatement that awakens modern readers to an awareness that the Bible speaks in relevant ways to contemporary issues in church and society is also necessary.[58] When Scripture is approached from this perspective, it will be necessary to determine underlying principles for all portions of Scripture that address the contemporary situation, even if the direct teaching of Scripture is somehow limited by cultural-temporal factors (cf. 1 Tim. 5:23; 1 Cor. 16:20; Eph. 6:5). Believers will recognize that this is the case because of the two-sided character of Scripture. Because it is authored by humans in specific contexts, certain teachings may be contextually limited, but because it is divinely inspired, the underlying principles are normative and applicable for the church in every age. When approaching the Bible, recognizing its authoritative and normative character, we can discover truth[59] and its ramifications for the answers to life's ultimate questions as well as guidelines and principles for godly living in the twentieth-century world.[60]

The Possibility of an Inerrant Scripture

Having affirmed the possibility of a normative Scripture, we must probe further and ask if we can also confess the truthfulness and reliability of Scripture. It is not the primary purpose of this chapter to discuss the issues relating to the dependability and inerrancy of God's Word. But we must address the issue because Scripture's inerrancy is the corollary and result of our affirmations about a plenary view of inspiration. While inerrancy is a "red-flag" word among some and subject to misunderstanding among others, it is still, when properly defined, an adequate term to describe the results of inspiration.

---

58. John Jefferson Davis, "Contextualization and the Nature of Theology," in *The Necessity of Systematic Theology,* 2d ed., ed. John Jefferson Davis (Grand Rapids: Baker, 1980), 169–85; Pinnock, *Scripture Principle,* 210–21; David Hesselgrave, "Contextualization and Revelation Epistemology," in *Inerrancy and Hermeneutics,* ed. Earl D. Radmacher and Robert D. Preus (Grand Rapids: Zondervan, 1986), 693–764.

59. Anthony C. Thiselton, "Truth," in *Dictionary of New Testament Theology,* ed. Colin Brown, 3 vols. (Grand Rapids: Zondervan, 1971), 3:874–902.

60. Anthony C. Thiselton, *The Two Horizons* (Grand Rapids: Eerdmans, 1980), 432–38.

The misunderstandings have resulted from false associations with a literalistic hermeneutic or dictation theories of inspiration. Additional problems have developed from careless statements on the part of advocates who have been overzealous in their defense of the doctrine (even denying the use of textual criticism) or who have concentrated unduly upon issues of "errors" when the focus should instead be placed upon issues of "truthfulness and falseness." Others have attempted to prove that inerrancy is a direct teaching of Scripture instead of acknowledging that it is the proper implication of inspiration. Still others have attempted to defend the issue from a "slippery-slope or domino theory" standpoint and have thus unintentionally moved the primary focus of the issue away from theological concerns to historical concerns. One additional matter that we should consider is related to the importance of inerrancy. It is important primarily for theological and epistemological reasons, and shifting the argument to the secondary realm of soteriological concerns has only confused the issue. Individual salvation is not dependent upon one's confession of inerrancy, but consistent theological method and instruction needs the base of inerrancy in order to continue to maintain an orthodox confession in salvific matters. Thus we see that inerrancy, as a corollary of inspiration, is a foundational issue upon which other theological building blocks are laid.

With these warnings behind us and an awareness of the complexity of the issue, let us suggest a definition of inerrancy.[61] Inerrancy means that "when all the facts are known, the Bible (in its autographs) properly interpreted in light of which culture and communication means had developed by the time of its composition will be shown to be completely true (and therefore not false) in all that it affirms, to the degree of precision intended by the author, in all matters relating to God and his creation (including

---

61. Very careful statements on the subject can be found in Erickson, *Christian Theology,* 221–40. Paul D. Feinberg has written two very helpful articles, "The Meaning of Inerrancy," in *Inerrancy,* ed. Norman L. Geisler, 267–304; and "Bible, Inerrancy and Infallibility of," in *Evangelical Dictionary of Theology,* ed. Walter A. Elwell, 141–45. Two volumes that advocate inerrancy and recognize the complexities of the issue are Carson and Woodbridge, eds., *Scripture and Truth;* and Nicole and Michaels, eds., *Inerrancy and Common Sense.*

matters of history, geography, science, and other disciplines addressed in Scripture)."

No doubt some will say that with the carefulness of the definition, which attempts to recognize the complexity of the issues, it is futile to carry on further discussion. But hopefully the exact opposite is true. We trust that the precision involved in the statement will set the tone for the type of dialogue desired by those who respond to this chapter in particular and to the entire book in general. The definition seeks to be faithful to the phenomena of Scripture as well as theological affirmations in Scripture about the veracity of God. It will be helpful at this point to offer some brief comments about our definition.

when all the facts are known The statement begins from the vantage point of faith, recognizing that we may not have all the data necessary on this side of the *eschaton* to bear on the Bible. It is also likely that our sinful, finite minds may misinterpret some fact that we do have.

the Bible (in its autographs) Inerrancy applies to all aspects of the Bible as originally written. A claim to complete inerrancy is limited to the original words of the text. A reference to the autographs is not restricted to some lost codex but is an affirmation relating to the original words that were written by the prophetic-apostolic messengers. Thus, our confession of inerrancy and inspiration applies to translations to the degree that they represent accurately the original words. It is our belief that we can express great confidence in our present translations. Therefore, the qualifying statement regarding the autographs is not intended as an apologetic side step but is a theological appeal to the providence and veracity of God in his superintending work of inspiration.[62] Such a statement is never intended to remove trust in our present-day translations (whether KJV, NIV, NASB, etc.) but to insure and confirm faith in these translations because they rest upon a sure foundation.

properly interpreted The definition recognizes that statements concerning the nature of the text cannot be separated

---

62. Cf. Greg L. Bahnsen, "The Inerrancy of the Autographa," in *Inerrancy*, ed. Norman L. Geisler, 172–89. See earlier comments in footnotes 18–21, where the same concepts applying to all canonical Scripture's inspiration are applicable to the discussion of inerrancy as well.

from hermeneutical issues.[63] Several other chapters in this volume underscore this assertion. Before falsehood can be recognized, it is necessary to know if a text has been interpreted properly. The author's intention must be recognized, and matters of precision and accuracy must be judged in light of culture and means of communication that had developed by the time of the text's composition. The text, as a guideline, should be interpreted normally, grammatically, historically, contextually, and theologically. The context, background, genre, and purpose of the writing must be considered in interpretational matters.

is completely true (and therefore not false) A very important aspect of the definition is to evaluate inerrancy in terms of truthfulness and falseness rather than in terms of error or lack of error. This removes the issue from grammatical mistakes or lack of precision in reports. Inerrancy, on the one hand, must not be associated with strict tests of precision in which careless harmonization attempts to bring about a precision uncommon to the text itself.[64] On the other hand, we cannot shift the emphasis to such general and meaningless definitions as willful deceit for inerrancy and infallibility.[65] Recognizing that the issue is truthfulness confirms what many have inferred when declaring inerrancy an improper term to describe Scripture. But inerrancy, like inspiration, has become embedded in the theological literature, and it is best to emphasize careful definitions rather than to attempt to change terms, especially in the midst of the ongoing controversy over Scripture.

63. This is one of the real strengths of Pinnock's recent work, *Scripture Principle,* 197–202; also cf. Radmacher and Preus, eds., *Inerrancy and Hermeneutics;* Carson and Woodbridge, eds., *Hermeneutics, Authority, and Canon.* It is for this reason (discussions of inerrancy are inseparable from hermeneutical issues) that several chapters in this volume are devoted to hermeneutical concerns.

64. It seems to me that Harold Lindsell's undue concern for excessive harmonization in *The Battle for the Bible,* 174–76, *hints* at an understanding of inerrancy in terms of extreme precision, even though he does not necessarily define inerrancy in such terms.

65. Rogers and McKim, *Authority and Interpretation,* 111, while not affirming inerrancy, but acknowledging infallibility, nevertheless, define their confession about the nature of Scripture in terms of a lack of willful deception. This is hardly an acceptable definition, for it says nothing about the essence of Scripture, but is only a very general statement about Scripture's intent. The weaknesses of the definition and the historiography behind it are ably discussed in John D. Woodbridge, *Biblical Authority,* 27–28.

in all areas The definition states that inerrancy is not limited merely to "religious" matters, thus creating, or at least providing the framework for, an improper dualism. We want to affirm that inerrancy applies to all areas of knowledge, since all truth is God's truth. Yet issues of history and science must be evaluated in light of the communicative means at the time of inscripturation. Modern canons of science and historiography and its concern for precision are not proper standards for first-century (and before) authors. These matters must be analyzed in light of the author's intended level of precision, which most likely should be seen in terms of phenomenological observation.

In light of this brief commentary upon our definition, we can maintain that inerrancy primarily points to theological and epistemological matters. In providing a statement about an inerrant Bible, we must be careful with "slippery-slope" theories or avoid them altogether. God can, and certainly does, overrule departure from orthodoxy, as church history bears testimony. We must avoid unnecessary associations with a literalistic, stilted hermeneutic, but we do not care to disassociate the issue from hermeneutics. It must be recognized that inerrancy is not a direct teaching in Scripture (although inspiration is a direct teaching) but is a direct implication and important corollary of a plenary, verbal, concursive view of inspiration.

We must seek a view of inerrancy that is consistent with the divine-human nature of Scripture. This means that the phenomena must be accounted for and Scripture's witness to itself and its divine character must be satisfied. Such an approach is not primarily dependent upon a correspondence view of truth, although many of the affirmations of Scripture can be verified. Most, if not all, of the theological and ethical statements lie outside the realm of verification, and thus a coherence view of truth is more encompassing and applicable for all of Scripture.[66] Realizing these issues, we can gladly confess that the Bible is a dependable, truthful, trustworthy, faithful, and thus inerrant, revelation of God to humanity.

---

66. John Jefferson Davis, *Theology Primer* (Grand Rapids: Baker, 1981), 20–21.

Conclusion

We saw in our previous sections that the Bible has a two-sided, divine-human nature. Equally, we observed that the Bible witnesses to its own divine character and inspiration. Divine inspiration should be understood as primarily referring to the final product, although we desire to avoid a conflict between the inspiration of the human authors of the text and the written text itself. But it is our conclusion that a view of inspiration limited to the human authors alone is insufficient.

While focusing on the product of inspiration—the inscripturated text—we do not want to ignore the purpose and process of inspiration. The purpose of inspiration is ultimately for salvific purposes, which, in its full understanding, includes teaching, reproof, correction and training in righteousness, so that believers can be equipped for service and good works. The process of inspiration is inclusive in the training and preparation of the authors, their research, and their use of witnesses. As a result we can posit that the Bible is simultaneously the Word of God and the words of men.

Having surveyed several approaches to the issue of inspiration, we noted that inspiration does not mean that God dictated all of Scripture, for this fails to account for the human activity. Neither can it be affirmed that the Bible is only a human book, whose authors, due to special spiritual sensitivity, produced inspiring works of literature. Not only must inspiration recognize the human authorship and the divine character of Scripture, but it must not divorce God's deeds from his words. Neither must we create dichotomies between thoughts and words, processes and product, writers and written word, God's initiating impulse and his complete superintending work. A plenary view is essential. This view affirms that inspiration applies to all of canonical Scripture (including the process, the purpose, and ultimately the product) and asserts that by the concursive action of God the Scriptures are, in their entirety, both the work of the Spirit and the work of human authors. Such a view of inspiration is not only plausible, but necessarily important for affirmations of truth. We believe that a plenary, verbal, inclusive view of inspiration alone does justice to the theological teachings and the phenomena within the text.

We examined these temporary conclusions in light of the

human authorship of the Bible. We recognized that a concursive view of inspiration accounted for the style, personality, background, and context of the human authors. We noted the possibility of confessing a concursive view because the human authors were not autonomous but were men of faith, functioning in communities of faith with an awareness of God's direction in their lives. Consistent with our view of the genuine humanness of the text is the need to notice the cultural-temporal factors involved in the issue. But recognition that the writers were bearers of the image of God opens up the possibility to qualify historical and cultural distance. This is due to the belief that they, along with their readers, had memories of the past, consideration of the present, and expectations of the future. This allows for the possibility of cross-cultural and cross-temporal communication. The reality of human authorship is evidenced by the variety of emphases in Scripture, the different writing styles, and the development within the Testaments and the writers themselves. It is our conclusion that this variety is complementary and not contradictory. Overarching the variety of Scripture is a genuine unity that is not forced upon the text but is present as a result of divine inspiration.

We have already noted the very real plausibility of maintaining the normative character of Scripture, while simultaneously affirming the historical situation of the human authors and the time-relatedness of the text. Because of basic needs shared by men and women of all ages and races in all times and cultures, the central message of Scripture can speak in a normative and authoritative way. Beyond this, we acknowledged that Scripture speaks not just to pietistic and religious needs but to the truth of and about God, and to the ramifications affecting all matters related to life and godliness. We saw that such a normative Scripture can be described as inerrant when inerrancy is carefully defined to avoid overstatement or improper association with a dictation view of inspiration. We believe, therefore, it is quite probable, even epistemologically necessary, that in the latter part of the twentieth century, we can carefully articulate a statement concerning Scripture that maintains with equal force both the humanity and deity of the Bible and, beyond articulation, commit ourselves to it by placing our trust and confidence in the truthful, trustworthy, and reliable Word of God.

2

Inerrancy as a Principle of Biblical Hermeneutics
Duane A. Garrett

*H**ermeneutics* is the term Christian scholars use to describe the methods and procedures of interpreting the Bible. In many ways, biblical hermeneutics is no different from any other form of literary criticism, for the biblical critic must ask many of the same questions and use many of the same tools as a critic of any other body of literature. For example: What is the genre of the text—legal, narrative, lyric, reflective discourse, or epistolary? If narrative, does the narrator participate in the action (first person), or is he detached from it (third person)? Also, if the original language of the text is not the native tongue of the critic, he must master the grammar and idiom of that language for his interpretations to have any real authority. He must also know something of the world out of which the text came. What were its cultural values and institutions, and what were the technical terms for these institutions? Was the text written in a time of political or historical crisis? Similarly, the critic must try to retain an awareness of his own cultural and historical situation. He cannot cancel out his own frame of reference (and indeed the ques-

45

tions he brings may discover new dimensions in the text), but he must guard against a bias that may cause him to pervert the meaning of a passage. Certainly the interpreter must not make his own values normative over the text.[1]

For all these similarities, however, the relationship between the Christian and his Bible is in one way profoundly different from the relationship between the literary critic and whatever text he happens to be studying. The Christian comes to the Bible with a commitment of faith in the God from whom, he believes, the Bible came. He studies the Bible, not primarily for pleasure or even "enlightenment," but for a direct word of instruction, admonition, or comfort from God. And this is especially true of Baptists because we, to a degree greater than many of our brothers and sisters in other Protestant groups, have consciously rejected the authority of ecclesiastical traditions and formulas and have tried to make Scripture our only rule of faith and practice.

How should this different perspective and purpose affect our hermeneutics? In what way should our method of interpretation differ from that of the secular critic? Simply put, the difference is that we approach the Bible with the presupposition that it is true. This presupposition is now commonly called the belief in the inerrancy of Scripture. The term *inerrancy* offends some and is said to be negative and divisive.[2] It is, of course, unfortunate that it is not enough to say simply that the Bible is true and authoritative; but in the present climate, in which the meanings of these words are not always clear, it is necessary to be as precise as possible. The word *inerrancy* therefore means full confidence in the trustworthiness of the Bible and is not used here for either polemic or schismatic purposes. Adherence to inerrancy is important, however, because it requires the believer to submit himself to the authority of the text and does not allow him the option of rejecting any of its teachings as erroneous.

One may note that the concept of inerrancy can be described

1. See D. A. Carson, "Recent Developments in the Doctrine of Scripture," in *Hermeneutics, Authority, and Canon*, ed. D. A. Carson and John D. Woodbridge (Grand Rapids: Zondervan, 1986), 41–42. Carson wisely warns against the recent trend in which interpreters give Scripture a feminist reading, a liberation theology reading, etc. The danger is that the reader will place a grid over the text.
2. Russell H. Dilday, Jr., *The Doctrine of Biblical Authority* (Nashville: Convention Press, 1982), 99; Clark Pinnock, "Three Views of the Bible in Contemporary Theology," in *Biblical Authority*, ed. Jack B. Rogers (Waco: Word, 1977), 67.

in two ways. One approach is from the perspective of the text it-self: The text of the Bible contains no errors. Another approach is from the perspective of the interpreter: The Christian must come to the text with the presupposition that it is true and the willing-ness to submit to it. Obviously, these two concepts are comple-mentary. It is utterly futile to approach the text with full confidence that it is all true if in fact it contains errors. The focus of this study, however, will be on the latter concept—the attitude the Christian interpreter should bring to the Bible.

The Bible and Authority

The assertion that inerrancy is a necessary rule of biblical hermeneutics is built upon certain presuppositions, all of which are hotly debated, but will not be discussed here in detail. The first of these is that the Bible is specially inspired by God and therefore has authority over the church.[3] The second is that this assertion of biblical authority is in accord with Scripture's de-scription of itself.[4] The third is that the sixty-six books of the Bible form the complete canon for the church. The early church properly received as canonical the Hebrew Scriptures and recog-nized as canonical the books of the New Testament.[5]

But is inerrancy the only approach to the Bible that main-tains biblical authority? Many assert that other formulas better describe the position the Christian should take vis-à-vis the Bible. For example, one approach is to assert that the Bible, while inerrant in its theological statements, contains factual and historical errors. This view affirms that in the Bible God has given us accurate doctrine, while it maintains that he has ac-commodated himself to human error and limitation. In doing this, however, it introduces a Kantian distinction between his-torical, scientific truth and theological belief that is utterly alien to biblical thought. The French Baptist scholar Henri Blocher re-

3. Assertions that inerrancy implies a dictation theory or a docetic Bible are properly questions about inspiration, not hermeneutics, and therefore are not discussed in this chapter.

4. Cf. Wayne A. Grudem, "Scripture's Self-Attestation and the Problem of Formulating a Doctrine of Scripture," in *Scripture and Truth,* ed. D. A. Carson and John D. Woodbridge (Grand Rapids: Zondervan, 1983), 19–59.

5. See David G. Dunbar, "The Biblical Canon," in *Hermeneutics, Authority, and Canon,* ed. D. A. Carson and John D. Woodbridge, 299–360.

fers to this approach as "fideism" and comments, "To oppose 'doctrine' and (factual) 'history' is to forget that biblical doctrine is first of all history."[6] This view, which bifurcates reality into the two realms of concrete, historical fact and esoteric, spiritual faith, is more at home in Buddhism or Manichaeism than in Christianity. Moreoever, its implications reach beyond mere historical fact. It renders theology both pliable (because doctrine that is only otherworldly has no basis on which to defend its claim to being absolute and exclusive truth) and irrelevant (because it has surrendered its point of contact with this world). Finally, a theology that so separates history from itself endangers the supreme historical and theological event of the Christian faith, the crucifixion and resurrection of Jesus. It has difficulty in ascertaining the theological significance of the death of Jesus for human guilt and forgiveness, and it cannot, with an easy conscience, confess the historical reality of Jesus' physical resurrection. But as Paul has said, without the resurrection Christianity is utterly devoid of power and significance (1 Cor. 15:12–18).

A second possible approach is to contend that the Bible contains the revelation of God or that it is the human record of the revelation of God. This view, which contrasts with the conservative assertion that the Bible *is* the Word of God, rather than *contains* it, is the approach championed by many followers of traditional historical-critical method. On the surface it appears strongly orthodox. What it means, however, is that the writers of Scripture recorded the fact that God spoke to them and that he acted for their salvation, but in the process of recording all this, they naturally intermingled their own ideas and interpretations with the original revelation of God. Moreover, subsequent interpolations by later editors of the books of the Bible further confused the matter. What we are left with in the Bible is a canon within the canon. Critical scholarship once claimed for itself the task of discovering this true, divine core beneath the errant, human husk, but that quest has now largely been abandoned as an acknowledged failure.

Although the terminology has somewhat changed, nevertheless, the fundamental perspective on Scripture is still one of allowing the interpreter to sift the material in the Bible and decide

6. Henri Blocher, *In The Beginning*, trans. David G. Preston (Downers Grove: InterVarsity, 1984), 24.

for himself what is normative and what is not. Hence, a true concept of authority has been jettisoned, and the reader is again master of the text. It is not surprising that many followers of this approach have difficulty in formulating a coherent statement on the nature of biblical authority.[7]

Another possible approach to Scripture is to assert that it is infallible in its purpose (i.e., to declare Christ). It does not fail to call man to Christ and demand a faithful response. A corollary of this is the assertion that the authority of the Bible rests on its effect on humanity and in particular on the believing community.[8] Biblical narrative, for example, is said to derive its authority from its ability to entice the reader into its world, shatter the reader's previous frame of reference, and bring him to acknowledge the new world of the kingdom of God.[9]

Pious as this approach may appear, it makes no significant statement and contains a redundancy. To assert that the Bible is infallible in fulfilling its purpose says no more than claiming that a book of American history is infallible in fulfilling its purpose (i.e., to describe American history). The book may have errors and omissions, but no one can deny that it describes American history. It is, after all, a history book and not a cookbook. And if it is well written, moves toward a carefully defined thesis, and contains logically compelling arguments, it will force the reader to rethink some of the old ways in which he may have looked at American history and restructure his political and historical frame of reference. Similarly, to say that the Bible is unfailing in its purpose to tell man about God and Christ says nothing more than that the Bible is a book about God and Christ. This hardly makes for a confession of faith. And to make the authority of the Bible dependent on how it inspires believers once again removes authority from the Scripture and places it in the mind (or feelings) of the believer. To assert that the stories of the Bible challenge the reader and force him to rethink his relationship with God actually may affirm nothing more than that the Bible is well written. Certainly the Bible tells the reader of his

7. Cf. Dunbar's critique of James Barr in "The Biblical Canon," in *Hermeneutics, Authority, and Canon,* ed. D. A. Carson and John D. Woodbridge, 345–48.

8. Paul J. Achtemeier, *The Inspiration of Scripture* (Philadelphia: Westminster, 1980), 159–60.

9. David L. Bartlett, *The Shape of Scriptural Authority* (Philadelphia: Fortress, 1983), 78.

need for Christ, and the reader, especially the believer, can feel its power. But that is only a testimony to, not the basis of, its authority.

Nor will it do to suggest that the Bible is authoritative because the Holy Spirit uses it in a special way. This approach says that the Bible becomes the Word of God as the Spirit uses it to speak to the reader and is especially associated with the neoorthodoxy of Karl Barth. Barth repeatedly stresses the central and unique place of authority the Bible holds in the church, and as Geoffrey Bromiley says, Barth's insistence on the role of the Spirit in empowering the written Word is laudable because it reminds us that God is present and working among us and that he has not abandoned us with nothing but a dead letter.[10] Nevertheless, to cite Bromiley directly, "Barth's dismissal of biblical inerrancy and his assigning of a special historical character to events like the Resurrection pose the question whether the biblical books can really enjoy the status of direct, absolute, material authority, except by a sacrifice of the intellect, if they do in fact contain demonstrably incorrect statements or tell of events that do not meet the test of normal historical verifiability."[11] More than that, Barth's position implies that revelation does not include rational communication, and, in Carl F. H. Henry's words, it "postulates a nebulous revelation behind the Bible."[12] These presuppositions are disastrous for the Christian faith because they render impossible the task of enunciating a theology that is in any meaningful sense authoritative.

In recent years another approach to the Bible, canon criticism, has been championed by Brevard S. Childs as an alternative means of maintaining biblical authority. In order to appreciate Child's position, one must know something of the position of modern biblical scholarship. Critical scholars, for the last one hundred years, have asserted that the books of the Old Testament contain numerous, and sometimes contradictory, theologi-

10. Geoffrey W. Bromiley, "The Authority of Scripture in Karl Barth," in *Hermeneutics, Authority, and Canon,* ed. D. A. Carson and John D. Woodbridge, 292–93.

11. Ibid., 291.

12. Carl F. H. Henry, *God, Revelation, and Authority* (Waco: Word, 1979), 4:199.

cal traditions. The historical accuracy of the Old Testament has been greatly discounted. This approach has naturally diminished the authority of the Bible in the eyes of many.

Childs seeks to avoid both the doctrine of inerrancy and the spiritual Death Valley of radical criticism. He explicitly accepts the major conclusions of historical criticism; for example, he considers the Documentary Hypothesis[13] to be a proper tool for explaining the origins of Genesis.[14] Nevertheless, he maintains that the proper area for Christian theological reflection and exegesis is not in the diverse fragments and strands discovered by higher criticism but in the canonical form of the Bible as we have it. In his discussion of Genesis, therefore, he gives considerable attention to the meaning of the book as it stands. He notes, for example, the importance of the theme of promise in Genesis and also observes that the whole book is structured around the phrase "These are the generations of . . ."[15] This is radically different from previous historical-critical exegesis, which, for example, concentrated on distinguishing the theology of the "Yahwist" from that of the "Priestly Document" and on describing the histories of the traditions behind the present text. Childs is to be commended for recognizing that theology must be done from the Bible we possess and not from hypothetical documents, and his numerous books are replete with profound insights and reflect massive learning. Nevertheless, his synthesis is not a success.[16] Acceptance of the Bible as a collection of myriad traditions of both doubtful historical value and contradictory theological perspective inevitably deprives it of canonical authority. James Barr, who also accepts higher critical theories about the origin of

13. A theory asserting that the Pentateuch is composed of materials from four different traditions, generally called JEDP. The theory implies that the Pentateuch is sometimes self-contradictory and, in its final form, a very late and historically inaccurate piece of literature.

14. Brevard S. Childs, *Introduction to the Old Testament as Scripture* (Philadelphia: Fortress, 1979), 140–50.

15. Ibid., 145–53.

16. Many critical scholars, no less than conservatives, have not found his arguments compelling. Cf. the *Journal for the Study of the Old Testament* 16 (May 1980), which is entirely devoted to responses to Childs. Cf. also Walter Harrelson, "Review of *Introduction to the Old Testament as Scripture,* by Brevard Childs," *Journal of Biblical Literature* 100 (March 1981): 99–103.

the Bible but allows no exaltation of the concept of canon, especially as applied to our present Bible, is more consistent here.[17]

Therefore, we can urge that no approach to the Bible that allows for inaccuracies and contradictions in the text can meet the fundamental requirement of biblical authority—enabling the reader to hear the voice of God. It is all well and good, however, for us to assert that only inerrancy allows us to stand under the authority of the Word of God, but what if inerrancy itself is a meaningless concept? Or what if it is so contradicted by brute facts as to be utterly untenable? It is to these questions we now turn.

Objections to Inerrancy

Perhaps the most frequently voiced complaint against inerrancy is that it dies the death of a thousand qualifications.[18] That is, the evangelical claims to believe that the Bible is without error, but when pressed, he so redefines, qualifies, and reformulates his position that his diluted doctrine of inerrancy becomes void.

One such qualification, frequently mentioned by moderates as rendering the notion of inerrancy meaningless, is that it refers only to the *Urtext,* that is, to the original copies of books of the Bible. Thus Paul J. Achtemeier wonders what the point is in claiming inerrancy for a book that no longer exists.[19] A similar position is voiced by William E. Hull in *The Baptist Program.*[20] A moment's reflection, however, reveals that conservatives are holding a position that is neither irrational nor absurd. The original copies of the books of the Bible were hand-copied thousands of times over. How could anyone possibly claim that inerrancy extends to all the variant copies of Scripture? The logical conclusion of such a formulation would be that every time someone copies a passage out of the Bible, that copy must be inerrant. Nor is it reasonable to assert that if God really cared about the inerrant original manuscripts, he would have preserved them. One

17. James Barr, *Escaping from Fundamentalism* (London: SCM, 1984), 41–50.

18. E.g., Pinnock, "Three Views," in *Biblical Authority,* ed. Jack B. Rogers, 64–65.

19. Achtemeier, *Inspiration of Scripture,* 52.

20. William E. Hull, "Shall We Call the Bible Infallible?" *The Baptist Program,* Dec. 1970, 17.

may just as well say that if God really cared about truth and Christian unity, he would never have allowed apostasy to enter the church. One cannot build a theology on prior assumptions about what God should have done.[21] Equally arbitrary is the assertion that a single textual tradition (e.g., that which underlies the KJV) preserved the true readings. But no inherent absurdity or improbability exists in the affirmation that God originally inspired his prophets and apostles in such a way that what they wrote was free from error and that the manuscripts and translations we now possess are a remarkably faithful (but not flawless) witness to the *Urtext*. Such a formula provides a rational basis for asserting that our present copies and translations of the Bible may be properly called the authoritative Word of God, while it includes the qualification that they may have errors of transmission and translation. This principle, we may note, is not a modern concoction but was recognized as early as the fourth century by John Chrysostom.[22]

This does not mean, however, that inerrancy as a hermeneutical principle refers only to the lost *Urtext*. Demonstrable scribal errors and alterations in the Bible are rare and do not affect its major teachings. The Hebrew Bible that has been preserved by the rabbis through the centuries is called the Masoretic Text. It is the basis for our modern translations of the Old Testament. The general reliability of the Masoretic Text has been amply demonstrated by the Dead Sea Scrolls,[23] and Old Testament textual critics are now far more hesitant to propose emendations than they once were.[24] Similarly, New Testament textual criticism attests to the great care with which ancient copyists handled the biblical documents[25] and gives us reason to believe that our present

21. Cf. Henry, *God, Revelation, and Authority* 4:241–42, for a discussion of this issue.

22. John Chrysostom, *De prophetarum obscuritate,* 2.2. Chrysostom is pointing out that the Septuagint is sometimes obscure because it is only a translation and not the original Hebrew.

23. Cf. IQIsa[a,b], the copies of Isaiah from Qumran, which lend considerable support to the Masoretic text tradition. Cf. John N. Oswalt, *The Book of Isaiah; Chapters 1–39* (Grand Rapids: Eerdmans, 1986), 29–31; and F. F. Bruce, *Second Thoughts on the Dead Sea Scrolls* (London: Paternoster, 1956), 61–62.

24. Cf. Ernst Würthwein, *The Text of the Old Testament,* trans. Erroll F. Rhodes (London: SCM, 1979), 113.

25. Jack Finegan, *Encountering New Testament Manuscripts* (Grand Rapids: Eerdmans, 1974), 55.

editions of the Greek New Testament are very close to the *Urtext*.
It should be noted that the wealth of good textual material available to New Testament scholars is the envy of classicists, who
must work with far inferior textual traditions. In contrast to the
thousands of manuscripts and fragments of the New Testament
that have survived from antiquity, major classical works (e.g.,
Caesar's *Commentaries*) only exist in a handful of copies.[26] And
as Achtemeier admits, conservatives, because of their desire to
work from a text that is as close as possible to the original, are
fully engaged in the tedious work of textual criticism.[27] Their appreciation for biblical authority has made them more careful as
scholars.

Most significant, however, is that conservatives do not use the
possibility of scribal error as a convenient escape hatch whenever they confront a problem passage. Difficulties are dealt with
as they stand and not shoved aside as textual corruptions.
Scribal error is invoked as the solution to a problem only where
solid textual evidence warrants it. Numbers and proper names
are especially likely to be corrupted in transmission. For example, the Masoretic Text indicates that 50,070 men of Beth She-
mesh were slain by God for looking into the ark of the covenant
(1 Sam. 6:19), but a number of Hebrew manuscripts say 70. The
larger number is probably an early corruption.[28] Inerrancy therefore is concerned with the Bible we possess; and textual criticism, standing as a natural and necessary corrective, is not
confined to lost originals.

Another qualification that occasionally meets criticism is
that inerrancy refers only to a text's intended meaning and not
necessarily to the words themselves as interpreted in their most
rigorously literal sense. The conservative insists that we must
recognize that biblical language is often either poetic or approximate, and that scientific precision is typically outside the biblical writer's purpose and cultural norms of truth. When the
conservative speaks of authorial intent, therefore, he is asserting that the biblical authors had freedom to use approximate

26. Cf. F. F. Bruce, *The New Testament Documents: Are They Reliable?*
(Grand Rapids: Eerdmans, 1960), 14–20.

27. Achtemeier, *Inspiration of Scripture*, 58.

28. Cf. also the apparent corruption in 1 Samuel 13:1, where Saul is said to
have reigned a mere two years.

and metaphoric language without bringing the charge of error upon themselves. To some, this is no more than another loophole for inerrancy. If the text as it stands seems to contain an obvious mistake, the conservative, so the argument goes, can always claim that the original author did not really mean for us to understand his words in that way. But again, the conservative can hardly be expected to disregard the matter of interpretation in his defense of the Bible. If the variety of the usage of language in Scripture and the need to discern the author's intended meaning cannot be taken into account, the only alternative is to insist that the Bible is true even when it has been misinterpreted! Certainly, no one can, or does, hold this position.[29]

Another criticism against inerrancy is that it has no real meaning for a great deal of the Bible, since many of its statements (e.g., "Rejoice in the Lord") cannot properly be called true or false. They are commands, not assertions.[30] D. A. Carson's reply is to the point: "Inerrancy does not mean that every conceivable sequence of linguistic data in the Bible must be susceptible to the term 'inerrant,' only that no errant assertion occurs."[31] More than that, inerrancy can be applied in a certain way even to commands. Recognition of the authority of the Bible implies acceptance of its commands as valid, binding (if one is in the command's target group), and morally proper.

A recent argument that seeks to falsify the concept of inerrancy on the basis of hermeneutics and epistemology emphasizes the problem of communicating across the ages and through cultural barriers.[32] How can we assert that a document written in an ancient culture by men with radically different presuppositions from our own communicates inerrant truth to us? It is undeniable that the mental framework of the modern man is very different from that of the ancient Semite. Similarly, the perspectives of the medieval Christian, the African, and the Chinese peasant are distinct, and these differences greatly increase the

29. Even the most rigid fundamentalists recognize that the Bible is not a history or science textbook. Cf. Moises Silva, "The Place of Historical Reconstruction in New Testament Criticism," in *Hermeneutics, Authority, and Canon,* ed. D. A. Carson and John D. Woodbridge, 109.

30. Dilday, *Biblical Authority,* 99.

31. Carson, "Recent Developments," in *Hermeneutics, Authority, and Canon,* ed. D. A. Carson and John D. Woodbridge, 31.

32. Achtemeier, *Inspiration of Scripture,* 95–98.

dangers of misinterpretation, but they do not make communication impossible. Carson notes that every human being has, to some extent, a distinct perspective on the world and that this argument, if pushed hard, eliminates the possibility of universal truth.[33] After all, no two people hold to concepts that are in all points exactly identical. Nevertheless, Christians believe that absolute truth both exists and can be communicated. Cultural and conceptual differences indicate that we must do careful research in our exegesis, but they do not invalidate the task itself.

Some scholars have also attacked the methods by which conservatives have tried to resolve various historical and theological problems in the Bible.[34] In particular, harmonization and the appeal to *sensus plenior* strike many critics as desperate and disgraceful moves by conservatives to acquit obviously guilty passages of the charge of error. Occasionally, the arguments of conservatives have deserved the scorn of their critics, and one can still find examples of obviously forced solutions to problems in some conservative literature.[35] Recent evangelical literature, however, has been characterized more by painstaking, honest analysis of all available data and thorough argumentation than by grasping at straws.[36] More frequently, it is now the critics who jump to the easy conclusion that every problem in Scripture represents an error or contradiction.

Craig L. Blomberg has recently given special attention to the question of harmonization.[37] Blomberg distinguishes between harmonization in the broad sense, which is simply an attempt to resolve an apparent contradiction, and harmonization in a nar-

33. Carson, "Recent Developments," in *Hermeneutics, Authority, and Canon,* ed. D. A. Carson and John D. Woodbridge, 40.

34. E.g., James Barr, *Fundamentalism* (Philadelphia: Westminster, 1978), 55–61; and idem, *Escaping from Fundamentalism,* 66–76; Achtemeier, *Inspiration of Scripture,* 66–69.

35. Cf. Harold Lindsell's widely criticized harmonization of the accounts of Peter's denial of Jesus in *The Battle for the Bible* (Grand Rapids: Zondervan, 1976), 174–76. Lindsell has Peter denying Jesus six times!

36. An excellent example of conservative research into a historical problem in the Bible is in John W. Wenham's *Easter Enigma* (Grand Rapids: Zondervan, 1984). Wenham deals with the apparent contradictions in the resurrection accounts, and his reconstruction of the events is highly plausible.

37. Craig L. Blomberg, "The Legitimacy and Limits of Harmonization," in *Hermeneutics, Authority, and Canon,* ed. D. A. Carson and John D. Woodbridge, 139–74.

row sense. The latter explains a contradiction by claiming either that a similar event happened more than once or that different narratives give partial, but not contradictory, accounts of a single event.[38] For example, Matthew says that Jesus and his family went to Nazareth after their time in Egypt to avoid living under Archelaus of Judea, whereas Luke says nothing about the flight to Egypt and indicates that the holy family simply returned to Nazareth sometime after Jesus' birth because that was where their home was. Harmonization resolves this by asserting that Jesus' family did indeed have a home in Nazareth and that they did flee to Egypt, but that Matthew and Luke each give only part of the story.

It is harmonization in this narrower sense that critics most frequently lampoon. Blomberg points out, however, that conservative scholars need to employ this stricter type of harmonization only in a minority of cases. Working primarily with historical problems in the synoptic Gospels, Blomberg shows eight different methods by which apparent contradictions are reasonably resolved. He uses tools that evangelicals have long employed, such as textual criticism (showing that an offending text has been improperly transmitted), linguistics (showing that certain words, clauses, or sentences have been misinterpreted), and historical context (showing that an apparent error in the text merely reflects our limited knowledge of the writer's historical situation).[39] But he also shows the value of certain approaches that evangelicals have been hesitant to follow. He asserts that form criticism, with its assumption that an oral tradition stands behind the written Gospels as we now have them, often provides us with the most reasonable solution to a problem. Oral tradition tends to streamline narratives with the result that one account leaves out details that appear in another. In this way he explains Matthew's omission of the Jewish embassy who interceded with Jesus on behalf of a Roman centurion.[40] Not all conservatives will agree with all of the form-critical solutions Blomberg offers,[41] but it is clear that in proclaiming the stories of Jesus in the early church, the apostles would naturally abbreviate and

38. Ibid., 144.
39. Ibid., 145–51.
40. Ibid., 152.
41. Cf. especially his analysis of Matthew 17:27, in ibid., 152–53.

omit detail, and that this in no way impugns their integrity or memory.

Following J. A. Baird, Blomberg also recommends a somewhat new approach—audience criticism. This method asserts that we must take seriously statements in the Gospels about the original audiences to whom Jesus spoke. It indicates that some passages appearing to be parallels are actually accounts of two different events.[42] For example, the two "versions" of the parable of the talents (Matt. 25:14–30; Luke 19:11–27) are not parallel versions at all but distinct presentations by Jesus of similar parables.[43] It is incontestable that Jesus, in his itinerant ministry, would have used similar sermon material many times, and naturally he must have varied the content and point of his illustrations from audience to audience. Therefore many form-critical attempts to demonstrate how the early church applied and transformed the primitive sayings of Jesus are fundamentally misguided.

Blomberg also asserts that evangelical scholars can make use of redaction criticism to defend the Bible. Here, too, many conservatives will want to be more cautious. Nevertheless, Blomberg has rightly pointed out that by observing an evangelist's apparent literary motives, we can solve a number of problems. Chronological problems, for example, sometimes disappear when we recognize that a writer does not always arrange his material chronologically; the sequence of events he presents may reflect a literary and theological purpose.[44]

Finally, Blomberg asserts that in some passages harmonization in the narrower sense is perfectly legitimate. For example, the question of whether Jesus was tried by the Sanhedrin in the night (Mark 14:53–65) or in the day (Luke 22:66–71) is resolved by assuming that Jesus was given more than one hearing, the first in the early, dark hours of the morning.[45] And he points out that harmonization is by no means the unique domain of conservative biblical scholars. Observing that the historians

---

42. Ibid., 142.

43. Craig L. Blomberg, "When Is a Parallel Really a Parallel?" *Westminster Theological Journal* 46 (1984): 91–96.

44. Cf. Blomberg's analysis of the chronological problem surrounding the conversion of Zacchaeus, "Legitimacy," in *Hermeneutics, Authority, and Canon,* ed. D. A. Carson and John D. Woodbridge, 157.

45. Ibid., 160.

A. B. Bosworth and P. A. Brunt have used harmonization to re-solve problems between Arrian's and Plutarch's respective his-tories of Alexander the Great, Blomberg aptly comments, "Here are two expert, contemporary classicists putting forward the very type of harmonizations that most biblical critics would re-ject out of hand if they came from Evangelicals."[46] Baptist scholars, we might note, have long been engaged in biblical re-search of this sort. In 1886, for example, John Broadus explained the apparent conflict between Matthew 27:63, which places the resurrection "after three days," and Matthew 16:21, Luke 24:7, and 1 Corinthians 15:4, which speak of the resurrection taking place "on the third day." He noted that the confusion was seman-tic; the ancients counted inclusively, so that something which took place on the third day could be equally well described as having happened after three days.[47] All of this makes clear that harmonization, both in its broader and narrower sense, is not some cheap trick to save the Bible, but is both a legitimate and reasonable enterprise that enables the conservative to maintain with good reason the trustworthiness of the Bible.

Not all of the problems, however, are historical or scientific. Theological difficulties are at least as serious, if not more so. The exegete must deal with both apparent contradictions (does James, in contrast to Paul, preach a salvation by works?) and, a related matter, apparent offenses to Christian morality (does the Bible endorse slavery and polygamy?). Critics accuse con-servatives of being dishonest with the text not only in historical areas but in theological areas as well. Barr, for example, says that conservatives pick and choose what passages they consider to be theologically normative. He says evangelicals consider Acts 16:31 ("Believe on the Lord Jesus Christ"), not Mark 10:21 ("Sell everything you have . . . give to the poor . . . follow me"), to be the correct answer to give to one seeking eternal life.[48]

In dealing with these questions, evangelicals stress the need to be aware of the genre and historical context in which a prob-lem text occurs. The importance of the historical context of a passage of Scripture may be illustrated by considering four ap-

46. Ibid., 170.

47. John Broadus, *Commentary on the Gospel of Matthew* (Philadelphia: American Baptist, 1886), 582.

48. Barr, *Escaping from Fundamentalism,* 112–13.

parently distinct and contradictory answers in the New Testament to the question of what a person must do to be saved. In the
two passages cited above, it appears that salvation is alternately
said to be gained by faith in Christ (Acts 16:31) and by giving all
one's possessions to the poor (Mark 10:21). In Acts 2:38 Peter
seems to add the condition of baptism ("Repent and be baptized
. . ."), while James seems to require works of obedience (James
2:14–26). Are there four different gospels here?

The dilemma is most easily resolved by giving close attention
to the situation of the recipients of each message. The Jewish
crowd who stood before Peter on Pentecost certainly knew of the
preaching and baptizing ministries of John and Jesus. They
knew that both had preached a message of repentance and acceptance of the coming kingdom of God and that baptism was the
sign of submission to their messages. More than that, they knew
that accepting baptism meant publicly joining the Christians
and turning their backs on the Pharisees. In this context, "Repent and be baptized" is virtually a hendiadys, and no sacramen-
tal requirement for salvation is implied. For the Roman jailer of
Acts 16, however, the ritual of baptism implied nothing about
faith and repentance. He was terrified by the events of the night
but deeply moved by Paul's faith and compassion. In the simplest
possible terms, Paul told him how to be free of fear and enter
God's kingdom: Believe in Christ. Only afterward did Paul explain the Christian practice of baptism (vv. 32–33).

The case of the rich young man who came to Jesus was
entirely different. Here was a man who, to all appearances,
believed himself sinless (Mark 10:19–20). Jesus' reply to his
inquiry indicates the severity of the demands of God—more than
just not breaking the law, God requires total renunciation of self-
ish concerns and absolute devotion to his service. It is important
to see that the man had not sought salvation or forgiveness (for
which he apparently felt no need), but the way to earn eternal life
(v. 17), and that Jesus answered this question. Evangelicals may
sometimes rightly be criticized for not giving due emphasis to
the cost of discipleship, but contrary to Barr, they are correct
in seeing faith in Christ, and not righteous deeds, as the way to
salvation.

Finally, the church to which James wrote had apparently
adopted a very casual view of sin. They were attributing their
temptations to God (James 1:13), were full of gossip and slander

(1:26; 3:1–12), and were obsequious to the rich but cruel to the poor (1:27; 2:1–7,16; 5:1–6). They arrogantly considered themselves to be in possession of a higher wisdom (3:13–18) and possibly tolerated adultery in the fellowship (1:21; 2:11). Therefore, James is telling them that their "faith" is no faith at all, but a lie. He is not, however, recommending a soteriology of works. In each of the above four passages, consideration of historical background is critical for theological exegesis.

Ecclesiastes 7:16–18 illustrates the importance of genre in interpreting a difficult passage. It reads: "Do not be overrighteous, do not be overwise; why destroy yourself? Do not be wicked excessively, and do not be a fool. Why die before your time? It is good that you hold to this and not let go of that, for the one who fears God escapes both of them."[49] Did not Jesus say that we are to strive for the perfection of God himself (Matt. 5:48)? Many interpreters say that Ecclesiastes 7:16–18 recommends a life of moderation[50] and implies that a little sin will not hurt.[51] Walter C. Kaiser, Jr., replies that the Hebrew of verse 16 means "Do not be wise in your own eyes" and therefore argues that Ecclesiastes is attacking a self-righteous spirit,[52] but his translation is unlikely.[53]

The verse must be understood in the genre and context of the book. In the world of wisdom, two polar opposites exist: wisdom and folly. The former refers to following a path of self-restraint and right behavior, and the latter refers to a life of self-indulgence and pleasure seeking. The former is said to lead to prosperity and life, the latter to poverty and death. But it is critical to see that the goal of wisdom is not justification before God or forgiveness of sin but a prosperous, happy life.

Ecclesiastes rebuts treating proverbs that are only general-

49. Translation mine. On the translation of verse 18b, cf. Michael A. Eaton, *Ecclesiastes: An Introduction and Commentary* (Downers Grove: InterVarsity, 1983), 114 n.2; Robert Gordis, *Koheleth, The Man and His Word: A Study of Ecclesiastes* (New York: Schocken, 1951), 277–78; and Charles F. Whitley, *Koheleth: His Language and Thought* (Berlin: Walter de Gruyter, 1979), 67. Cf. also the Vulgate.

50. E.g., R. B. Y. Scott, *Ecclesiastes* (New York: Doubleday, 1965), 237. Cf. also the NIV.

51. George Aaron Barton, *Ecclesiastes* (Edinburgh: T and T Clark, 1908), 144.

52. Walter C. Kaiser, Jr., *Ecclesiastes: Total Life* (Chicago: Moody, 1979), 86.

53. Cf. Gordis, *Koheleth,* 277.

izations as invariable absolutes. It shatters the view that a life of wisdom and the regular observance of religious ceremony (cf. 8:14; 9:2) guarantees good fortune, affluence, and happiness. The book recognizes the importance and value of wisdom but also sees its limitations (2:12–16). In this passage the terms *righteous* and *wicked* do not refer to theological concepts of sin but to wisdom and folly.[54] The text rejects the view that one can use moral behavior to seize prosperity or force God to bless and protect, a view that is self-destructive because it is bound to be disappointing. It insists that God is sovereign and dispenses his benefits according to his own will (9:1). This view anticipates the New Testament concept of grace. Also, verse 17 does not recommend a little sinning but does encourage the reader to allow for "folly" in the sense of enjoying the good things of life. Among these are the pleasures of friendship (4:8–12), food, clothes, marriage, and work (9:7–10). The reader is exhorted to both follow the teachings of wisdom and enjoy the good things of life (v. 18). A similar thought is found in Ecclesiastes 4:5–6, where two apparently contradictory proverbs are juxtaposed. The first indicates that the fool "consumes his own flesh" by laziness. In other words, he falls into poverty. The second says that one handful of contentment is better than two fistfuls of labor and trying to catch the wind. In other words, it is better to have a little and be content than to have great wealth at the expense of a life of endless work and frustration. Both proverbs are true. The one who fears God will neither be a lazy fool ("overly wicked") or a slave to hard work ("overly righteous").

In this sense, Ecclesiastes may be said to reject practical asceticism. Just as Paul exhorts his readers to a life of faith and not works of the Law, so Ecclesiastes encourages the reader to place fear of God above the promises of wisdom (7:18; cf. 12:13–14). "The one who fears God," like the New Testament believer, recognizes that since God is sovereign, his favor and protection are freely given; they cannot be grasped. Like God, the believer too has become free. The teachings of wisdom keep him away from self-destructive patterns, but at the same time his recognition of his dependence on God frees him to rejoice in the good things he has received, since he does not live in fear that any relaxation

---

54. Cf. J. A. Loader, *Polar Structures in the Book of Qoheleth* (Berlin: Walter de Gruyter, 1979), 47–48.

and enjoyment of life will inflict calamity on himself. J. A. Loader's assessment is to the point: "He who fears God is the one who escapes both the danger of seeking welfare in the practice of wisdom and the danger of indulging in folly."[55] The passage rejects legalism but does not recommend immorality. The "moderation" recommended here is not the Greek ideal ("Nothing in excess") but is in accord with biblical teaching on the value of wisdom and on the sovereignty and grace of God.

The teaching of Jesus that we must be perfect, however, falls within a different context and genre. In the Sermon on the Mount, Jesus is teaching his audience about the standards God uses in judging humans. He is, in effect, giving the Law of God in its purest form. Anyone who would dare claim himself to be righteous before God must be completely free from sin in both action and thought (Matt. 5:17–48). He reveals how deeply sin has penetrated the human psyche and shows how far we are from being able to gain God's favor apart from an act of grace and mercy, even as he also gives us a practical standard by which we live and judge ourselves. Here, the question is, not How do I obtain a prosperous and happy life? but What does God require of me? The two passages seek to answer two entirely different questions, but their answers contain no real contradictions. Even the most difficult theological problems, like the historical problems of which Blomberg speaks, can be resolved if the interpreter continues to work patiently with the text and does not simply assert the Bible to be self-contradictory.

Another major problem is the use of the Old Testament in the New. As Douglas J. Moo comments in his penetrating article on the subject of *sensus plenior*,[56] the appearance that the New Testament writers fundamentally misunderstood the meanings of certain Old Testament passages creates a "potentially legitimate objection to the inerrancy of Scripture."[57] Moo asserts that such apparent misinterpretations of the Old Testament in the New can be explained in several ways. For example, a New Testament writer's casual citation of an Old Testament text may not be intended as a definitive interpretation,[58] nor is his moral applica-

---

55. Ibid., 48.

56. Literally, "fuller meaning."

57. Douglas J. Moo, "The Problem of *Sensus Plenior*," in *Hermeneutics, Authority, and Canon*, ed. D. A. Carson and John D. Woodbridge, 186.

58. Ibid., 188–89.

tion of a passage necessarily meant as definitive exegesis.[59] But Moo also contends that we must take the possibility of *sensus plenior* seriously. That is, the Spirit who inspired the prophets may have intended more than the prophets themselves realized. After the revelation of God in Christ, the church realized the deeper, fuller meanings pregnant in various Old Testament passages. Moo is aware of the various objections to this view, and he deals with each in detail.[60]

Two other ways of dealing with the relationship between the Testaments deserve mention (Moo is aware of both): theological exegesis typified by Walter C. Kaiser, Jr.,[61] and typological exegesis. The use of Hosea 11:1 in Matthew 2:15 serves as a helpful test case.

Hosea 11:1 reads, "When Israel was a child I loved him, and out of Egypt I called my son." At first reading, the text seems to be no more than a retrospective look at the Exodus event. Matthew 2:15, however, takes the verse as a prediction of Jesus' childhood sojourn in Egypt. Barr therefore asserts that Matthew has ignored the context of Hosea 11:1 and, like other first-century sectarian Jewish groups, has interpreted the passage according to chauvinistic principles of hermeneutics.[62] But Kaiser, who believes that the New Testament writers understood and adhered to the original meanings of the Old Testament passages they cited, interprets the problem in an altogether different way. He argues that Hosea's choice of the word *son* is particularly significant. It looks back to the designation of Israel as God's son in Exodus 4:22–23 and to the Davidic-messianic use of the word in 2 Samuel 7:14 (see also Ps. 2:7; Prov. 30:4).[63] Furthermore, he believes that the point of Hosea 11:1 is to testify to God's covenantal, preserving love. He then argues that Matthew's citation emphasizes more the concept of God's preservation of his "son" in a time of oppression than the geographical location of Egypt and that therefore he used the verse in exactly the sense as Hosea himself did.[64] Kaiser has made a valuable contribution here, but

59. Ibid., 189–90.

60. Ibid., 201–11.

61. Cf. Walter C. Kaiser, Jr., *The Uses of the Old Testament in the New* (Chicago: Moody, 1985).

62. Barr, *Escaping from Fundamentalism*, 98–99.

63. Kaiser, *Uses of the Old Testament,* 49.

64. Ibid., 51–53.

in reading the text it is hard to avoid the conclusion that the geography of the passage is important and that Matthew believed Jesus had to come out of Egypt in order to somehow "fulfill" Hosea 11:1.

Application of typology to the text, however, may resolve the dilemma. At the outset we must insist that, contrary to the popular misunderstanding, typology is completely different from allegorization. The latter is the interpreting of accidental parallels between the Old Testament and the New as spiritually discerned, hidden pictures of Christ. Thus, the scarlet cord Rahab hung from her window in Joshua 2:18 is taken as an allegory of the blood of Christ. Allegorization is based on Hellenistic and Alexandrian models of interpretation[65] and cannot be considered as serious exegesis. Genuine typology, however, is built upon real history and a theology of history, and it follows careful, specific rules of exegesis.[66] More than that, the Old Testament prophets themselves spoke from a typological perspective. Joel, for example, saw in the locust plague of his day (1:4–20) a type for an invasion by a human, apocalyptic army (2:1–11). He saw the end of that locust plague as a type for the destruction of the apocalyptic enemy and judgment on all nations (cf. 2:20; 3:1–21), and the restoration and blossoming of his land after the plague as a picture of the pouring out of the Spirit of God (2:21–32). He unites all of these events typologically under the theme of the day of the Lord.[67] Typology is therefore not just a theological fuse that jumps the gap between the Testaments; it is the manner of prophesying in the Old Testament itself. Even Jesus prophesied typologically. Note how he blended the picture of the fall of Jerusalem in A. D. 70 with images of the last judgment (Matt. 24). Typology is the biblical way of describing historical patterns in the way God works.

Jesus was keenly aware that major events in his life and ministry were fulfillments of Old Testament precursors, and he com-

---

65. In these models literature was interpreted allegorically, either for moralizing purposes or to show how the earthly realm corresponded to the heavenly realm. Cf. G. W. H. Lampe, "The Reasonableness of Typology," in *Essays on Typology*, by G. W. H. Lampe and K. J. Wollcombe (London: SCM, 1957), 32–33.

66. Cf. Richard M. Davidson, *Typology in Scripture* (Berrien Springs, Mich.: Andrews University, 1981), 421–22.

67. Duane A. Garrett, "The Structure of Joel," *Journal of the Evangelical Theological Society 28* (1985): 289–98.

municated this awareness to his disciples (Luke 24:26–27). He deliberately and explicitly set out to fulfill Old Testament types. For example, his forty days in the wilderness parallel Moses' forty years,[68] even as his Sermon on the Mount recalls the giving of the Law on Sinai.[69] He applied the Davidic-messianic motif of the Good Shepherd to himself,[70] and certainly he was aware of fulfilling the Isaianic image of the Suffering Servant in his death.[71] It is no surprise, therefore, that Matthew should see it as a typological fulfillment that Jesus, like the nation of Israel, spent part of his childhood in Egypt. Whether or not Hosea himself had any idea that Hosea 11:1 would have messianic fulfillment is impossible to say (and appreciation for *sensus plenior* is helpful here). But it is significant that Hosea, by his own intent or by God's, used the theologically charged word *son* for Israel. Moreover, insomuch as both the prophets and Jesus understood God's dealing with Israel typologically, Matthew cannot be accused of having introduced an alien concept. His interpretation of Hosea 11:1 is fully in keeping with normative biblical theology. Evangelicals are now pursuing this and similar approaches to resolving dilemmas with regard to the New Testament's use of the Old and cannot be accused of foisting artificial interpretations on the text.

Despite all the progress that has been made in dealing with problem texts, there remains a frequently voiced objection that inerrancy still leaves the Bible in a particularly vulnerable position since a single error in the Bible invalidates the doctrine. Many argue that conservatism needlessly forces the whole concept of biblical authority to run the gauntlet of a thousand trivial tests. And should the Bible fail even one of these tests, the whole evangelical theological framework collapses.[72] This argument may be the most serious of all, especially since the number of historical problems in the Bible is not small.[73] But this argument

68. Leonhard Goppelt, *Typos,* trans. Donald H. Madvig (Grand Rapids: Eerdmans, 1982), 99.

69. Ibid., 67–68. Note Jesus' many references to the Law in the sermon and his stress on fulfilling it (Matt. 5:17).

70. Ibid., 88–89.

71. Ibid., 96.

72. Cf. Barr, *Escaping from Fundamentalism,* 82.

73. On the other hand, the number of problems is not especially large considering that the Bible was written book by book over a period of over a thousand years by more than a few writers.

precisely illustrates what we mean by asserting that inerrancy is a principle of hermeneutics. We are making a practical and foundational declaration on how we approach God's Word.

Inerrancy means that we, as believers, have submitted ourselves to the authority of Christ, his apostles, and the Old Testament Scriptures that they themselves were under. And we cannot be under their authority while at the same time we consider ourselves free to declare what they assert to be wrong or erroneous. When we encounter historical or theological problems in the text, we deal with them honestly; happily, Christians of the present and former generations have already satisfactorily resolved many of the thorniest problems. But when we begin to say of the text, "This is in error," we have radically altered our position vis-à-vis the Word of God. We have assumed the position of its judge. Inerrancy is thus more than a theological domino theory. It is submission to God's revelation and a confession of our own inadequacy to speak meaningfully about God or the history of his work in the world without that revelation. But when we say that the Bible has errors, we have placed ourselves over it, for we set ourselves in the position of deciding what parts are erroneous and what parts are not. Unresolved problems remain, but that is exactly what they are—unresolved problems. They are far from being compelling proofs of inaccuracy in the Bible. Therefore, we do not abandon our faith that the Bible is true just because problems exist, but we continue to study it with faith and trust while we rejoice at how past and present research vindicates that trust.

Inerrancy and the Priesthood of the Believer

Another question, one with which Baptists are especially concerned, is whether or not inerrancy somehow violates the concept of the priesthood of the believer, or of *soul competency*, in religion. The doctrine of the priesthood of the believer teaches that every individual Christian is free to approach God directly with prayer and intercession, and indicates that no one needs to seek God's forgiveness through a humanly ordained priest or saint in glory. It has nothing to do with the question of what a Christian is free to believe or disbelieve. A Baptist who comes to reject the doctrine of the incarnation, for example, is not exercising his priestly rights; he has simply become apostate. Other doctrines may be less important than the incarnation (e.g., baptism by immersion), but this is not the place to attempt to rate Christian teachings according to importance, if, indeed, such is possible. The point is that the concept of the priesthood of the believer is not germane to the present discussion, since it has to do with access to God and not with freedom to believe as one chooses.

The concept of soul competency does indicate the believer's right, under the leadership of the Spirit, to interpret Scripture free of dogmatic guidelines imposed by ecclesiastical authority. No one disputes this. There is no orthodox Baptist commentary on the Bible with which all must agree. This does not imply, however, that Baptists believe Christians are free to regard a biblical teaching as false or erroneous. As E. Y. Mullins wrote, "The Scriptures are the rule of faith and practice and the omnipresent Spirit the interpreter."[74] It is hard to see how the Bible is the "rule" if soul competency actually frees the believer from its authority. More than that, even in the realm of interpretation, freedom is not absolute; no Baptist could accept an interpretation of Acts 2:38 that asserted water baptism to be necessary for salvation.

Inerrancy and Critical Scholarship

A final issue is whether or not commitment to the belief that the Bible is true promotes antagonism toward the tools of critical scholarship. It is true that conservatives have been slow to accept the advances of modern scholarship, sometimes to their own loss. On the other hand, as Carson says, these tools are not really as precise as the word implies.[75] Often it is the interpreter's preconceptions, not his use of form criticism or structural exegesis, that determine his views on the history and meaning of a text. Also, conservatives have often rightly wondered whether the gains of modern scholarship were really gains at all. With good reason they have been alarmed at how critical scholarship has shredded the books of the Bible into myriad contradictory tradi-

---

74. E. Y. Mullins, *The Axioms of Religion* (Philadelphia: American Baptist, 1908), 131.

75. Carson, "Recent Developments," in *Hermeneutics, Authority, and Canon,* ed. D. A. Carson and John D. Woodbridge, 32.

tions and theologies, has treated many of its stories as myths and legends, and has uniformly treated its prophecies as *vaticinia ex eventu*.[76] This is not just sentimental distress at seeing the Bible subjected to attack; conservatives recognize that as the integrity of the Bible is compromised, its theology shrivels and dies.

The case of the Book of Daniel is illustrative here. The book describes incidents from the life of its hero, Daniel. He is said to have been a young man taken captive to Babylon in 605 B.C. (1:1) and preserved by God through various trials (e.g., being cast into a pit of lions, chap. 6). He is also said to have been an interpreter of dreams and a recipient of visions, and considerable attention is given to describing his visions.

Until the last century, Christians and Jews have assumed that the book accurately described the life of its protagonist (and indeed that it may have been written by him) and that the visions in the book are genuine predictions from God. Higher criticism, however, has radically changed the picture. Most modern scholars now consider it to be beyond doubt that Daniel, in its present form, was written about 165 B.C., that its stories are at best legends without historical basis that began to circulate around the third century B.C., and that its prophecies are *vaticinia ex eventu* written during the Jewish war with their hated enemy, Antiochus IV Epiphanes, the Greek king of Syria. In other words, Daniel is simply a piece of religious fiction that, with stories of heroic triumphs over paganism and with artificial prophecies of a final victory, encourages the Jews to persevere in their fight for survival against the Greeks.

Critical scholars did not come to this conclusion without some good reasons. The classic English expression of the argument for the late date and fictitious nature of Daniel was given by S. R. Driver. Driver gave historical, linguistic, and theological reasons why he believed Daniel had to have been written around 165 B.C. Among these are the arguments that the second-century B.C. Jewish sage Jesus ben Sirach never mentioned it, the fact that Daniel erroneously regards Belshazzar as a king of Babylon, the book's peculiar use of the term *Chaldean,* and the pres-

---

76. I.e., asserting that a prophecy was actually written after the event it professes to predict. New Testament critics, for example, frequently assert that the prophecies of Jesus, such as that found in Luke 19:42–44, were actually written by the early church after the events described had transpired.

ence of loanwords from Persian and Greek.[77] The case seems so strong that most recent critical introductions to Daniel scarcely bother to argue the point.

Of course, no a priori reason exists why Daniel cannot be fictional. The parables of Jesus are certainly fictional, but no one asserts that they are therefore not genuine revelation. A significant point, however, is that the parables are explicitly presented to the reader as fiction. Can the same be said of Daniel? Is this the perspective that the New Testament has about Daniel? To these questions, any honest student must say no. The book itself gives no hint that it describes anything other than true history, and the New Testament, to all appearances, shares that view of Daniel (cf. the evident reference to Daniel in Heb. 11:33). Most significant is Jesus' assertion that a divine revelation came "through the prophet Daniel" (Matt. 24:15). This is not just to say that if Daniel were not really a historical prophet, then Jesus, as the Son of God, should have known better (although that argument is not nearly as weak as many claim) but to point out that the uniform perspective of Scripture is that Daniel is true as history and prophecy.

For this reason conservatives have been unwilling to follow the critical line and have defended the historicity of the book. Outstanding among these is the apologetic writing of R. K. Harrison, whose *Introduction to the Old Testament* is a standard for conservative students of the Old Testament. Harrison has answered the critical attacks on Daniel point by point and has argued forcibly that the historical credibility of Daniel has been supported, not eroded, by modern research.[78] Other conservative scholars have done similar work. John C. Whitcomb, for example, has done important research on the knotty problem of the identity of Darius the Mede.[79] Curiously, critical scholars do not bother to answer conservative arguments but simply ignore them or dismiss them as the ravings of fundamentalists.

More is at stake here, however, than the emotional comfort of

77. S. R. Driver, *An Introduction to the Literature of the Old Testament* (Edinburgh: T and T Clark, 1898), 497–510.

78. R. K. Harrison, *Introduction to the Old Testament* (Grand Rapids: Eerdmans, 1969), 1110–27. A more recent conservative introduction is C. Hassell Bullock, *An Introduction to the Old Testament Prophetic Books* (Chicago: Moody, 1986), 281–92.

79. John C. Whitcomb, *Darius the Mede* (Grand Rapids: Eerdmans, 1959).

being able to say with some assurance that Daniel is true. If the book is fictitious, then not only is its place in the canon inexplicable but biblical theology is far poorer. The critical treatment of Daniel 2 illustrates this point.

In that chapter Nebuchadnezzar has a dream in which he sees an image made of four metals: gold, silver, bronze, and iron. A rock "that was not cut out by human hands" strikes the image on the feet and demolishes it, and then the rock grows into a great mountain. Daniel interprets the dream and says that the four metals represent four human kingdoms (Nebuchadnezzar's being the first), and that the rock represents the final victory of the kingdom of God (Dan. 2:36–45). Unfortunately, Daniel did not give us the names of the other three kingdoms.

Christians of previous generations and present conservatives interpret the four kingdoms to be the empires of Babylon, Persia, Greece, and Rome and assert that the rock in the vision represents the coming of the kingdom in the person of Christ. They point out that each of these four kingdoms, in succession, had dominance over the Jews from the time of Daniel to the time of Christ and assert the text to be a remarkable messianic prophecy.

For critical scholars, however, this interpretation is out of the question. Since the book is a religious and political tract that addresses the crisis of 165 B.C., it is inconceivable that it proclaims the still distant military triumph of Rome, much less the birth of Jesus. Therefore, the first three kingdoms of the vision were not Babylon, Persia, and Greece but Babylon, Media, and Persia. The fourth part—iron and clay—represents not Rome but the Greeks, with whom the Jews were then (ca. 165 B.C. according to the critical theory) engaged in a life-and-death struggle.[80] A problem here is that the Median empire is itself a fantasy of earlier critical scholarship invented to provide a missing fourth kingdom to replace the Rome of the rejected older interpretation.[81] Aware of this, modern scholars now either assert that the author of Daniel

---

80. Cf. James A. Montgomery, *The Book of Daniel* (Edinburgh: T and T Clark, 1927), 59–63; R. H. Charles, *A Critical and Exegetical Commentary on the Book of Daniel* (Oxford: Clarendon, 1929), 46; Georg Fohrer, *Introduction to the Old Testament,* trans. David E. Green (Nashville: Abingdon, 1968), 478; Norman W. Porteus, *Daniel* (London: SCM, 1965) 47–48; and Andre Lacocque, *The Book of Daniel,* trans. David Pellauer (Atlanta: John Knox, 1979), 50–53.

81. Cf. Montgomery's attempt to prove the existence of a Median empire, *Book of Daniel,* 61–62.

himself held to a mistaken belief that a Median empire had ex-isted[82] or propose alternate interpretations of the passage.[83] Still, the traditional understanding is considered impossible.

What this means theologically is that Daniel has scarcely any message for the church. Childs has assessed the present situa-tion as follows: "Although I do not contest for a moment the genu-ine insights which have emerged from this history of critical research—the destruction of the rationalism implicit in the older orthodox position was a major contribution—it remains a per-plexing phenomenon that the theological insights into the Book of Daniel have not increased proportionately. One could almost wonder whether there is an inverse ratio."[84] At most, critical scholarship could only yield a few theological crumbs—Daniel encourages faithfulness in the face of adversity and hails the coming of the kingdom of God (albeit on the basis of a strange, sectarian, and now discarded eschatology).[85] For Christians the book can be meaningful only through "a new hermeneutic of the prolongation of the times."[86]

For conservatives Daniel 2 yields far more theological riches. Not only did this chapter tell the ancient Jewish reader some-thing of when the messianic age (and hence the Messiah) would come, but it also gives the Christian reader the key to under-standing what it means to live "between the times." From the time of the Babylonian captivity of the Jews, four earthly king-

82. Porteus, *Daniel,* 47–48, attempts to explain how a second-century B.C. Jew could have made such a blunder.

83. E.g., P. R. Davies, *Daniel* (Sheffield: JOST, 1985), 48. Davies says that the interpretation of the dream in Daniel 2 is secondary, and that it originally de-scribed the degeneration of the kings of Babylon, the first being the mighty Neb-uchadnezzar and the last being either Nabonidus or Belshazzar.

84. Childs, *Old Testament,* 613.

85. E.g. Fohrer, *Introduction to the Old Testament,* 478. Childs, *Old Testa-ment,* 615–27, has attempted to develop the theology of Daniel in greater detail in accordance with canon criticism, and a number of his insights are helpful. But it is very questionable whether his theological construction can stand on the historical-critical foundation he accepts. He argues that Daniel 7–12 is a later canonical expansion of Daniel 2 and the seventy years of Jeremiah. But cf. Otto Eissfeldt, *The Old Testament,* trans. Peter Ackroyd (New York: Harper and Row, 1965), 518–19, 524, on the unity of Daniel.

86. Norman Gottwald, *The Hebrew Bible: A Socio-Literary Introduction* (Philadelphia: Fortress, 1985), 594.

doms were ordained to rule the people of God until he established his own kingdom. During the fourth kingdom the Christ did come and begin his reign. But just as the rock slowly grew into a great mountain, so the kingdom of God did not suddenly appear in all its glory. Moreover, the fourth kingdom is itself diverse in nature. It is both iron and clay. It manifests itself in various forms, as illustrated by the ten horns it has in a subsequent, related vision (7:19–22). It suffered a fatal wound, and yet it continues to live (Rev. 13:3). The fourth kingdom is Rome, but it is more than Rome; it is the power, oppression, messianic pretension of the kingdom of man. It has existed, and continues to exist, in many places under many names. Already defeated by the risen Messiah, it nevertheless continues to war with the kingdom of God. Already crushed and broken in the eyes of God, the idol still stands before the eyes of man and receives his worship and devotion.

The Christian reader understands that he lives in the apocalyptic climax of history. He views the Jewish warriors who struggled with Antiochus as precursors to the present age, but looks upon the Christian martyrs both of Rome and of other ages in church history as fellow strugglers in the conflict of which he is a part. The struggle with the fourth kingdom is not a matter for historical appreciation or curiosity about the future but is, for the Christian church, always in the present tense. Nevertheless, the victory has already been won. The Savior, the "stone cut out of the mountain without hands," appeared when the fourth kingdom was in the apex of its glory, in the Augustan Age. Inescapably beaten, the fourth kingdom can only become progressively more monstrous as it approaches final annihilation.

The question of the historicity of Daniel is therefore a matter of crucial theological importance. Far more is at stake than whether or not a Jewish official in Babylon once interpreted some dreams for a king and was later miraculously saved from some hungry lions. More is at stake than whether or not stories we learned in Sunday school are true. The issues are embedded in the very theological foundations of the meaning of the kingdom of God.

The point of what we are saying is simple: The Christian must study the Bible with the presupposition that it is true. Without that commitment of faith, his interpretations will be misguided and his theology will be shallow at best, if not altogether wrong. Problems exist, but by studying those problems instead of casting them aside as evident errors and proofs of confusion in the text, new levels of meaning will appear, and the interpreter will find himself better able to grasp and proclaim the Word of Truth.

3

On Taking the Bible Literally
L. Russ Bush

Once in a while someone will argue that biblical inerrancy is not a Christian doctrine at all, since this exact terminology is not found in the Bible itself nor in the historic confessions of faith. The concept of biblical truthfulness, however, is so axiomatic for historic Christian theology that to quibble over terminology is almost to miss the point entirely. Terminology often changes through the years because of varying circumstances, but in each case words are chosen to express certain ideas that need to be emphasized at that time. The term *inerrancy* has come into common usage in recent years, because it strongly affirms the fundamental presupposition of consistent Christian orthodoxy precisely at the point where it has been so strongly attacked in our day.

To call the Bible inerrant is to say that the Bible always tells the truth; it is not errant. This terminology sets forth the doctrinal concept plainly. I am not suggesting that the term *inerrancy* is not subject to semantic confusion. It has, in fact, been soundly criticized exactly because of the semantic difficulties that have grown up around it. Terms can be defined, however, and the term *inerrancy* has been clearly and carefully defined. Few doctrinal affirmations are more clearly set forth than this one.[1]

Thus, I consider as false the continuing charge that inerrancy is not a clear concept. It is only unclear to those who lack the ability or the desire to understand. Just as election may be thought by some to mean that our salvation is somehow tied to a democratic political process in heaven, so inerrancy may be misunderstood as well. But clear definitions of the doctrine of election can be and have been produced by scholarly Reformed theologians. It is simply dishonest for critics to continually criticize caricatures rather than to direct their comments to the actual meaning of the doctrine.

Could anyone imagine the historic Christian confessional affirmations apart from their axiomatic foundation in biblical truthfulness? Surely if anything is unambiguous and obvious, it is that Christians historically have built their doctrines out of biblical teachings. The necessary assumption that allowed this process to have intellectual integrity has been that the biblical teachings were authoritative, sufficient, and inerrant (that is, completely truthful).[2]

Why do we believe in the virgin birth? It is, scientifically speaking, quite unlikely. The resurrection is equally unlikely. Election, redemption, salvation, heaven and hell—all of these doctrines and more—are known, understood, and believed primarily because they are biblical teachings. If the Bible always

---

1. Cf., for example, the "Chicago Statement on Biblical Inerrancy" (1978), available from ICBI, P. O. Box 346, Walnut Creek, CA 94596.

2. The most serious recent attempt to demonstrate that historic Christian orthodoxy built itself on something other than the axiom of biblical inerrancy has come from Jack B. Rogers and Donald K. McKim, *The Authority and Interpretation of the Bible: An Historical Approach* (San Francisco: Harper and Row, 1979). The Rogers and McKim thesis, however, is a serious distortion of the historical facts. John D. Woodbridge, in *Biblical Authority: A Critique of the Rogers/ McKim Proposal* (Grand Rapids: Zondervan, 1982), has produced a definitive critique and an effective rebuttal to this rather strange contention that denies a necessary relationship between biblical inerrancy and historic orthodoxy. The historic claim for biblical truthfulness most certainly did apply to all biblical teachings and affirmations, and it was not limited only to so-called matters of salvation.

teaches truth and not error, then these biblical teachings are true, and they are not erroneous. That is the foundational premise of historic Christian orthodoxy.

It is false to suggest that the theological method implied by belief in biblical inerrancy leads to untenable theories of biblical inspiration (e.g., mechanical dictation) or to incredible hermeneutical tactics (e.g., refusing to recognize or acknowledge literary genre, semantic forms, such as figures of speech, or cultural parameters of expression or meaning).

As far as Baptist theologians are concerned, my own research in the primary sources led me to conclude that over the last several centuries, the mainstream of outstanding Baptist theologians solidly held to the theological method described by the contemporary term *biblical inerrancy*. This conclusion was so obvious and the theme was so consistently a predominant factor in the Baptist theological literature that I found one could only argue a contrary position by concentrating one's attention on certain twentieth-century and a few late nineteenth-century writers.[3]

Baptist theologians have historically affirmed the full truthfulness and supreme (even sole) authority of the properly interpreted authentic text of the Bible. As I understand it, that is precisely what is meant by the contemporary usage of the term *biblical inerrancy*.

Yet some will raise the issue of terminology in another way. If truthfulness is the real issue, then why insist on the negative term *inerrant*? Has not that term become a code word for some anti-intellectualists to use politically against some theological scholars who may simply interpret the Bible differently?

It must be admitted that the term *inerrant* has been applied to the Bible by all sorts of people, and perhaps it has been misused by some for political purposes. Some people have used the term *patriotism* as a code word to permit and condone bigotry and prejudice. That hardly destroys the real and legitimate meaning

3. That this modern non-inerrancy stance is indeed a break from the historic Baptist tradition is documented somewhat in L. Russ Bush and Thomas J. Nettles, *Baptists and the Bible* (Chicago: Moody, 1980). The evidential support for the thesis of the book is significantly more extensive than the limited documentation in the book can show.

of patriotism. So it is with inerrancy. Misuse of the term by some does not destroy the actual meaning of the term (unless the misuse were to become the dominant usage). The affirmation of the inerrant truthfulness of the Bible is an attempt by modern evangelical scholars to rule out and deny legitimacy to any interpretation that assumes or claims that biblical teachings or affirmations are contradictory, false, or erroneous. The negative term *inerrant* is not, for me, the most preferred term, but for several important reasons it has found a place of significance in modern theological discussions. The language of inerrancy, however, by no means implies that there can be no variety of interpretative models or viewpoints concerning the specific or systematic meaning of some particular biblical passage.

Biblical inerrancy is a confessional affirmation of dispensationalists and covenant theologians, of Calvinists and Arminians, of Baptists, Lutherans, Presbyterians, and Wesleyans, of liturgical and nonliturgical churches, of premillennialists and amillennialists, of charismatic and noncharismatic theologians, and others. But inerrancy inevitably seems to draw a line between evangelicalism and neoorthodoxy, between conservatives and liberals, between those who submit to biblical authority and those who subject the Bible to their own critical judgments.

One of the quite false and yet deliberate rumors being spread of late against the doctrine of biblical inerrancy is that inerrancy implies hermeneutical insanity. In other words, some modern opponents of this historic Christian doctrine claim that anyone who holds to biblical inerrancy must interpret the Bible in some kind of crazy way. If the Bible is inerrant, they say, then we must believe that some people were born from a lion's womb (Gen. 49:9), that the Red Sea parted when God blew his nose (Exod. 15:8), that Jesus encouraged us to become cannibals (John 6:52–53), or that Jesus taught us to hate our mothers (Luke 14:26). If in amazement we reply that we take these passages to be examples of truth expressed in figures of speech, the critic smiles and with a hearty chuckle accuses us of being dishonest. But something is wrong here. Why would the important discussion of biblical authority and truthfulness degenerate into a debate over such matters as whether or not truth can be expressed by figures of speech? Have there ever been serious interpreters of the Word of God who did not recognize that biblical literature often uses symbolic language, metaphors, types, poetic phrases, and other figurative materials?

To really understand the meaning of inerrancy for biblical studies, we must first examine the standard pattern of biblical interpretation used by most evangelical theologians. Then we can ask what hermeneutical functions the doctrine of inerrancy has for discovering the authentic meaning of the Bible. Perhaps we will at last be able to discover the real meaning of the doctrine of inerrancy.

Evangelical Interpretation of the Bible

In his prologue to *Protestant Biblical Interpretation: A Textbook of Hermeneutics,* 3d revised edition (Grand Rapids: Baker, 1970), Bernard Ramm claims "to present the system of hermeneutics which most generally characterizes conservative Protestantism." Ramm explicitly denies that he had "defended any specific school of thought within Protestantism." In equally explicit terms, however, he designates it as his purpose "to lay bare the essential features of the literal system" (p. ix).

Ramm is well aware that "the word 'literal' is offensive to some even within the conservative circle," and thus it must be clearly defined. But "there is no other word that can serve our purposes," he concludes, "except possibly 'normal'" (p. x).

For Ramm, divine inspiration is "the foundation of historic Protestant hermeneutics and exegesis" (p. 93). In fact, Ramm emphasizes that for evangelicals "only a full-fledged, intelligent biblicism is adequate to the present-day situation in science, philosophy, psychology, and religion" (p. 95). Accepting the plenary inspiration of Scripture, an evangelical interpreter "severs company with all forms of rationalism, for example, neoorthodoxy, religious liberalism, or Reformed Judaism" (p. 94). Belief in plenary inspiration leads evangelical interpreters to approach the Bible in an attitude of faith and trust, to be patient when confronted with critical problems, and to search out the true text and the best interpretative methods, so that the word of man does not intrude into the Word of God. Historic evangelicalism "therefore does not indulge in the wholesale reconstruction of texts, histories, and documents which characterizes liberalism" (p. 95).

The goal of the true scholarly spirit in biblical interpretation is "to discover the original meaning and intention of the text" (p. 115). Competent exegesis, then, must be done in the original languages, and for Ramm, this clearly implies the necessity of literal interpretation. Hermeneutics, he says, must start with the literal meaning of words, that is, with the basic, customary, socially designated meaning of the language. "The spiritual, mystical, allegorical, or metaphorical usages of language," says Ramm, "reflect layers of meaning built on top of the literal meanings of a language. To interpret Scripture literally is not to be committed to a 'wooden literalism,' nor to a 'letterism,' nor to a neglect of the nuances that defy any 'mechanical' understanding of language. Rather, it is to commit oneself to a starting point and that starting point is to understand a document the best one can in the context of the normal, usual, customary, tradition[al] range of designation" (p. 121).

Ramm further argues that "the literal method of interpretation is the usual practice in the interpretation of literature" (p. 123). "All secondary meanings of documents depend upon the literal stratum of language" (p. 124), and "only in the priority of literal exegesis is there control on the exegetical abuse of Scripture" (p. 124).

No fair reading of Ramm, nor of any evangelical textbooks in hermeneutics, nor of scholarly exegetical works by evangelicals would ever lead one to believe that the literal method of interpretation overlooks or denies figures of speech, symbols, types, or even allegories that are actually found in Scripture.[4]

4. Baptist theologian A. Berkeley Mickelsen, in *Interpreting the Bible* (Grand Rapids: Eerdmans, 1963), a widely accepted evangelical textbook, lists and illustrates more than twenty types of figurative expressions from the Bible including allegories, fables, and riddles. He gives five chapters to figurative language and then devotes a separate chapter to prophecy and another to poetry. He is careful to affirm, however, that "in order to understand any figure, one must of course first recognize the literal meaning and then, by reflecting on the relevant points of similarity, interpret the significance of the figure" (p. 198).

Benjamin Keach (1640–1704), an outstanding Baptist theologian, is typical of many classical expositors. He speaks of the Bible as "the infallible storehouse of heavenly verities" in his essay, "Divine Authority of the Bible," which prefaced his comprehensive *Tropologia: A Key to Open Scripture Metaphors, Together with Types of the Old Testament* (currently available from Kregel Publications under the title, *Preaching from the Types and Metaphors of the Bible,* 1972). The Bible, he contends, "is of divine [origin], inspired by the Spirit of God, and therefore of infallible truth and authority. . . ." Keach then spends 240 pages describing the figurative nature of biblical language.

In summary, then, we discover that the so-called literal method of interpretation is nothing more than the traditional grammatical-historical method in which meaning is found by normal interpretative rules. This is not to downplay the highly complex structure of language, but it is to acknowledge that language has a divinely ordained purpose—the communication of ideas, feelings, and concepts—and to recognize that language successfully accomplishes that purpose.

The Hermeneutical Function of Inerrancy

Evangelical Christians are often caricatured as naive literalists who never think beyond the surface meaning of a text. James Barr has quite astutely recognized, however, that "the point of conflict . . . is not over *literality* but over *inerrancy*."[5] For the conservative theologian, "the truth of the Bible, its inerrancy, understood principally as correspondence [of textual meaning] with external reality and events, is fed into the interpretative process at its very beginning."[6] If the literal interpretation of a passage would result in an affirmation of error, or if it would create a theological inconsistency or challenge the truthfulness of God's Word in any way or raise some other serious problem, such as turning the passage into nonsense, another kind of interpretation would be given. Inerrancy, not literalness, is a constant factor in evangelical hermeneutics.

The Nile Turned to Blood: An Exemplar

Recently in Southern Baptist life, some vocal critics have attempted to ridicule inerrantists by pointing out that the commentary notes in the *Criswell Study Bible* (Nashville: Nelson, 1979) do not always reflect a naive, literalistic reading of the text. The most notable example, perhaps, is the suggestion in the

5. James Barr, *Fundamentalism* (Philadelphia: Westminster, 1978), 40.
6. Ibid., 51. Morris Ashcraft, in "Response to Carl F. H. Henry, 'Are We Doomed to Hermeneutical Nihilism?'" *Review and Expositor* 71 (1974): 221, argues that the acceptance of propositional revelation and the identification of the Bible as being that revelation is a presuppositional stance that makes "genuine interpretation" impossible. Henry's essay had, of course, argued cogently that only those very assumptions could prevent the loss of genuine interpretation. Ashcraft wants to use the "living tradition" of "the church" as a hermeneutical bridge to transmit "the meanings of the written symbols" (pp. 222–23).

Study Bible's interpretive notes that the Nile River may not have turned into literal human or animal blood (Exod. 7:17–25) but that the term *blood* may be a term literally describing the color of the miraculously polluted water rather than the substance of the pollution. (The *Study Bible* note itself mentions two other Old Testament references where the words seems to be used in exactly that way, as a reference to color rather than substance.)

The point of this criticism toward the *Study Bible* seems to be based on the false identification of inerrancy with crass or naive literalism, and on the mistaken belief that neoorthodoxy's characteristic denial of the historicity of the miracles is nothing more than a form of figurative interpretation. The Exodus 7:17–19 note in the *Study Bible,* however, in no way denies the historical reality of the event—the God-caused, miraculous, poisonous change in the water—or the fact that it was a judgment of God on the river god beliefs of the Egyptians. Rather, it affirms all of those things.

As to the legitimacy of a figurative interpretation at this point, the question of whether or not the blood is the literal substance that normally flows in human or animal veins seems to be raised in the text itself: (1) Egyptian magicians (v. 22) duplicate the effect (surely not by creating red corpuscles, nor does it seem likely that they were slaying animals and secretly mixing real blood into their water sources); and (2) fresh water could be found (v. 24) by digging in the sandy banks of the polluted rivers (whereas real blood would not, under normal circumstances, be filtered out or changed into drinkable water by sandy soil).

Moreover, blood was sacred in Israel because it carried and sustained life (Lev. 17:11). This blood in the Nile River is never said to have carried or sustained life in any creature; it made no atonement, nor did it serve any liturgical purpose. It was simply a judgment on Egypt and then was apparently dumped into the Mediterranean after several days to dissipate.

I think it is interesting to notice how seldom this miracle is explicitly mentioned in the rest of Scripture (the most explicit passages are in the Psalms). The parting of the Red Sea and, of course, the Passover itself (which did involve an innocent lamb's blood, which was shed and sprinkled on the doorposts as a sign that the lamb's death was being substituted for the required death of the firstborn son) are the liturgically remembered events. Many biblical miracles are only mentioned once, but in this case (of the river turning to blood) such treatment as that seems a bit odd, given the significance of blood in Israelite religion.

A further contextual point to notice is that the miraculous plagues seem to be grouped together in definite patterns and are ordered in such a way that their intensity increases until they reach a climax in the death of the firstborn sons (see the *Study Bible*'s note on Exod. 7:14). Turning the entire Nile River into actual blood would seem to be a greater and more significant miracle than any of the other plagues except the last one, yet this is the initial plague in the series of ten.

Those who take the term *blood* as a reference to substance rather than color often appeal to the acknowledged fact that the Hebrew word used in the text usually refers to actual human or animal blood. They also point to the parallel between this plague and the account in Revelation 16:1–6.

The interpretive note on Exodus 7:17–19 in the *Study Bible* may be mistaken. The river blood of the first plague may have been literal human or animal blood. But it is certainly no necessary denial of inerrancy to suggest otherwise in light of the contextual descriptions (summarized above) given in the biblical text itself. This is especially so when the historical and scientific reality of the miraculous event is so strongly affirmed in the contextual notes of the same *Study Bible*. Those who use this example to ridicule inerrancy simply do not understand what inerrancy means. The criticism that evangelicals are given over to literalism was clearly intended to be damaging to the conservative position, yet Barr thinks it granted far too much to it. "People tended to say, yes, the Bible is of course right, but not in the literal sense. . . . But at many points the reverse must be said: the text should indeed be understood 'literally,' in that the literal sense was the one intended by the author, but this must mean that, in passing from the sense of the text to the statement of what happened, or to a statement of the real theological entities involved, one must make a critical reconstruction which does not follow the exact lines of the text: in other words one must take a line that for the fundamentalist means that the text is 'wrong.'"[7]

7. Barr, *Fundamentalism*, 54.

Barr does not accept the doctrine of inerrancy. He believes that some actual (properly interpreted) teachings of the Bible are wrong. Evangelicals reject the theological stance of modern biblical critics such as Barr. We believe that the teachings of the Bible are all true. Modern critics clearly disagree on that point.[8]

Other Hermeneutical Issues

Harmonization, a characteristic hermeneutical procedure used by evangelicals, is in no sense acceptable to the modern critic. If inerrancy implies that biblical statements correspond to a sequence of actual events or to the actual relationships between existing realities, then modern critics will and can have no sympathy for such a principle.[9]

It is common for evangelicals to assert that we should, as disciples, hold the same views of "biblical criticism" that Jesus held (including his obvious acceptance of traditional authorship

8. Paul J. Achtemeier, in *The Inspiration of Scripture: Problems and Proposals* (Philadelphia: Westminster, 1980), 76, writes, "Perhaps the most important single issue that separates the modern critical view of Scripture from that of the conservatives lies in the fact that critical scholars take Scripture far more literally." For Achtemeier this "literal" approach leads him to find numerous errors in the Bible including theological errors and discrepancies (cf. pp. 60–66, for a fairly extensive list of supposed errors arising from what he calls the "plain and obvious" sense of Scripture).

9. Achtemeier, *Inspiration of Scripture,* 76, suggests that "critical scholars are not so much perturbed by discrepancies and errors which a preconceived notion of the nature of Scripture would force them to explain away or harmonize, as they are interested in accounting for them." On page 79, he continues, "Critical scholars assume that when the same phenomena appear in the Bible and in other ancient literature, *they have the same cause,* and thus the scholars seek to isolate the various traditions which have been woven together in our Bible" [italics mine]. To me, it is utterly incredible that Barr, Achtemeier, and other recent scholars are actually claiming literal interpretation to be the sufficient cause to explain modern critical theories that depend upon the supposed existence of multiple sources known and recognized only by comparative literary discrepancies. These hypothetical autographs solve all interpretive difficulties, it seems. But are these men seriously claiming, for example, that the central rationale behind the Documentary Hypothesis is concern for a logically noncontradictory narration? Are they also demanding that there be "inerrant autographs" of J, E, D, or P? No! They are not suggesting any such thing. So why must "discrepancies" be signs of sources at all?

claims and historicity).[10] While there is nothing wrong with that in principle, it is nevertheless true that some modern critical questions of date or authorship or interpretation of biblical materials may not be able to be finally settled strictly by an appeal to the teachings of Christ. In the first place Jesus did not directly comment on all of these matters, and in the second place he often did speak in, what seems to be, ordinary cultural terms rather than with modern technical precision (e.g., the mustard seed reference of Matt. 13:32). But on the question of scriptural authority and truthfulness, Jesus does make explicit affirmations of his own view. He leaves no ambiguity in the minds of his apostles as to the normative attitude he expects his disciples to take. The Scripture is the truthful Word of God and is to be believed, understood, obeyed and fulfilled.

Modern critics, however, like Barr, see no reason to presuppose the didactic truthfulness of Christ in all his recorded utterances.[11] In fact, Barr argues that it is "nonsense" to speak about "the Bible" claiming to be inspired. There is only "this or that source" claiming something about some other writing. Apparently, Barr sees the Bible as nothing more than a collection of great, but diverse, religious literature. Evangelicals believe that such a stance is the logical result of modern biblical criticism coupled with the denial of inerrancy. (On the other hand, critical methods under the normative authority of full biblical truthfulness can be very helpful in our quest to discover the real meaning of divine revelation.) The real issue, then, is still inerrancy.

No evangelical would ever argue for the necessary inerrancy of a purely human writing (such as a systematic theology textbook). Only God is infallible; only what God says will always be true. Thus, only a word from God can properly be thought of as

10. Leon Morris, in *I Believe in Revelation* (Grand Rapids: Eerdmans, 1976), 49, is by no means atypical when he writes: "For the Christian the critical thing in this whole subject is the attitude of Jesus Christ. He is the norm for the Christian and by definition the way he regarded Scripture is the Christian way." (See further his entire chapter, "Christ and Scripture," 49–67.) Perhaps the two most significant recent studies of this question from the standpoint of both content and methodology are John W. Wenham, *Christ and the Bible* (Downers Grove: InterVarsity, 1972); and R. T. France, *Jesus and the Old Testament* (London: Tyndale, 1971; Grand Rapids: Baker, 1982).

11. Cf., for example, Barr, *Fundamentalism,* 72–85.

infallible. Holy Scripture is said to be fully truthful and without error because it is an inspired record of divine revelation. Jesus— God's word in flesh, the divine Son of God—would for those very reasons be considered to be an infallible teacher, an unerring spokesman, and a sinless Savior. Reading an inerrant (because inspired) record of his teachings is the moral equivalent of actually hearing Jesus teach. An inspired record of revelatory events is the epistemological equivalent of direct participation in the event if the record is accepted with unqualified belief.

If we are interpreting a truthful word from God, we then have some normative guidelines for interpretation that flow directly from the claim that we do have truth. Nevertheless, we must interpret even truthful propositions. Prior knowledge of (or reason to believe in) their truthfulness will rule out some interpretations that could be offered, but interpretation must still occur. Gordon Fee even contends that "the battle for inerrancy must be settled in the arena of hermeneutics."[12]

Surely the first principle of interpretation must be to determine the intention of the author. Until we know what the author intended his readers to understand by his words, we can never rightly or fully understand the passage. Assuming that we can detect by philological and historical methods the original message, we then must try to apply that same message to the modern cultural situation. Whether or not the author used figurative language, he did intend to convey some meaning. Precisely because that meaning is believed to be completely true and to have come to us with divine authority, the evangelical is concerned to discover that exact original meaning and carefully apply it today. Without this hermeneutically axiomatic assumption of authority and inerrancy, what ultimate motivation is there to discover this original intention of the canonical text other than the academic interest of the religious historian?

It will not do to locate the authority of the Bible only in its firsthand or eyewitness relation to Jesus Christ,[13] because there is then no apparent way to determine whether or not these human (and thus fallible) witnesses are reporting the truth about

12. Gordon Fee, "Hermeneutics and Common Sense: An Exploratory Essay on the Hermeneutics of the Epistles," in *Inerrancy and Common Sense,* ed. Roger R. Nicole and J. Ramsey Michaels (Grand Rapids: Baker, 1980), 161.
    13. Cf. Ashcraft, "Response to Carl Henry," 221.

Christ accurately. Authority must finally be located in God alone. Authority may then be mediated to us by divine revelation. That Scripture is the direct product of that revelation is the affirmation of evangelical theology.

The evangelical doctrine of biblical inspiration is that the Holy Spirit conveyed the message and meaning of God's revelation so effectively, and guided the biblical writers so appropriately, that without violating their personality or their integrity, he moved them to convey God's truthful message in writing (in Scripture) without any mixture of legitimate error therein.

It does sound properly spiritual to affirm that Christ himself, and not the record about him, should be central to our theological method, but epistemological criteria that will provide authentic knowledge of Christ apart from (especially prior to) acceptance of the validity of the historical records are less than obvious to say the least.

Is the Bible Literally True?

Modern biblical critics assume (they believe that this assumption has been forced upon them by the nature of the biblical materials) that the biblical literature "has been composed in many instances of the combination of earlier traditions; that in the transmission of those traditions as well as in their combination, theological reflection and appropriation have continued to occur; and that Scripture therefore reflects the dynamic process at work in the community of Israel, and in the church, as those who stood within these communities sought to understand the significance of their God-directed history."[14]

That some portions of the biblical books are based upon previously written sources is not the point of controversy (see 1 Kings 11:41 and 15:31 for two references to apparent source materials no longer extant). Modern critics, however, often conclude that the Scripture is generally a compilation of diverse traditions, that these sources were primarily of human origin, and that they

---

14. Achtemeier, *Inspiration of Scripture,* 79. John D. W. Watts, in "The Historical Approach to the Bible: Its Development," *Review and Expositor* 71 (1974):165, speaks of source analysis in the Pentateuch and in the synoptic Gospels saying, "The recognition that more than one source had been used in compiling these books has explained many discrepancies in the finished text."

were collected, edited, and arranged by the religious leaders of Israel and the early church to make political as well as theological points.

This process of working and reworking these stories to modify and revise their teachings is thought to have been a historical process in which many authors and/or editors contributed. Chronicles is said to be a recasting of 1 and 2 Kings (in this instance the older version survived). Matthew and Luke are thought of as perhaps the most successful early commentaries on the Gospel of Mark, but they are not thought of as authentic documents composed by the actual authors claimed in their canonical titles. New Testament books bearing the name John are at best thought to be collections of materials produced by those who were perhaps most closely associated with the congregations led and taught in an earlier time by John himself. Genesis is thought to have been finally composed eclectically (probably by Ezra) from several (perhaps seven) earlier, conflicting sources (some of which may have had Mosaic traditions woven into them).

Is this the literal meaning of the biblical text? Do modern critical conclusions follow from the consistent application of the "analogy of faith?"[15] Is redaction criticism[16] going to postulate an inner logical congruity of the postulated sources to be able to distinguish (infallibly?) the original from the edited copy from which the canonical text has come? Do the supposed redactors in-

15. Evangelical theologian R. C. Sproul gives a very fine discussion of this subject in "Biblical Interpretation and the Analogy of Faith" in *Inerrancy and Common Sense,* ed. Roger R. Nicole and J. Ramsey Michaels, 119–35.

16. Watts, "The Historical Approach," 166–67, describes redaction criticism as "the study of the editorial processes by which the sources, traditions, and books have been prepared for a place in the Bible." By isolating the parts of the text where the redactor departs from his sources, the modern interpreter is said to be better able to discern the particular purpose and message each editor wanted to convey.

In the 18 October 1985 issue of *Christianity Today,* the Christianity Today Institute published a twelve-page study entitled "Redaction Criticism: Is It Worth the Risk?" Participants in the dialogue included D. A. Carson of Trinity Evangelical Divinity School; Harold W. Hoehner, Dallas Theological Seminary; Vern S. Poythress, Westminster Theological Seminary; David M. Scholer, Northern Baptist Seminary; and Kenneth S. Kantzer, Trinity Evangelical Divinity School. This is an excellent discussion of the issues relating to biblical criticism in the context of evangelical commitments to the Christian faith and to biblical authority and biblical truthfulness.

errantly and consistently project their purpose through their handling of the (edited) traditional material handed down to them? How do we know yea or nay?

Historical-critical methodologies are not by definition wrong, however. Marvelous insight has come from literary studies, from form-critical studies that have recognized, for example, the related styles in the Psalms, and from the redactional and structural studies that have helped us to discover some special theological elements in the text, such as the unique emphases of Luke compared with those of Matthew or Mark.

Many critical (analytical) study tools can be very effectively used by evangelical as well as nonevangelical biblical scholars.[17] The evangelical's consistent use of these methods is guided by the normative principle that the authentic canonical text is inspired by God's Spirit and thus is properly understood as affirming the truth and only the truth (without any mixture of legitimate error). Such a parameter does not exist for nonevan-

---

17. Standard introductory textbooks for biblical studies within the evangelical tradition include the following: Gleason Archer, Jr., *A Survey of Old Testament Introduction,* rev. ed. (Chicago: Moody, 1974); Robert H. Gundry, *A Survey of the New Testament,* rev. ed. (Grand Rapids: Zondervan, 1981); Donald Guthrie, *New Testament Introduction,* 3d ed. (Downers Grove: InterVaristy, 1970); Everett F. Harrison, *Introduction to the New Testament,* rev. ed. (Grand Rapids: Eerdmans, 1971); R. K. Harrison, *Introduction to the Old Testament* (Grand Rapids: Eerdmans, 1969); William Sanford LaSor, David Allan Hubbard, and Frederic William Bush, *Old Testament Survey* (Grand Rapids: Eerdmans, 1982); Merrill C. Tenney, *New Testament Survey* (Grand Rapids: Eerdmans, 1961); and Edward J. Young, *An Introduction to the Old Testament,* rev. ed. (Grand Rapids: Eerdmans, 1964).

For the sake of comparison, the student may want to carefully study the following nonevangelical sources that advocate modern critical conclusions: Bernard W. Anderson, *Understanding the Old Testament,* 3d ed. (Englewood Cliffs: Prentice-Hall, 1975); Otto Eissfeldt, *The Old Testament: An Introduction,* trans. P. R. Ackroyd (New York: Harper and Row, 1965); Paul Feine and Johannes Behm, *Introduction to the New Testament,* re-ed. Werner Georg Kümmel and trans. A. J. Mattill, Jr., 14th ed. (Nashville: Abingdon, 1966); Henry Jackson Flanders, Jr., Robert Wilson Crapps, and David Anthony Smith, *People of the Covenant: An Introduction to the Old Testament,* 2d ed. (New York: Ronald, 1973); Reginald H. Fuller, *A Critical Introduction to the New Testament* (New York: Harper and Row, 1963); Robert M. Grant, *Historical Introduction to the New Testament* (New York: Harper and Row, 1963); Walter Harrelson, *Interpreting the Old Testament* (New York: Holt, Rinehart, and Winston, 1964); and James L. Price, *Interpreting the New Testament* (New York: Holt, Rinehart, and Winston, 1961).

gelical theologians, and their guiding principle for critical studies seems to be nothing other than the credulity limits of the
individual interpreter.

Critics of evangelical scholarship seem to have made a fundamental error in their efforts to force literal interpretation on
those of us who are actually arguing for literal truth. Parables,
similes, metaphors, and other figurative language forms may
not (in fact, do not) pretend to literally depict some factual aspect
of present or past reality, but the author or spokesman surely did
intend to convey some actual, definable idea. That idea, if it is
really true, is surely literally true whether the interpretive
principle used to recognize and comprehend it was directly literal or not.[18]

In one sense all language is symbolic, and perhaps all interpretation is figurative. But there is only one God; he is the source
and the standard for defining truth. Thus, literal truth (real
truth) exists as surely as the thoughts of God exist. Carl F. H.
Henry is quite correct when he writes: "The alternatives to the
historic evangelical insistence that Christianity conveys literal
truth about God are hardly convincing and lead invariably
toward skepticism. There is only one kind of truth. Religious
truth is as much truth as any other truth. Instead of being de-
vised for tasks other than to express literal truths about God, human language has from the beginning had this very purpose in
view, namely, enabling man to enjoy and to communicate the un-
changing truth about his Maker and Lord."[19]

Modern critics have given up the prophetic model of biblical
authorship altogether.[20] The new *community model* of authorship completely eliminates any concept of an original autograph, and thus traditional orthodox affirmations of biblical
inerrancy (built, as they must be, on traditional concepts of a
prophet or an apostle producing a divinely inspired written ac-

18. When someone says that literal truth is not possible for finite minds, I
wonder if they mean that literally?

19. Carl F. H. Henry, *God, Revelation, and Authority* (Waco: Word, 1979),
4:128. Henry discusses anthropomorphism, cultural relativity, the finitude of
human language, analogical theories of religious knowledge, and several other
crucial aspects of this question in his chapter "Is the Bible Literally True,"
103–28.

20. The most explicit recent explanation of this modern paradigm shift is in
Achtemeier, *Inspiration of Scripture,* especially 99ff.

count of the revelation God granted to them) are considered by modern critics to be incredible and impossible.

No precanonical documents have yet been found, however, and orthodox harmonizations are no more speculative than critical reconstructions. Rather, harmonizations at least take the text and seek to explain it as it stands. Modern critics seemingly explain the text primarily in terms of how they think it *might* have originated. Surely the former procedure (harmonization) is more likely to be able to discover the literal meaning of a passage and reapply it to the modern situation without compromising the integrity of the source.

Modern theological scholars would do well to take seriously (and more generally) Otto Eissfeldt's emphatic reminder in *The Old Testament: An Introduction* (pp. 240–41) that "the whole of Pentateuchal criticism is a hypothesis. . . ." Endeavors to solve the Pentateuchal question by other methods have not shaken the critical consensus, in his opinion, but they should and do stand "as a warning against too great reliance upon the results of Pentateuchal criticism itself."

Eissfeldt, of course, does not expect alternative theories to undo the essential critical understanding of the material in terms of its eclectic source composition. He could never conceive of going back to a view of biblical inerrancy (the "flat picture of the Pentateuch" as he mistakenly calls it). Evangelicals, on the other hand, affirm inerrancy precisely because they do want to deny the negative, critical, naturalistic conclusions drawn by the modern critical school of thought in both Old and New Testament studies.

To make Christ truly central in our lives and in our thoughts, we must have some way of knowing truly who he is. If we recognize that he surely is the Christ, the Son of the living God, it will not be flesh and blood that will have revealed this to us, but it will be God, our Father who is in heaven.

God's Word is truth; Scripture (God's Word written) does not teach error. On this rock of divine revelation, on this confession of the uniquely revealed deity of Christ, the Lord has built his church, and even death itself *(hadēs)* cannot destroy the new people of God.

4

Contemporary Hermeneutics and Biblical Authority
Richard R. Melick, Jr.

What is the meaning of any statement? The question is not answered as simply as many have thought. In fact, many thousands of pages have been written in an attempt to analyze the nature of the term *meaning*. It has been studied linguistically, psychologically, philosophically, and existentially. Any attempt, therefore, to be exhaustive in a discussion of intent or meaning would be foolish. It is necessary, however, in a work like this to say something about meaning, since many of the difficulties encountered in biblical studies, particularly in the authority of the Bible, reflect a diversity of understanding here. David Scholer's comment expresses something of the tension experienced in the minds of biblical students when they are confronted with a course in exegesis or hermeneutics. He says, "The widespread naivete represented by the person who said to me, 'Professor, it's all right if you want to interpret the Bible; however, I'll just ac-

cept what it says' is, obviously, an impossible situation."[1] Many
are torn between wanting to accept what it says and knowing
they must interpret to determine what the Bible means.

There have been several responses to the necessity of interpretation. Many, like the case cited above, would like to dismiss the
hermeneutical problems and simply "take what is said," that is,
the letter of the word. In actuality, while many may claim to employ such a principle of operation, inevitably and subtly, hermeneutics is taking place. "If theology is to make sense *now* about
the meaning of Jesus Christ whose career took place *then*," says
Paul J. Achtemeier, "it has in that moment engaged in a transfer
of meaning. It has carried out a hermeneutic. Rather, the question is whether that hermeneutic, or the principle on the basis of
which it has been carried out, is to be the object of deliberate
theological reflection, or whether it is to be assumed and allowed
to operate without the benefit of theological clarification."[2] The
question, therefore, is what kind of hermeneutic will guide the
interpreter, not whether or not he will engage in hermeneutics.

The subject has another dimension in the current debate over
biblical authority. Many times the reply to questions about the
nature of the controversy over the Bible is, "It's all hermeneutics." While this is true from one perspective, it is also a decep-
tive reply for at least three reasons. First, when someone replies
in that fashion, the impression is that the issue is relatively un-
important, certainly not worth all the current discussion. Such
is not the case. There is much at stake in both theoretical and
practical areas. Second, the reply may suggest that the greater
issues are really a point of unity, that is, that all agree on the
larger issues and that we should agree to disagree in minor matters. In fact, however, a study of current hermeneutical issues reveals that there are still major differences on crucial points.
Although the language may be the same for both (or many) sides,
the meanings are radically different. To say, "It's only hermeneutics," therefore, is to gloss over some very rough areas. Third, few
people understand philosophical hermeneutics and thus are

    1. David M. Scholer, "Unseasonable Thoughts on the State of Biblical Her-
meneutics: Reflections of a New Testament Exegete," *American Baptist Quarterly* 2 (June 1983): 134.
    2. Paul J. Achtemeier, *An Introduction to the New Hermeneutic* (Philadel-
phia: Westminster, 1969), 14–15.

prone to misunderstand the statement anyway. To many, hermeneutics is simply a matter of understanding such things as metaphors and idioms. The focus of this chapter, therefore, is on some of the important aspects of hermeneutics that prevail in contemporary discussions about the Bible. The language is nontechnical, and sometimes the issues have to be grossly simplified. Nevertheless, such an overview is needed to enable one to get one's bearings in the world of biblical studies.

Until recent times the study of meaning was relatively simple. One studied the historical, lexical, and linguistic data and reached a conclusion about the meaning. Anthony C. Thiselton says: "Traditionally hermeneutics entailed the formulation of rules for the understanding of an ancient text, especially in linguistic and historical terms. The interpreter was urged to begin with the language of the text, including its grammar, vocabulary, and style. He examined its linguistic, literary, and historical context. In other words, traditional hermeneutics began with the recognition that a text was conditioned by a given historical context."[3] This meant, of course, that the reader was able to study the text objectively and, theoretically, was able to understand its meaning "perfectly." J. I. Packer points out that this method is the heritage of Aristotle and that it was the prevailing principle of interpretation until the time of the Reformation. This approach still persists in many of the Protestant textbooks on hermeneutics.[4] Even the liberal scholars of the eighteenth and nineteenth centuries worked on this basic assumption regarding interpretation. They read and interpreted rather literally and then, because of their own world-view, discarded much of the Bible. The fact that they could debate the nature of the supernatural elements of Scripture, and reject them, indicates that they understood the Bible to affirm these matters. In other words, the words were taken to mean "what they said."

This view of meaning, however, was to change. The science of interpretation, like most other disciplines, has been heavily influenced by both philosophy and natural science. Until the time

---

3. Anthony C. Thiselton, *The Two Horizons: New Testament Hermeneutics and Philosophical Description* (Grand Rapids: Eerdmans, 1984), 11.

4. J. I. Packer, "The New Hermeneutic: Response," in *Hermeneutics, Inerrancy, and the Bible,* ed. Earl D. Radmacher and Robert D. Preus (Grand Rapids: Zondervan, 1984), 562.

of the Reformation, two basic approaches prevailed. Many advocated a historical-grammatical approach, which stressed the objective nature of the text, and that a lexical, syntactical, and grammatical study would reveal its meaning. Others utilized a dogmatic, or doctrinal, approach. Here the dogma of a church or group provided the principle for interpretation. The dogma often kept interpreters from developing wild interpretations if they followed a spiritual or allegorical exegetical method, which some tended to do.

After the Reformation, however, biblical studies were cut loose from the controls of the church, and the historical-critical method arose. The basic tenet of this approach was "correspondence with empirical actuality."[5] Seeking to integrate biblical truth, natural science, and current philosophy, this approach engendered source and literary criticism, form criticism, and, perhaps to a lesser degree, redaction criticism. It was the method of eighteenth- and nineteenth-century liberalism, which disregarded the supernatural elements found in the Bible.

The historical-critical method has had significant impact on biblical studies and remains a dominant factor. It has been praised by its own for "rescuing the Bible from theology" because of its insistence that truth must conform to modern man's understanding. Thus, the accounts of the miracles and the redemptive terminology of the Bible were to be classified as "faith statements," the product of theology, and of little value in establishing the actual historical events surrounding the birth of Christianity. It was this method that launched the quest for the historical Jesus in an attempt to understand him apart from the eyes of faith. This did not mean that all who applied this method distrusted the faith of the early church. They were very concerned with it for a variety of reasons. Some were even personally committed to it. But as an outworking of this philosophy, many were led to distrust the historical and biographical material in the Gospels and therefore attempted to understand Jesus through other means.

The Subject-Oriented Approach

In more recent times, largely because of the spiritual sterility of the historical-critical method, there has been the emergence of

5. James Barr, *Fundamentalism* (Philadelphia: Westminster, 1978), 49.

a *subject-oriented hermeneutic,*[6] which stresses the role of the interpreter himself in the process of interpretation. Although actually dependent on earlier ideas, this approach has come of age in the last twenty years. It takes many forms, but all have one basic intention: to make the Bible relevant to contemporary needs. Many would express themselves like Karl Barth, who found that his heart was warmed as he read the Bible, even though his head was filled with the sterile conclusions of critical scholarship. They therefore turned to the message of the Bible (variously interpreted and understood) to find meaning for existence.

Each of these approaches has representatives today, but this chapter focuses on the last—the subject-oriented approach. For our discussion it is noteworthy that many biblical scholars have been profoundly influenced by the philosophers Francis Bacon, Immanuel Kant, Friedrich Schleiermacher, Martin Heidegger, H. G. Gadamer, and Ludwig Wittgenstein.[7] These influences have led them into a strongly subjective view of language and meaning and, in our opinion, a different concept of biblical authority.

The analogy has often been drawn to the work of an artist and the writers of the works of literature. It might be easy to appreciate the differences in the models by following the analogy. The philosopher H. G. Gadamer, in *Truth and Method,* develops this comparison.[8] When an artist produces a painting, he has a defi-

6. It is common today to distinguish between the plural *hermeneutics,* as principles of interpreting language, and the singular *hermeneutic,* as the philosophical approach to language. While that distinction is generally helpful, it is not strictly maintained here. The focus of this chapter is on one's approach to literature, his *hermeneutic,* rather than principles of interpretation, his *hermeneutics.*

7. Since many excellent histories of hermeneutics have been produced, it is needless to recap them here. Rather, some casual observations will help establish the direction of thought. For brief but helpful historical reconstructions, one might read, among many good surveys, J. I. Packer, in *Hermeneutics, Inerrancy, and the Bible,* ed. Earl D. Radmacher and Robert D. Preus, 561–64; Roger Lundin, "Our Hermeneutical Inheritance" in *The Responsibility of Hermeneutics,* ed. Roger Lundin, Anthony C. Thiselton, and Clarence Walhout (Grand Rapids: Eerdmans, 1985), 1–29; Thiselton, *Two Horizons;* and, from a literary perspective, Roy J. Howard, *Three Faces of Hermeneutics: An Introduction to Current Theories of Understanding* (Berkeley: University of California, 1982).

8. H. G. Gadamer, *Truth and Method* (London: Sheed and Ward, 1975). Although often used, perhaps a better analogy is offered by Sandra Schneiders, in

nite picture in mind, which he attempts to reproduce through his medium. Assuming he is relatively successful in his reproduction, others may come to view his work. When they see it, however, they may have quite a different sense of appreciation and impact. The viewers may see in the picture elements the artist did not foresee, emphasis he did not intend to make, and relationships that he did not build. The reason for this is that the viewer views the painting from his personal perspective. He brings the painting into his world of understanding and evaluates it through his own sense of appreciation, that is, his own insight.

The artist, then, has become the producer of a catalyst for a response in the experience of the viewer, and the significance of his art will be measured in large part by the kind of response it brings. The technical precision of his work may be well appreciated, but it is subordinated to its aesthetic value. To these critics the permanent value of the painting is that the product has the capability of producing an experience by itself. In that sense art is an unfinished product, since every viewer completes the project in his own viewing of it. The artist cannot predict the response of the viewer, and he need not argue about the finer points of emphasis. He is satisfied if the viewer appreciates his work, is drawn to and into what he sees, and thereby experiences it.

The analogy is well chosen. Through critical studies of the Bible, many scholars have classified the Scriptures as some form or collection of forms of literature. Their rationale is that the Bible has been utilized primarily by a religious community as central to its faith, and it should, therefore, be classified like the religious literature of other groups. This, of course, reduces the historical value of the Bible since, according to them, precise history is not its central focus. The Bible must be measured by its spiritual value alone. When this literary appraisal is combined with a philosophy that cannot accept the miraculous accounts of the Bible, a plausibly strong case is made. The liberal scholar reasons as follows: The Bible was never intended to be history, and its language and records reflect a different world-view that

---

"The Literal Sense of Scripture," *Theological Studies* 39 (1978): 719–36, who argues that the text is to be perceived as a musical score that must be rendered with fidelity to the score but will have a personal aspect, depending on the artist.

includes the magical and miraculous, which modern men cannot accept. Therefore, we are told that we must classify this as religious literature, not true history.

This approach also means that methods of study appropriate to other forms of literature should characterize biblical studies. For example, Rudolph Bultmann insists that "the interpretation of the biblical writings is not subject to conditions different from those applying to all other kinds of literature."[9] The Bible, then, must first be read to determine its value quite apart from its (theological) claim to be divine revelation. That is, the message of the Bible is not as significant as the experience of the men who wrote it and the motivation they had while writing it. The content, it is said, is not an end in itself but a means to understanding their insights.

At the heart of the analogy between the Bible and a work of art is the assumption that the viewer of a painting and the reader of the Bible are the same. That is, just as the painting may be seen differently from the painter's intention because of the perspective of the viewer, the Bible may be viewed differently from its intended meaning because of the perspective of the reader. Furthermore, no two readers will view it the same way. Ultimately, one's perspective is not as important as the effect it produces. If the Bible brings one into a new religious experience, it is valuable to the reader regardless of his particular understanding of its nature. The logic of this leads ultimately to a position that the Bible has as many meanings as readers, and that even the author himself may not or cannot know what he meant.

Two obvious questions emerge from this view of the nature of hermeneutics. First, from where does the reader get his personal perspective, and what form does it take? Second, is there any way to test the reader's response so that it can be determined whether or not it is valid?

The Nature and Source of One's Perspective

The first question may be answered rather easily. The perspective comes from the reader's world-view—the way he views him-

9. Rudolph Bultmann, *Essays: Philosophical and Theological* (London: SCM, 1960), 53.

self and his environment. It is, in short, his perspective on everything. This is both acquired by heredity (from such things as the location of birth, race, nationality, sex) and by his cultural education (used in the broadest sense, i.e., everything learned). Since these factors vary from person to person, so does the response to any given object or experience. Language expresses and measures our responses to our world, and these are often conditioned responses over which we have no little control. Recently, some scholars have suggested that language can only reveal what a person thinks. Since what he thinks is highly conditioned by his background (world-view), it is suggested that it is impossible for man to make meaningful statements about reality. All one is capable of doing is making a statement about the way *he* feels about reality.

Reality must then be understood as evasive (perhaps impossible to gain) or as extremely relative (hence suited to anyone's version of it). It is evasive because no one could possibly know whether or not he has it. At the other extreme, it must be considered relative because every interpreter has equal claim to have apprehended reality. This may be illustrated by the following parable: "There were four blind men in this parable—one touched the trunk of the elephant, and said that reality is a tree; the second touched the elephant's tail, and concluded that reality was like a rope; the third touched the leg and said that reality was like a pillar; the fourth touched the elephant's skin and declared that reality was like a desert."[10] The men had varying perceptions and descriptions, but ultimately they examined the same thing. In the religious world, it may mean that neither the Buddhist nor the Christian can have certainty about his faith, and that ultimately they both experience reality through diverse forms. That is, they have the same elephant even though they speak of it differently. Everything relates to one's perspective.

The matter of personal perspective was brought to biblical studies largely through the work of Rudolph Bultmann, considered by many nonevangelicals to be the most significant biblical scholar of the twentieth century, and although much of his exe-

10. This parable was first promulgated by Vardhaman, or Mahavira, the founder of the sixth-century B.C. reformed movement in Hinduism known as Jainism.

getical and theological work is outdated, his hermeneutic lives on in his followers. He remains, therefore, a significant figure in contemporary biblical studies. He championed the idea that the New Testament message must be translated into language and concepts that modern man can appreciate. For him the modern scientific age differs so radically from the world of the New Testament with its prescientific orientation that the message of the Bible cannot be understood as it stands. He developed a now-famous approach to the Gospels called demythologizing. He says that "the historical method includes the presupposition that history is a unity in the sense of a closed continuum of effects in which individual events are connected by the succession of cause and effect."[11] "This closedness," he says, "means that the continuum of historical happenings cannot be rent by the interference of supernatural, transcendent powers and that therefore there is no 'miracle' in this sense of the word."[12]

The Bible could not be taken at face value because of the supernatural elements in it, which are now "known" to be impossible. The language and literature of the Bible is therefore to be classified as myth. Since mythical language expresses the faith of a religious community, such as the primitive church, it should be heard. What it says, however, cannot be understood by the (surface) words, which purport to communicate the message. Rather, one must get behind the literary forms of the story to the faith written by the author (or the community). Bultmann's exegetical method reinforced the development of form criticism, a hermeneutical method that seeks to classify, analyze, and interpret the different forms of the text. Bultmann stated that many of the forms of the stories did not originate with Jesus or the disciples. Rather, the church took many previously existing stories and legends and inserted their "hero figure"—Jesus of Nazareth—into them. By a comparative study of the various forms of the New Testament Christianity and other religious writings, one could arrive at an understanding of the real meaning behind a particular story.

11. Rudolph Bultmann, "Is Exegesis Without Presuppositions Possible?" in *Existence and Faith,* selected, translated, and introduced by Schubert M. Ogden (London: Hodder and Stoughton, 1960), 291.
    12. Ibid.

According to Bultmann, once the story is understood, it is necessary to translate its meaning to modern man without the miraculous content. Naturally, one would think that he would favor the Epistles because they explain the events of Christianity. But there is a strange distrust of biblical explanations, since they are only the way the writers of the New Testament understood the events, and they, too, were locked into their own world-views, which must be demythologized. The focus, therefore, is on events and their meaning once the supernatural elements are removed and the interpretative statements themselves (Epistles, for example) are explained. Bultmann realized that the supernatural elements cannot be totally discarded because they are a vital part of the biblical literature. He therefore stated that they are to be considered as "internal (spiritual) history" (but not real events—simply a part of the religious history of the church), while the other events are history as we know it. As Paul J. Achtemeier says: "It is clear, for example, that the New Testament does not intend to be a historical record in any modern sense of the word. To analyze the New Testament as though it were such a record can only result in distortion of its intention. Rather, the text intends to be proclaimed. It is meant to confront men with the decision as to whether or not they are willing to speak the language of faith, i.e., to let Jesus' relation to God become event in their lives as well."[13]

If one accepts this approach, he must find some means of opening the meaning of the New Testament for himself, since the language, taken at face value, no longer communicates. For Bultmann it was his commitment to existentialism. He was influenced by the strain of thought that assumed that the individual was the center of the world and his existence was everything. Therefore, he taught that the Bible must speak to one's existence if it is to be of value to man, and everything should be interpreted in light of one's own personal existence. This is not as egocentric as it may seem, since for Bultmann every statement about self is a statement about God. The writers of the Bible found their lives enriched by their understanding of God, and we must seek to understand what it was that did that for them. Even so, the expression of their faith is not as important as their faith itself. The end of this Bultmannian process is that one is left with a nonsuper-

13. Achtemeier, *New Hermeneutic,* 118.

natural perspective towards an obviously supernatural book, and with a skepticism about the Bible's own explanation of what it means because it is from an outdated era.

This attitude radically alters the traditional view of the authority of the Bible. Rather than being a body of revealed truth, it is a model of responses to the truth. Rather than being a message of redemption from sin, it is only an example of redemption from the supposed (or real) problems of that day, which the writer defined as sin. This is not the view of authority that the church has historically held. Yet, one who approaches the Bible in this contemporary fashion may also claim that it is authoritative, and to anyone unfamiliar with the recent trends in biblical and theological studies, the language employed sounds very much the same.

The New Hermeneutic

The *new hermeneutic* develops this subjective approach. The reader is not an objective investigator of the past, viewing it through unbiased eyes. Everyone comes to the text with some perspective and is therefore subjective in his study. Actually, all interpretation is the conclusion of a subjective reader who is attempting to understand a piece of subjective writing. This opens the door to two problems to which we have alluded, but not directly addressed. The problems are those that are now commonly called horizons. "The world of our own existence," explains Magda King, "is the horizons in which our everyday understanding moves, so that from it and in reference to it the things we come across are intelligible *as* . . . things that can be useful for some purpose. The horizon of our world is primarily 'meaning-giving.'"[14] Thiselton defines the word *horizon* as "a technical term in hermeneutical theory. Even in popular parlance *horizon* is used metaphorically to denote the limits of thought dictated by a given viewpoint or perspective."[15] Both definitions reveal that a person perceives and understands anything and everything by the horizons of his own world-view.

There are two horizons. The world in which we live is one, and the world of the biblical writer is the other. It is common to speak

14. Magda King, *Heidegger's Philosophy: A Guide to His Basic Thought,* quoted in Thiselton, *Two Horizons,* 31.
15. Thiselton, *Two Horizons,* xiv.

of them as the inner horizon (of the reader) and the outer horizon (of the writer).

The inner horizon affects the reader in two crucial ways. First, it affects the way he approaches the Bible. Each reader seeks to find answers to the questions he has about life. However, he cannot formulate questions to ask of the text except through his own perspective. Thus, he comes to the Bible seeking answers to questions he formulates (from his own perspective), but these are not necessarily the questions asked by the original audience. The answers the Bible provides, therefore, are not necessarily the answers to the questions the reader of today is asking. This means, simply, that the careless reader *may* construct a theology of living based entirely on a weak, if not fallacious, foundation. Second, the reader will receive answers to his questions whether or not they are the correct questions. Thus, there is a reinforcement of belief that prompted the questions in the first place and a confirming of one's own theology. Of course, the outworkings of this are that any reader may come to the Bible genuinely and have it speak to him, but he may hear a far different message than what another reader hears from the same document. Advocates of the new hermeneutic call this the hermeneutical circle, and this is, in fact, what is happening in biblical studies.

It is easy to understand how an individual's perspective affects his reading of the Bible. It has to be emphasized that no one can come to the Bible with pure objectivity. Conservative biblical scholars approach the Bible with a certain mind-set of their own, as do more liberal scholars. Everyone has a perspective that enables him to make sense out of his life experiences. This is the point of Magda King's statement, "The horizon of our world is primarily 'meaning-giving.'"[16] Without this perspective no one would be able to function consistently, and no one would be able to handle new learning or new personal situations. John P. Newport and William Cannon identify several factors that affect or reveal a person's perspective.[17] They helpfully identify some of the sociological, ideological, and theological causes of disagreement and identifies some of the basic areas of conflict, such as

16. Quoted in Thiselton, *Two Horizons,* 31.
17. John P. Newport and William Cannon, *Why Christians Fight over the Bible* (Nashville: Nelson, 1974).

prejudice, world-view, the definition of truth, the historical nature of the Bible, and methods of interpretation. Unfortunately, they approach these matters purely descriptively. There is no help provided to enable an evaluation of the issues or for comparing which models may be the most biblical. After finishing their book, the reader is left with the impression that either one's perspective does not matter, or that there is no escape from his perspective. Neither of these conclusions is necessary. The Bible was written to change natural perspectives into biblical perspectives and to provide a biblical world-view in which to operate.[18]

One's perspective also has the capacity to influence one's theology, so that he sees in the Bible what he wants to see. Thus, the Bible is either quoted to support theology (for conservatives) or used to illustrate theology (for many liberals), but often these are mere extensions of the way people want to see it or have been conditioned to see the text. This point is supported by a former colleague of mine who taught psychology. Each year he had his students search the Bible to support various theories about man—from the behavioral models to the "spontaneous." Amazingly, his students repeatedly found they could support multiple models by appealing to the Bible itself! One could *prove* almost anything from the text. The same conclusion is reached by Thiselton in a remark about liberation theology. "The fact that Marxist interpreters do in fact tend to arrive at Marxist interpretations of the Bible, even when they are aware of their own preunderstanding, sharpens the problem of objectivity in biblical interpretation."[19] The same could be said of some conservative interpreters as well. Obviously, it is impossible to avoid having a perspective before undertaking biblical study, but it is necessary to be willing to change perspectives if the Bible is the authority for faith and life.[20]

18. The authors obviously did not intend to address this point, but it is crucial to the subject matter addressed.

19. Anthony C. Thiselton, "Hermeneutics and Theology: The Legitimacy and Necessity of Hermeneutics," in *A Guide to Contemporary Hermeneutics: Major Trends in Biblical Interpretation,* ed. Donald K. McKim (Grand Rapids: Eerdmans, 1986), 170.

20. Achtemeier says, "It soon becomes apparent that one's preunderstanding must be allowed to be corrected or the text simply cannot be understood" (*New Hermeneutic,* 119).

Hermeneutical Keys to Interpretation

The crucial question here is, What perspective best unlocks the meaning and message of the Bible? Various keys have been suggested. Naturally, each reader advocates some principle that opens the Bible's meaning for him. In a recent paper by Professor Yandall Woodfin, several such keys are discussed.[21] Many of these are theological; others are philosophical or sociological. The paper illustrates and categorizes various interpretive keys well, but it fails to provide a vehicle for evaluating the respective positions. In the denominational situations addressed, Woodfin demonstrates that the interpretation actually rests upon the theological tradition of the group. Thus, the tradition of the denomination becomes the authority. This is no more than a dogmatic approach to the problem of verification.

Many ideas have been suggested as keys to the understanding of the Bible. One recent approach, which has far-reaching repercussions, is the *sociological model*.[22] Assuming the bankruptcy of the historical-critical method of exegesis, these men have looked to sociology, anthropology, and comparative religions to provide the model for understanding. They compare the Christian community to other religious communities in the world in similar historic circumstances and use this comparison to explain the meaning of Christianity.[23] The Christian message, then, is one

21. Yandall Woodfin, "The Bible and a Christological/Encounter Hermeneutic" (Unpublished paper). The author's work is descriptive rather than evaluative, thus he does not intend to provide an evaluative vehicle. Nevertheless, that would be a helpful contribution.

22. Its so-called value is now recognized by the Society of Biblical Literature, which has sessions devoted to this movement.

23. This, too, generally assumes that the message as interpreted by the apostles had no ultimate and exclusive truth value. For recent discussions, see, for example, the following major contributions to this approach: John G. Gager, *Kingdom and Community: The Social World of Early Christianity* (Englewood Cliffs: Prentice-Hall, 1975); Gerd Thiessen, *The First Followers of Jesus: A Sociological Analysis of Earliest Christianity* (London: SCM, 1978); Bengt Holmberg, *Paul and Power: The Structure of Authority in the Primitive Church as Reflected in the Pauline Epistles* (Philadelphia: Fortress, 1978); Howard Clark Kee, *Christian Origins in Sociological Perspective: Methods and Resources* (Philadelphia: Westminster, 1980); Abraham J. Malherbe, *Social Aspects of Early Christianity* (Baton Rouge: Louisiana State University Press, 1977); Ronald F. Hock, *The Social Context of Paul's Ministry: Tentmaking and Apostleship* (Philadelphia: Fortress, 1980); and John H. Elliott, *A Home for the Homeless: A Sociological Exegesis of 1 Peter: Its Situation and Strategy* (Philadelphia: Fortress, 1981).

example of how religion is a part of man's basic outlook, which surfaces with various distinctives according to differing circumstances. Jesus is often compared to another "hero figure" or "charismatic prophet" to describe his specific value to the church. If this is so, the words used by the biblical writers to explain the meaning of Jesus are not considered as normative.

In the past two decades *liberation theology* has arisen in the search for the significance of Christ. This theology of the Third World seeks to understand Jesus in terms of the political and economic needs of the day. There are various forms of liberation theology with religious connotations: political, economic, ethnic, cultural, personal, and sexual. In each of these the Bible is not the only Christian authority, and this is freely acknowledged by liberationists. One spokeswoman, Elisabeth Schussler Fiorenza, clearly expresses the hermeneutical dilemma of the feminist movement, for example.[24] Her comments could well be applied to other wings of the movement as well. "Is being a woman and being a Christian," she asks, "a primary contradiction which must be resolved in favor of one to the exclusion of the other?"[25] Her problem is the fact that the Bible is written from a male perspective and, thus, represents a male-dominant society. She finds that "a feminist theologian must question whether the historical man Jesus of Nazareth can be a role model for contemporary woman, since feminist psychological liberation means exactly the struggle of women to free themselves from all male internalized norms and models."[26] For that reason, both the Bible and biblical faith must be understood as "sources alongside other sources." Even more pointedly she explains: "The canon and norm for evaluating biblical traditions and subsequent interpretations cannot be derived from the Bible or the biblical process of learning within and through ideologies but can only be formulated within and through the struggle for the liberation of women and all oppressed people. It cannot be 'universal,' but it

24. Elisabeth Schussler Fiorenza, "Toward A Feminist Biblical Hermeneutic: Biblical Interpretation and Liberation Theology," in *A Guide to Contemporary Hermeneutics: Major Trends in Biblical Interpretation,* ed. Donald K. McKim, 358–81.

25. Ibid., 371.

26. Ibid., 378.

must be specific and derived from a particular experience of oppression and liberation."[27]

Fiorenza, therefore, calls for a "new paradigm of biblical interpretation that does not understand the Bible as archetype, but as prototype," (something that is open to the necessity of its own transformation).[28] This new way of interpreting must "evaluate biblical traditions and their political function in history in terms of their own canons of liberation."[29] Clearly, for Fiorenza, reaction to the specific situation of oppression is the key that unlocks the meaning of Scripture. Both the theology of liberation and the political and economic situation are authoritative.

This principle, which establishes a norm for interpretation, produces what has been called a canon within a canon. The canon may vary among liberationists. James Cone, for example, wrote concerning black liberation that it is "Jesus as the Black Christ who provides the necessary soul for black liberation. . . . He is the essence of the Christian gospel."[30] For some it is the Marxist model. In each case the movement is supported by a principle they see taught or illustrated in the Bible that makes the Bible meaningful for them. Thus, in the liberation movement, the Bible is authoritative only in that it serves as a sanction for violent social reform.

The principle of subject-interpretation may also be seen in the *existence model* of interpretation as presented by Ernst Fuchs, a German scholar who subscribes to the new hermeneutic as described above. Achtemeier describes Fuch's position by stating that the hermeneutical principle allowing the Bible to speak is "the question about the self, prompted by the estrangement of the self from itself, an estrangement every man knows in terms of a gulf between him and his true self. . . . It is this question that allows the text to function as it intends to function: as an address to the self, not as information about some historical event or cosmological structure. . . . This is the hermeneutical principle that allows the text to 'happen,' that allows it again to become a

27. Ibid.

28. Ibid., 379–80.

29. Ibid., 381.

30. James Cone, *Black Theology of Liberation* (Philadelphia: Lippencott, 1970), 80, quoted in Fiorenza, "Biblical Hermeneutic," 378.

language-event. When that happens, those addressed by the text may respond by themselves learning the language of faith summoned forth by the language-event underlying the text, namely, Jesus and his proclamation. And when the language of faith is learned, man may respond to life, in faith, as Jesus did."[31]

One may see how radically this understanding of Jesus differs from the concept that he is the divine Son of God, the agent of salvation, and the object of faith. In this approach he is the model of faith. Even the prophetic nature of Jesus' ministry must be changed to conform to the ever-present "now" of existence. Achtemeier continues: "Jesus' relationship to the future must therefore be understood in a different way, namely, through his words, his language. Jesus' gift to his hearers is not insight into the future course of history, not information about how or when it will end. Rather, his gift to them is his own words, formulated in such a way that the hearer has something to hold on to when troublesome times occur, something that can function as a model of faith for him. . . . It was Jesus' language, then, that constitutes the way in which he would be effective also in the future."[32]

Here Jesus' words have authority, but this authority is in what those words model, not in the explanations they provide for the questions of life. In effect, Jesus becomes no more than a spiritually sensitive man with unusual spiritual insight. Yet even there, his insight is confined to the limitations of his perspective, or world-view. His pronouncements about the end of the world, the redemptive nature of his work, and the uniqueness of his person are to be discarded, replaced by the expressions of his own faith in God that helped him in times of trouble. This is little more than nineteenth-century liberalism.

The subtlety of this is that there is here an element of truth that everyone affirms. Jesus was, in fact, a model of commitment to God, and the Scriptures consistently present him as such. The Book of Hebrews, for example, presents the highest claim for the humanity of Jesus. Passages such as 5:7–10 present a very human side of his life, and even 12:1–2 presents him as the "champion" and, therefore, chief model of our faith. There is a precedent for understanding him this way because the early

31. Achtemeier, *New Hermeneutic,* 126–27.
32. Ibid., 134.

church's outlook included it, too, even though Jesus' humanity was a source of struggle in the church for many centuries. But it is equally important to note that the Book of Hebrews presents Jesus as more than an example; it also presents him as a sacrifice, sinless, and totally sufficient *of himself* to provide atonement for our sins (Heb. 7–10). The point is, the writers of the New Testament took him as a model, but they also understood him as the provider of eternal life and forgiveness because of his unique ability to atone for sins. These modern interpreters quite clearly accept some elements of the text but reject others. The reason for this, of course, is that their world-view allows them this freedom. This means that the individual himself, or his perspective, is in actuality the authority, not the text.

This hermeneutical method is not confined to the Gospels. Achtemeier provides an insightful example from Fuchs' exegesis of Philippians 2:5–11. Historically, Christians have understood this pericope to have a dual role in the Epistle. First, it provides an example of the proper attitude for the church. If each would focus on the self-giving attitude displayed by Christ, the church would indeed be the kind of Christian community desired by God. Second, it illustrates this attitude by appealing to well-known and traditional theology (Christology). Therefore, the church understood this to reflect a real movement of Christ that added humanity to deity and servanthood to majesty.[33] Most modern commentators accept this as a hymn—known, sung, and appreciated by the early churches. The fact that Paul can appeal to its content so easily, assuming they would know and accept it, evidences the fact that the church agreed on its theological content, even though they had to learn its moral significance in their own experience.

Fuchs, however, handles the hymn in a different way. He correctly sees the death of Jesus as the focus of the passage, but his death is merely a revelation to us of how we, too, should face

33. Many conservative interpretations reflect the work of J. B. Lightfoot, whose commentary provides a good locus for understanding most of the issues involved as well as providing a generally accepted interpretation among conservatives. Cf. *The Epistle of Paul to the Philippians* (London: Macmillan, 1913). One might also see the recent discussion by Ralph P. Martin, *Carmon Cristi: Philippians 2:5–11 in Recent Interpretation and in the Setting of Early Christian Worship* (Grand Rapids: Eerdmans, 1983).

death and find love and freedom from it. Thus "a poem that, on the face of it, seems to speak of some kind of metaphysical-historical events (Jesus, present with and equal to God, sheds that divinity to become man, dies obediently on a cross, and for that is then raised up to heaven, given God's name and accorded universal worship) is revealed, upon confrontation with the hermeneutical principle, to speak of the necessity of the self to admit that what happened to Jesus happened to inform and instruct us to abandon all security . . . and exalt Jesus, who willingly underwent humiliation in death for us."[34]

The death of Jesus becomes an example for us, rather than the place where God's justice is vindicated and his love displayed. The death of Jesus must be taken in terms of "me," that is, of the self and its existence. With this goal in mind, therefore, the passage is explained existentially. "In light of the question of the self, the cross of Jesus means, in simplest terms, that Jesus opposed the self-assertion of men who feel compelled to ground and justify their existence for and to themselves, and that he died as the final act of that opposition."[35]

The individual, therefore, according to Fuchs, is to learn to die to his own self-assertion, thus allowing the love of God and the freedom of God to come to him. The cross of Jesus is also a judgment on us. Because of Jesus, we are able to see God's ideal and are compelled to allow that to happen in us also. If we do not, it is the cross (example) of Jesus that will be used to judge us. Therefore, we must be "willing to let the crucifixion of Jesus function as judgment on us."[36] By maintaining the faith of Jesus, we are able to accomplish what he did and, thereby, die to self.

Everyone will agree that the passage before us calls Christians to think and act like Christ. The differences emerge in specifically how that is pictured and what it means. For one who denies the supernatural elements here and is forced to demythologize, the passage must be studied with a focus on the psychological aspects. Since Paul calls to mind the death of Christ, the interpreter must bring to bear the psychological import of that death and must read into it the demythologized interpretation.

34. Achtemeier, *New Hermeneutic*, 132.
35. Ibid., 143.
36. Ibid.

For him, that means learning to die as Jesus showed us. There
can be nothing of a moral, legal, and metaphysical aspect of
Jesus' death, for that belongs to an outdated era. The only way to
reclaim the message of Jesus' death is to translate it into some
form of the example theory of the atonement (that Jesus only
showed us how to die, rather than died in our place). The problem
is, of course, not so much the psychological *application* of the passage, as with forcing this as the *meaning* and as the *paradigm* for
the early church's understanding of Christ.[37]

These examples illustrate how a different hermeneutic approaches the authority of the Bible. To this point we have discussed the problem of meaning, the fact that many today view
the Bible in a highly subjective manner (as a work of art, perhaps!), that they claim the need to demythologize or make the
meaning of the text relevant, and we have illustrated the approach of three modern movements. All of that has been the subject of the first question, Where does a perspective come from and
what form does it take? We may now address the second question, Is there any way to test the perspective or the response
brought by it?

Testing One's Perspective

Problems with the Subject-Oriented Hermeneutic

We have alluded to the fact that these approaches basically
differ on the nature of the Bible's authority. Biblical authority is
the crucial point because it opens the door to many other differences. The highly subjective approaches, those which place the
emphasis on the reader rather than on the object written, come to
the text as though it were some type of catalyst. This is true to a
large extent in the new hermeneutical approaches but is also
characteristic of the less subjective approaches as well. The new
hermeneutic basically looks to some other source of authority be-

---

37. This passage is complicated by the fact that example is prominent here.
That does not mean that this is the passage that best explains Paul's understanding. He uses it illustratively. His understanding of the death of Christ must be
gained from didactic passages where the subject is directly taught. Here he illustrates an attitude.

hind the text. It may be some supposed reaction to God described by the text, such as the model of Jesus or, to a lesser degree perhaps, of Paul or David. It may be to some religious feeling that authenticates personal existence, or it may be a sensitivity to larger ethical issues that concern society today. Although the Bible may be superior to other sources in producing the desired responses, in actuality, the real authority lies in the interpreter's own idea or the ideas of the religious group to which he belongs. Even the prevailing philosophy of the age can be the ultimate authority. Thus, it is hardly honest to call the Bible an authority, or the sole authority, in the traditional sense of the word.

One must recognize, first, that for these interpreters the Bible "masks" as authority, while something else actually rules. Apart from the fact that this is contrary to historic Baptist (and Protestant) beliefs and statements about the nature of biblical authority, it also suggests that the perspective fails because it is an inherently doomed approach. More will be said about this later.

Second, those who take a highly subject-oriented approach to the text disregard the intent of the author. This does not mean that the text is disregarded, at least ostensibly. Some, including Bultmann, have at times displayed a remarkable ability to do exegesis, but the intent of the author is set aside to make room for the intent of the reader and his interests. The message was adequate for that day, but the author was so confined to his own world that he has no relevant message for us today. It is said that the author's intent is basically anachronistic, and that if we desire meaning from the Bible, it will differ from what that author intended.

Discovering the Meaning of a Text

How does one discover the original meaning of a given writing? One initial problem in our thinking is that the word *meaning* may be used in a variety of ways. C. B. Caird discusses the theological implications of this and lists several different meanings of the term *meaning*.[38] Therefore, some clarification is in order.

---

38. C. B. Caird, *The Language and Imagery of the Bible* (Philadelphia: Westminster, 1980), 37–61.

The ultimate meaning of a text must be understood in at least three dimensions. First, there is the level of definition, or what we may call general meaning. This level deals with the lexical, grammatical, and syntactic relationships of words to themselves and other words within and outside their sentences. Second, there is the point of the statement, or the intent, of the author. Third, there is the level of significance. This is the point of the combinations of words that comprise a statement. Obviously, there are times when a statement does not mean what it actually says, such as in the employment of idiom or irony, and much of that is found in the Bible. Each of these makes a contribution to the exegesis or interpretation of a text.

Theoretically, everyone can understand these elements and arrive at some understanding of the intent of the author. Otherwise, society could not exist, since it could not communicate. We previously discussed the matter of subjectivity interfering with knowledge, but not even one's perspective entirely prevents him from the ability to see the author's intent. This is why Bultmann can exegete Scripture with some degree of accuracy, that is, he can understand the author's intent. As E. D. Hirsch says: "If all interpretation is constituted by the interpreter's own cultural categories, how can he possibly understand meanings that are constituted by different cultural categories? . . . We can understand culturally alien meanings because we are able to adopt culturally alien categories."[39] Tracing this ability to the basic makeup of man, he continues: "Cultural subjectivity is not innate, but acquired; it derives from a potential, present in every man, that is capable of sponsoring an indefinite number of culturally conditioned categorical systems. It is within the capacity of every individual to imagine himself other than he is, to realize in himself another human or cultural possibility."[40]

This has a bearing on the interpretation of the Bible. While it is obviously impossible to identify completely with the culture of the Bible, it is not impossible to appreciate the cultural perspectives that prevailed then. It is even possible, though difficult, to adopt the cultural values and perspectives of that era, if one should so choose.

39. E. D. Hirsch, Jr., *The Aims of Interpretation* (Chicago: University of Chicago Press, 1976), 46.
40. Ibid., 46–47.

The discovery of events in the past, however, brings with it increased difficulties. Some general assumptions prevail in many circles, which need to be challenged because of their bearing on biblical studies. Hirsch draws attention to "three relativistic fallacies."[41] The first is the "fallacy of the inscrutable past."[42] This fallacy states that the past is known only to a few who can actually sympathize with it. Therefore, it is basically unknowable for most men. Certainly biblical scholars deny this, since it logically destroys any biblical study. The second is the "fallacy of the homogeneous past."[43] This fallacy assumes that everyone who lived in a certain age shared a common perspective imposed by his culture. If this were the case, no advancements could be made because improvements come from men with ideas that transcend their cultures. The argument may be stated syllogistically:

Medieval man believed in alchemy.

Chaucer was a medieval man.

Chaucer believed in alchemy.

Obviously that is incorrect. Yet that fallacy persists in biblical studies. Interpreters often confine, even imprison the writers within their ages so that they cannot think, speak, or write differently from their age as it is perceived by the interpreter. Using the apostle Paul as an example, a syllogism could be stated as follows:

First-century people were idolatrous.

Paul was a first-century person.

Paul was idolatrous.

Obviously, this conclusion is wrong because the premises are wrong. We know better. Not all first-century people were idolatrous, and Paul is one who was not. Many, however, will reason the same way:

41. Ibid., 38.
42. Ibid., 39.
43. Ibid., 40.

First-century people believed in a three-story universe.

Paul was a first-century person.

Paul believed in a three-story universe.

This is no more demonstrable than the other. All we know is that some people of that time *did* believe that way, but we do not know that all did. One complicating factor here is that our information about the prevailing ideas of the past is too sketchy to formulate accurately every element characterizing an era. That leads to the third fallacy. It is "the fallacy of the homogeneous present-day perspective."[44] This fallacy assumes that all men of the present time share the same perspective and are, therefore, culturally bound. This simply is not the case. There is a wide variety of perspectives in any nation and even greater diversity worldwide. If these are indeed discarded as fallacies, then many objections to recovering the ideas and values of the past are overcome.

Let us return to the task of evaluating perspectives. Anyone can understand the cultural situation of another (although incompletely), and the past in and of itself is not a barrier to our understanding. Now a third element may be added. All men understand a piece of writing through the same "preperspectival" viewpoint. For example, if one is to understand Homer accurately, he must begin at the same point any other person does. He must learn Greek and study the Greek text of Homer, and by doing so, he will arrive at a meaning ("definitional meaning," see previous discussion). If he has access to enough literature of that period, he may also understand significance, since other data will be available. Assuming he can gain a close knowledge of the total situation, he can even know the intent of the writing and the specifics of it. These are basically objective in nature *regardless of the subjective elements brought to bear by the reader*. The text has an objective nature to it. We can easily see that by the response to our communication when we are misunderstood. We reply, "But I didn't mean that!"[45] The author's meaning, then,

---

44. Ibid., 41.

45. "No matter how much critics may differ in critical approach," says Hirsch, "they must understand a text through the same pre-critical approach if they are to understand it at all" (ibid., 44).

may be understood. To take a different approach and suggest that one cannot understand the meaning of a text because of his perspective is called by Hirsch cognitive atheism.[46]

The real problems in evaluating perspective occur at this point. Once the meaning is understood, the interpreter must enter into a dialogue with the text. In this manner one may be brought to a perspective outside his own. Thiselton remarks, "The text progressively corrects and reshapes the interpreter's own questions and assumptions."[47] Nearly all interpreters discuss this stage, but many dangers abound. In fact, this is the greatest tension in the debate over biblical authority.

We have discussed the highly subjective view of interpretation, which actually appeals to basis of authority other than the biblical text. It will be helpful to pursue that again. Bultmann, a representative of this view, rejects the authority of the Bible and its world-view, and opts for an interpretation that revolves around the self. While seeking to understand the text, he refuses to submit to the teaching of the text. His view of the ultimate meaning of the Bible is, therefore, greatly altered.

Bultmann was a product of this age and his personal response to his theological studies. Having embraced radical critical scholarship and German philosophers, he sought to select elements of thought from a variety of sources and put them together. "What makes Bultmann foreclose in advance certain possibilities of interpretation," explains Thiselton, "is not his hermeneutical theory as such, but the theological response which he makes to the legacy of neo-Kantian thought."[48] Clearly, his perspective therefore conditions his explanation of the ultimate meaning. Rather than listening to the text, he subordinates the text. Nothing can change his idea of things, for, as Thiselton says, "it is difficult to see what, on the basis of Bultmann's assumptions, could have counted as evidence against his interpretation."[49] Thus, in Bultmann's interpretation, "it remains true that Christ . . . can only be what he is *for me*."[50]

---

46. Ibid., 36.
47. Thiselton, *Two Horizons,* 439.
48. Ibid., 284.
49. Ibid., 266.
50. Ibid., 291. [Thiselton's italics]

Toward an Evangelical Approach

What, then, is an evangelical approach? It is found through several methodological principles. First, one must derive his theology from the text of Scripture itself, not from his environment or even his theological tradition. Discerning the meaning the writer intended involves allowing the Bible to be the source of theology, including our understanding of the nature of the Bible itself. The biblical teaching may be rejected, but if the Bible is the authority, dialogue with it will bring the interpreter closer to the meaning of Scripture. J. I. Packer refers to this process as the hermeneutical spiral (rather than hermeneutical circle) because progress is attained in this interaction.[51]

As evangelicals allow the Bible to determine their concept of inspiration, they focus on the attitude and teaching of Jesus concerning Scripture. Whether Jesus was God in flesh, as evangelicals affirm, or simply a model for our faith, as liberals teach, his view of Scripture cannot be taken lightly. In fact, in either case what he taught (and displayed) must be taken as normative and as a model for our understanding. Sometimes people protest that the phenomena of Scripture do not bear out the teaching about its own integrity, and others state that the Bible never claims inerrancy for itself. These objections have been handled thoroughly elsewhere in this book (see, e.g., chapters 1 and 2). Evangelicals believe that they must accept the views of Jesus. He was uniquely approved by God in his life, death, and resurrection, and his words were the very words of God. Leon Morris states the case well: "The fact is that nobody comes to regard the Bible as the book that gives us God's word because he has worked through it and come up with acceptable solutions to all the difficulties. He accepts it thankfully and regards it as reliable because that was the view of Christ and his apostles. It is just this, and not our ability to explain difficulties, that is the justification for our holding the Bible to be God's authoritative revelation."[52]

From one standpoint, then, the failure to accept the Bible's perspective is a failure to accept the Bible's own witness to the

51. J. I. Packer, "Infallible Scripture and the Role of Hermeneutics," in *Scripture and Truth*, ed. D. A. Carson and John D. Woodbridge (Grand Rapids: Zondervan, 1983), 348.

52. Leon Morris, *I Believe in Revelation* (Grand Rapids: Eerdmans, 1976), 140.

truth. Some scholars overlook the statements of Jesus and the apostles. Others dismiss them by their critical orientation to the text and by their conclusions that we do not in fact have the words of Jesus for our guide. These are related problems but must be left to other studies. The least that can be said is that this attitude is a failure to accept the teaching of Jesus as normative for all of faith and practice.[53] As such, it is a failure to accept the authority of Jesus over both life and thought.

The second step in an evangelical approach is to engage in serious dialogue with the text. This is the crux of the matter, and the battle for authority comes into focus here. The questions are: Do I know better than they? Am I "inspired" in the same way or to the degree that they were? Has God chosen for each man to place his own approval on the word, as though God's Word is subject to man's acceptance?

There are only three possibilities for authority. First, we can accept the Bible as the objective revelation of God's truth and the Holy Spirit as the guide to its interpretation. Second, we may submit to theological traditions. This model has been consistently criticized by Baptists who affirm the Bible as the only authority, although many liberal and conservative theologians are related to a Christian community only because of their relationship to its tradition. Often their exegetical methods are highly subjective and, if followed consistently, would not lead to the theology of the denomination. This inherited tradition is a persistent problem. Third, we may appeal to reason or to personal experiences, so that everything is evaluated by one's intellectual perception or his personal experiences. Some will claim that God is the authority rather than the Bible, tradition, or reason and experience, but this begs the question by moving into an unverifiable and indefensible position. God is always understood through some medium of communication, and that is what must be tested.

Although there are many problems in accepting the tradition

53. Geoffrey Bromiley's comment regarding those who reject inerrancy and seek to retain the Bible as revelation of God's truth remains a relevant problem. "While it is no doubt a paradox that eternal truth is revealed in temporal events and witnessed through a human book," writes Bromiley, "it is sheer unreason to say that truth is revealed in and through that which is erroneous" (quoted in Morris, *I Believe in Revelation,* 139).

as authority, the focus of this chapter is on subjectivism as a method of interpretation. To make personal experiences or reason alone the authority is both crassly egocentric (idolatrous?) and extremely pessimistic. It is egocentric because ultimately the "I" is the final court of appeal in any matter. What seems good to me rules the life, and Thiselton's appraisal of Bultmann may be justly applied: "It remains true that Christ . . . can only be what he is *for me*."[54] Even though others may arrive at the same conclusions "I" do regarding the nature of spiritual experience, and thereby provide some support and intellectual comfort, it is ultimately my interpretation that matters.

This egocentric view is also basically pessimistic for the same reasons that it is crassly egocentric. As Morris correctly observes: "It means that we have nothing from which to correct our errors, no way of knowing what is true or false once we have accepted the idea. If man's mind is the measure of things there is no way of getting back to the right way once that mind has gone off on the wrong track. Only the most pessimistic among us can be comfortable with such a view."[55]

In light of this appraisal, one might wonder why anyone would approach the text in this fashion. Those who practice this method defend it both spiritually and hermeneutically. Spiritually, they justify it by their conception of faith. Since the days of Soren Kierkegaard, the Danish theologian of the early nineteenth century, it has been popular to define faith as "leaping into the arms of God without objective or rational basis for doing so." Kierkegaard understood that faith grows out of a moral dilemma, which has no logical solution. It has been characterized, therefore, as a "leap into the dark." For these interpreters, this means that the attempt to verify the facts of the Bible is totally unnecessary and might even prohibit genuine faith. For them, faith must be (1) intensely personal, (2) without objective support, and (3) experientially verifiable. The final test, therefore, is not conformity to the descriptions of faith found in the Bible, to the experiences of others, or to objective historical fact. The authority is in whether or not it speaks to my experience and brings meaning to me (hence, Bultmann's egocentricity). Of course, this

---

54. Thiselton, *Two Horizons*, 291. [Thiselton's italics]
55. Morris, *I Believe in Revelation*, 142.

approach is far different from that described in the Bible and the expectations of biblical writers, who accepted an objective basis for faith as well as the subjective personal aspects. (This also makes faith more epistemological—a means of knowing or a way of "seeing"—than moral—a means of submitting to Christ, whose lordship is independent of man's seeing or understanding it. Our primary responsibility is to accept it.)

The hermeneutical justification relates to the nature of language. Words spoken or written become public domain, and the individual who hears them places his own meaning on them, since initially that is all he can do. Thus, some of these interpreters have suggested that the words need not even mean what the author intended. Some have even argued that the author himself cannot be sure of his meaning once the words are used.[56] When this approach to language is fully developed, the result is what Hirsch calls the "banishment of the author."[57] These literary critics say that even if we were able to consult the author, it would make little difference ultimately, and certainly it would matter little to us in our world.

Often an objection is raised that the biblical culture was too far removed from ours to make the text normative, but the cultural differences between the two eras have been magnified beyond necessity. Although they exist in the scientific and technological dimensions of society, they are less pronounced in the moral aspects of life. Leon Morris suggests that the interpreter consider the following factors in evaluating the cultural distinctions between the biblical times and ours: (1) The miraculous inference is wrongly drawn. A correct reading of the Bible suggests that miracles occurred only at certain times in history and these were for specific reasons. (2) It should not be assumed, as it too often is, that men of Bible days could not handle language as we can. They also spoke phenomenologically (e.g., the "sun sets"). (3) God does in fact work in history. The question is, which way? But if we believe in the intervention of God in history, the Bible's record can be accepted as an adequate model. (4) There are always more explanations of events than are utilized

56. A good simple discussion of this situation occurs in E. D. Hirsch, Jr., *Validity in Interpretation* (New Haven: Yale University Press, 1967), 1–23.
57. Ibid., 1.

to describe them.[58] It should also be noted that the writers were speaking of unusual phenomena when they spoke of the intervention of God in history. The apostles were no more accepted in their day than modern men who hold to the supernatural and miraculous. This may be seen in Acts 17:16–31, where Paul addresses the philosophers on Mars Hill. They had great difficulty believing in the resurrection. Thus, although the cultures differ at significant points, the differences need not mean that the biblical descriptions of supernatural events were more easily understood then than now.

A third suggestion regarding the proper approach builds on the other two. We have said that, first, one must come to the text for his theology, which includes his understanding of the nature of the Bible. Second, one must submit to the authority of the text and enter into serious dialogue with it, and allow God through his Word to have prominence over one's mind or experience. The third principle is to recognize the categories of truth statements in the Bible and to accept them for what they are. There are patterns of communication that must be observed and understood.

This suggestion does not mean there are different levels of truth in the words of the Scriptures. For example, the genealogy of Matthew 1 is as inspired and, therefore, as true as Jesus' words in John 14. The point is that we must recognize how the biblical writers chose to verify their statements.

There are three distinct categories of statements. Some are correspondence statements. That is, they correspond to some clearly objective reference point. For example, one might say "The car is green" or "John died." Both of these may be tested and verified regardless of one's personal interpretation or perception. This enables us to speak in a fashion that is easily understood, so that we are not forced to qualify ourselves ad infinitum. There are many of these statements in the Bible. They are empirically verifiable statements, which can be understood readily. For example, someone might say "Jesus went up to Jerusalem" and the reader is to understand the words in a geographical context.

Second, there are statements that correspond to reality by coherence. That is, they are rationally intelligible and make sense from the perspective of the group that uses them. These are

58. Morris, *I Believe in Revelation,* 144–45.

tested by logical consistency. They are verified by their relationship to other statements in the system. The philosopher Ludwig Wittgenstein did a significant study on language games and sought to prove that much of our language makes sense only to those "in the know." He suggested that those outside the group may be totally unfamiliar with the meaning of a given word or expression. While anyone can see the validity of his study and its helpfulness, it is imperative that one should also see its limitations. The fact is, we can understand what others mean by the language they use, and we can project ourselves into their frame of references (at least enough to communicate). Otherwise, we could only communicate when our statements were empirically verifiable, or used in a correspondence framework as described above. But society communicates in many more intricate ways than empirically verifiable words would allow. (In fact, no one could understand Wittgenstein's philosophy if he could not accept this type of language framework.)

Finally, there are experientially verifiable statements. These are statements like "Turnip greens are good" or "I love Joan." The statements may be true or false, depending on the experience of the speaker. In the same way, a statement like "I found hope in Jesus" is experientially verifiable and true for the speaker, but another may as truthfully say "I found hope in Wall Street." No one can deny the claim that is made by either one.

The Bible contains all three kinds of truth statements. It is important to recognize the nature and intent of the statement in order to understand its significance. Both fundamentalists and liberals have been guilty of trying to translate all statements into experiential statements. Thus, for example, the resurrection becomes a statement of "truth for me," rather than "true at face value." That is, the resurrection of Jesus is a matter of one's religious experience, not a truly historical event. This leads to great confusion and misunderstanding of original intent. The biblical writers intended that the historical reality would have personal dimensions as well, but the resurrection, for them, was historical.

Some examples of this in Scripture will help. In 1 Corinthians 15 we find Paul's greatest and most extended discourse on the resurrection. He begins his case with a statement about the resurrection of Jesus, then moves to the prospect of the believer's resurrection, and concludes with the nature of the resurrection body.

He states the essentials of the gospel in verses 3–5. They may be structured as follows:

> Christ died for our sins according to the Scriptures
>   and that he was buried
> and that he rose again the third day according to
>   the Scriptures
>   and that he was seen. (KJV)

This passage has several correspondence statements—statements that are intended to be empirical: (1) Christ died, (2) he was buried, (3) he rose again the third day, and (4) he was seen. Paul approaches each of these with an awareness that they belong to the public; they are events that were verifiable with human eyes. Interestingly enough, and more importantly, these events are the foundations for the entire Christian message.

Several other statements such as the following are coherent: (1) for our sins and (2) according to the Scriptures (twice). No one would be able to understand the significance of the death of Christ unless Paul explained it as he did. Although a vicarious death cannot be proven *empirically* (by correspondence), it is a perfectly natural deduction when the biblical evidence is considered. The entire sacrificial system, the traditions predicting the Messiah's work, and the prophetic passages of Scripture anticipate such an event and explanation. In that light, it is difficult to see how Fuchs and those like him can state that Christ's death means only the end of "self-assertion." That makes nonsense of all of Old Testament history, and one wonders why Christians have appreciated the Old Testament as they have. Certainly it is not for its moral value alone. The statement "according to the Scriptures," found twice here (vv. 3–4), functions to show the logical whole, that is, the system, of which Paul is persuaded. For the most part, the remainder of chapter 15 is based upon a coherence model of understanding, which came to Paul by divine revelation.

Finally, there are also some experientially verifiable statements in 1 Corinthians 15, although they are not as frequent or clear here as in some other passages. In verse 19 Paul explains that he has hope in Christ, that is, that Christ is his hope. Verse

15 assumes that the testimony of Jesus is that which brings meaning to Paul's life. Therefore, in this one important chapter, all three types of statements are found.

There is a natural progression in this passage, however, which is typical of Paul's thought. The order is correspondence, coherence, experience, or events, explanation, personal understanding. Although this order is not strictly found everywhere in Scripture, the writers clearly base their understanding of the gospel upon both historical events (described by correspondence statements) and divine interpretation by revelation (described by coherence statements). These are the bases of the appeal to experience and personal dimensions of truth found in the Bible.

Understanding these patterns helps in understanding the author. Those who say the resurrection is purely spiritual, or that it is simply a part of the death of Christ (as does Fuchs) in freeing the self to experience life, have disregarded the author's meaning and use of language. Paul intended the readers to understand that the death, burial, and resurrection of Christ belonged to the public domain. They were facts of history. In order to appreciate them, however, one must also understand the divine explanation provided in both the Old and New Testaments.

A similar problem arises with the records of Jesus' life. The accounts of his life contain historical statements. They are handled in the same way as other empirically verifiable statements, that is, as correspondence statements with coherence explanations. To say that they were intended to be understood only experientially, as only true in one's experience, is to violate the entire structure of language and meaning. The authors intended to write historically, at one level, and hoped it would change the reader's experience, at another level. The life of Jesus may be verified the same way any event of the past is known empirically—by the record of those who were there. Any other approach makes the individual the center of perception, so that "if I did not see it, it did not happen." It is true that the records may be rejected, but in rejecting the records of the Bible, one is accepting another authority over his life. It may be his world-view, or it may be his experience. In either situation, the Bible is not the authority for life.

These three elements point to the proper approach to Scripture. First, one must go to the Bible for his understanding. In so doing, he will be confronted with the words of the living Lord,

under whose authority he must live. Second, one must submit to
the authority of the Bible and engage in serious dialogue with it.
Great care must be exercised so as not to subject the Bible to human understanding, but rather to submit human understanding
to the testimony of the Word. Third, one must understand the nature of the language used by the various writers. Propositions
may be analyzed according to the nature of their verification, by
correspondence, coherence, or experiential criteria. Figurative
language must remain figurative and symbolic, but straightforward, nonfigurative language must also be recognized for
what it is. These principles help the interpreter to evaluate his
perspective and to break from his own world-view to recapture
that of the Scriptures.

In the modern debate about religious authority, the pendulum
has moved to the subjective end of the spectrum. For many, personal and individual experience determine the validity of ideas,
philosophies, and life principles. No Christian would doubt the
subjective aspects of divine revelation. The authority for Christian living resides in the Word of God and the Spirit who lives
within. Further, the nature of the gospel compels us to flee from
our natural understandings and values and to embrace a relationship with the living Lord, who calls us to security in him and
him alone. As a part of the adventure of discipleship, we must
accept the perspective of Jesus and of those commissioned by him
to write the Scriptures. Only then will the Bible be the objective
authority for our faith and life.

5

Inerrancy in History
Something Old, Something New
Thomas J. Nettles

For how long have the people of God had to exercise their faith and their minds over apparent contradictions and other monumental problems in what was presented to them, with strong evidence, as the Word of God?

Commitment to noncontradiction of divine revelation began much earlier than either Augustine or Origen. Abraham, the father of our faith, experienced a greater severity in this struggle than any of us. God specifically promised Abraham, "Sarah thy wife shall bear thee a son indeed; and thou shalt call his name Isaac: and I will establish my covenant with him for an everlasting covenant, and with his seed after him" (Gen. 17:19 KJV).

The promise was as astounding as it was specific. It appeared physically impossible for Abraham and Sarah to produce a child. Yet, the child was to come from the union of Abraham with Sarah. Isaac was to be his name. He was to live to have seed. God's faithfulness was bound up in the fulfillment of this everlasting covenant through Isaac and "his seed after him."

127

The beginning of the fulfillment of this covenant is recorded in Genesis 21:3 with the birth of Isaac. Before Isaac marries, however, God comes to Abraham again with a requirement in obedience that apparently contradicts absolutely the earlier promise. Isaac is to be offered as a sacrifice: "Take now thy son, thine only son Isaac, whom thou lovest, and get thee into the land of Moriah; and offer him there for a burnt offering upon one of the mountains which I will tell thee of" (Gen. 22:2, KJV).

No greater contradiction exists in Scripture. Everything else is mild compared to the obvious contradiction of promise and requirement that Abraham faced. So what options existed? First, Abraham could have concluded that he misunderstood either God's promise of a seed or God's demand for a sacrifice. But the promise was too clear, had come too often, had set aside all other options, and had already received miraculous confirmation. On the other hand, the demand was too recent; it was still ringing in Abraham's ears. He knew the voice of God and clearly understood it.

Second, Abraham could have concluded God was deceiving him. But God's holiness and faithfulness had already been demonstrated very clearly to Abraham. Could God cease to be holy, and would he now, after so long, prove unfaithful? No, these conclusions were impossible.

Third, Abraham might have said: "God wants me to use my reason in this situation to determine if it is possible and beneficial to obey such a command. The promise was prior, and its fulfillment is at least initiated; the requirement, therefore, besides being too brutal and too opposed to personal sentiment, would interrupt what is begun. God is merely testing my ability to use my reason and judge the likelihood of his requiring this of me in this particular situation. The most loving action, therefore, toward God, Isaac, and myself is to ignore the requirement." Such sophist reasoning, if it came to Abraham's mind, was from the old serpent himself.

Abraham could have believed that there was a way to harmonize promise and requirement. Only one thing could dispel the apparent contradiction. Would Abraham dare be so presumptuous and affirm such an answer, even in the deepest recesses of his mind? Could he, even at this stage of divine revelation, draw a conclusion from these two problematic realities that would thrust him into the most mature understanding of the power and purpose of God?

"By faith Abraham, when he was tried, offered up Isaac; and he that had received the promises offered up his only begotten son, or whom it was said, that in Isaac shall thy seed be called; accounting that God was able to raise him up, even from the dead; from which also he received him in a figure" (Heb. 11:17–19 KJV). The necessity of affirming the full truthfulness of apparent contradictions brought Abraham to an astounding maturity of faith because he saw the curse of the fall defeated and the power of death overthrown in the purpose of a faithful God, who cannot lie. For this reason Abraham is the father of the faithful and an example of how the faithful must treat the Word of God.

The thesis of this chapter is that virtually every objection to the doctrine of inerrancy had been raised and answered adequately before the middle of the nineteenth century. In addition, most current defenses of inerrancy are so obviously biblical and logically consistent that they have been used far prior to the conflict with liberalism in the last 100 years. Both of these realities are old. What is new is that these defenses now must be used, not against avowed pagans and infidels of various sorts, but against those who claim to be Christians or even evangelical Christians.

This presentation does not aim to demonstrate that our forefathers believed in an inerrant Bible (which they did), but seeks to discover their *modus operandi* in dealing with the larger practical concerns of such a claim.

The Patristic Period

Church historians are well aware that the Fathers of the early church believed in the inspiration of the Scriptures to such a degree that it could be affirmed as inerrant. Such is the conclusion of J. N. D. Kelly: "Their general view was that Scripture was not only exempt from error, but contained nothing that was superfluous."[1]

Not only did the Fathers affirm inerrancy, but they affirmed it in the face of many of the same objections that are raised today

---

1. J. N. D. Kelly, *Early Christian Doctrine* (San Francisco: Harper and Row, 1978), 61.

against that doctrine. In their debates with heretics and pagans, Fathers such as Justin Martyr, Tertullian, Athenagoras, Clement of Alexandria, Origen, Irenaeus, Augustine, and others affirmed the divine inspiration of Scripture. The pagans reasoned that if they could prove one error in Scripture, they would disprove the inspiration of Scripture and thus destroy the veracity and credibility of Christianity. For the Fathers, therefore, the defense of divine inspiration was not the protection of an esoteric and sectarian view of Scripture but was for the maintenance of the Christian faith itself.

Porphyry (233–304), a neo-Platonist philosopher, shared the neo-Platonist scorn toward Christianity and wrote fifteen books under the title *Against the Christians*. Methodius and Eusebius of Caesarea answered Porphyry adequately and sought to show the regrettable character of Porphyry's philosophy. It was Augustine, however, who dealt most precisely with the implications of Porphyry's thought for the doctrine of biblical inspiration.

To Porphyry's claim that the Gospels contradict each other and that they claim more for Christ than he claimed for himself, Augustine answered with his massive *Harmony of the Gospels*. The purpose of this work was to demonstrate the veracity of the gospel accounts of Christ and to demonstrate their eyewitness character. All that they say of Christ is true and all that they say Christ said of himself is true, Augustine claimed.

Augustine's *Harmony* is divided into four sections. In the first section, he argues against the pagan critics who had claimed that the disciples invented the gospel portrait of a divine Christ. In the second and third sections of the book, he argues for the real harmony of apparent disagreements and contradictions in the four Gospels. The reason for this method by Augustine is obvious. First, if Christ is not divine, then Christianity fails to be more than just a refined paganism. Furthermore, if it can be shown that the disciples of Christ were indeed inventors of embellished views of Christ, then the Bible is demonstrated to be a book of mere human authorship and not of divine revelation. In addition, the efforts of Augustine to harmonize apparently contradictory passages of Scripture show his conviction that if real contradictions existed, one could not claim that the whole Scripture was inspired of God. Thus, the simple arrangements of his book on the harmony of the Gospels is testimony to his and the early church's conviction that God's inspired Word has no error and, of necessity, must be consistent with itself. It also demonstrates that the historicism of modern criticism has introduced no surprises or substantial problematic data in this area.

Augustine defends the careful historical style of the writers of the Gospels and indeed says that they not only kept in remembrance the words heard from Christ's lips and the deeds wrought by him before their eyes, but that they were also careful to acquaint their readers with the events of his life that took place before they became his disciples. The account of these events— Christ's nativity, infancy, and youth—came from careful historical investigation; none of the things they said were false. Augustine argues that it is absurd to reject the historical veracity of these portraits of Jesus, who was a greater man than Pythagoras or Socrates, who were also wise men but did no writing. Augustine concludes with this notable passage:

> What reasonable ground, therefore, have they for believing, with regard to those sages, all that their disciples have committed to record in respect of their history, while at the same time they refused to credit in the case of Christ what his disciples have written on the subject of his life? And all the more, may we thus argue, when we see how they admit that all other men have been excelled by him in the matter of wisdom, although they declined to acknowledge him to be God. Is it, indeed, the case that those persons whom they do not hesitate to allow to have been by far his inferiors, have had the faculty of making disciples who can be trusted in all that concerns the narrative of their careers, and that he failed in that capacity? But, if that is a most absurd statement to venture upon, then in all that belongs to the history of that person to whom they grant the honor of wisdom, they ought to believe not merely what suits their own notions, but what they read in the narratives of those who learned from this sage himself those various facts which they have left on record on the subject of his life.[2]

After having discussed various complaints made against the historical accounts of the life of Jesus and the absurdity of alter-

2. Augustine, *The Harmony of the Gospels,* in *A Select Library of the Nicene and Post-Nicene Fathers of the Christian Church,* trans. S. D. F. Salmond, 1st series, 14 vols. (Grand Rapids: Eerdmans, 1956), 6:82.

native interpretations of Jesus' ministry and words, Augustine
closes part 1 of his *Harmony* with this strong affirmation of the
complete accuracy of the accounts:

> Moreover, in virtue of the man assumed by Him, He stands to all
> His disciples in the relation of the Head to the members of His
> body. Therefore, when those disciples have written matters which
> He declared and spake to them, it ought not by any means to be
> said that He has written nothing Himself; since the truth is, that
> His members have accomplished only what they became ac-
> quainted with by the repeated statements of the Head. For all that
> He was minded to give for our perusal on the subject of His own
> doings and sayings, *He commanded to be written by those disci-
> ples, whom He thus used as if they were His own hands.* Whoever
> apprehends this correspondence of unity and this concordant ser-
> vice of the members, all in harmony in the discharge of diverse
> offices under the Head, will receive the account which he gets in
> the gospel through the narratives constructed by the disciples, in
> the same kind of spirit in which he might look upon the actual
> hand of the Lord himself, which he bore in that body which was
> made His own, were he to see it engaged in the act of writing. For
> this reason let us now rather proceed to examine into the real
> character of those passages in which these critics suppose the
> evangelists to have given contradictory accounts (a thing which
> only those who fail to understand the matter aright can fancy to
> be the case); so that, when these problems are solved, it may also
> be made apparent that the members in that body have preserved a
> befitting harmony in the unity of the body itself, not only by iden-
> tity in sentiment, but also by constructing *records consonant* with
> that *identity*.[3]

Augustine would answer critics within the tradition of the
synoptic problem today with the same affirmation. It is nothing
new to attack the credibility of Scripture on the basis of supposed
discrepancies within gospel accounts, and it is nothing new to
show the harmony in these accounts and to affirm that, indeed,
the biblical writers were expressing the mind of the Lord in what
they wrote. As early as A.D. 180 the Muratorian Fragment had
called Luke "one zealous for correctness" and concerning the different gospel accounts had explained: "And so to the faith of be-

3. Ibid., 6:101. [emphasis mine]

lievers there is not discord, even although different selections are given from the facts in the individual books of the Gospels, because in all of them under the one guiding Spirit all the things relative to his nativity, passion, resurrection, conversation with his disciples, and his twofold advent, the first in the humiliation arising from contempt, which took place, and the second in the glory of kingly power, which is yet to come, have been declared. What marvel is it, then, if John adduces so consistently in his epistles these several things, saying in person: 'What we have seen with our eyes, and heard with our ears, and our hands have handled, those things we have written.' For thus he professes to be not only an eye-witness but also a hearer and narrator of all the wonderful things of the Lord in their order."[4]

In his prologue to book 2 of the *Harmony*, Augustine affirms with confidence that the Gospels can be discussed "with the view of seeing how self-consistent they are, and how truly in harmony with each other."[5] In the prologue to book 3, which contains the demonstration of the harmony of the evangelists from the accounts of the Last Supper to the end of the gospel records, Augustine arranges the entire narrative in a sequential way, including all the particulars, of each gospel account. He claims that this "is done in such a manner, moreover, that all these statements, *in regard to which we have to prove an entire freedom from contradictions,* are taken as made by all the evangelists together."[6]

This tension between historical truthfulness and distinctiveness in the selection and arrangement of historical events in the Gospels continues to be an important issue in Christian apologetics and New Testament studies. Grant Osborne has summarized the present state of discussions among evangelicals and has offered suggestions for reaching a consensus in evangelical use of redaction criticism. His description of the issues could, with only minor alterations, be transported into the third or fifth century as descriptive of current biblical studies.

There are several types of editorial activity: selectivity, arrangement, modification and creativity. The first two are viable for the

4. Theodore Zahn, "Muratorian Canon," in *The New Schaff-Herzog Encyclopedia of Religious Knowledge* (Grand Rapids: Baker, 1964), 8:53–56.

5. *Harmony of the Gospels* 6:102.

6. Ibid. 6:177. [emphasis mine]

evangelical, and minor modifications (such as reading later Church issues or teaching back into Jesus' ministry; wholesale creation of accounts) are clearly inimical to inerrancy. The problem is that evangelical scholars have found it difficult to remain within the allowable areas, because for [some] the methodology draws one inexorably toward the more radical conclusions. When done properly the approach is little different from the time-honored techniques of the divines down through the ages. Therefore, these scholars argue, the term "redaction criticism," as well as its techniques, are inappropriate for evangelicals.

These concerns are valid, and any evangelical approach must remain cognizant of such dangers. I believe, however, that they can be avoided and that any proper study of the gospels must adopt a nuanced form of redaction criticism. In fact I perceive a growing consensus. While [some] are leery of the term "redaction criticism" they are not opposed to the techniques of selection, arrangement or modification so long as they do not impinge upon the historical veracity of the gospel material.[7]

It is important for us to realize that historical and literary criticism played an important part in the conflict between Hellenistic paganism and the early Christians. If Christians were to make claims about the person and work of Christ, then they had to do it on the basis of true history and must not invent their own accounts out of misguided memory or existential self-affirmation. Their accounts had to be substantiated by an appeal to the same criteria used in establishing any document as reliable or any event as historical. Christians were not afraid to argue that the history of the Gospels could be verified by objective data and, in light of the majesty of their content, the claims of their subject, and many other evidences, that they must be inspired of God.

Even earlier than Augustine, Origen had defended the full truthfulness of the biblical text in opposition to a noted Celsus, who had written a generation prior to Origen. In *De Principiis* Origen had affirmed without equivocation the absolute unity of the Old and New Testaments. He stated that "the Scriptures were written by the Spirit of God and that Christ, who worked within Moses and whose words are recorded in the Gospels, worked also in Paul and Peter and the other apostles. Thus, the

7. Grant Osborne, "Round Four: The Redaction Debate Continues," *Journal of the Evangelical Theological Society* 28 (1985): 399–410.

just and good God, the Father of our Lord Jesus Christ himself, gave the Law and the Prophets and the Gospels, being also the God of the apostles and of the Old and New Testaments."[8]

Origen was also convinced that the inspiration of Scripture guaranteed an absolute coherence in its teaching from beginning to end. Although many of us would be appalled at the great liberties that Origen took with his principles of interpretation, we would share his conviction of the coherence of the divine revelation. Such a conviction can exist only where one accepts the Bible as unconditionally true, as Origen did. Origen's commitment to coherent truth guides his discussion of the necessity of a systematic theology: "Everyone, therefore, must make use of elements and foundations of this sort according to the precept 'enlighten yourselves with the light of knowledge' if he would desire to form a connected series and body of truths agreeably to the reason of all these things that by clear and necessary statements he may ascertain the truth regarding each individual topic and form, as we have said, one body of doctrine by means of illustrations and arguments—either those which he has discovered in Holy Scripture, or which he has deduced by closely tracing out the consequences and following a correct method."[9]

Origen is so confident of the inspiration of Scripture that he can state that the one who reads it and understands it "will feel his mind and senses touched by a divine breath, and will acknowledge that the words which he reads were no human utterances, but the language of God."[10] In introducing an extended section of illustrations from Scripture, Origen makes a distinction between the bodily and spiritual principles of interpretation and rejects the literalness of some things. He affirms that such careful interpretative attention must be given because every reader must reverently understand "that the sacred books are not the compositions of men, but that they were composed by inspiration of the Holy Spirit, agreeably to the will of the Father of all things through Jesus Christ."[11]

8. Origen, *De Principiis,* in *The Ante-Nicene Fathers,* trans. Frederick Crombie, 10 vols. (Grand Rapids: Eerdmans, 1956), 4:241.

9. Ibid. 4:241.

10. Ibid. 4:354. [from the Latin]

11. Ibid. 4:357. Though Origen contended Scripture should be understood in a threefold manner and dealt with some passages in order to illustrate the threefold meaning, he normally divided passages into only literal and spiritual (or fig-

In spite of Origen's tendencies toward allegorization, he nevertheless realizes the absolute importance of the historical reality of the Christian faith. Virtually his entire book against Celsus is a refutation of Celsus' arguments against the historical veracity of the events of Scripture. When Celsus accepts Greek and Egyptian and Roman myths rather than biblical accounts, Origen consistently challenges the basis of Celsus' criticisms and claims that Celsus' reasoning about the gospel accounts is absurd. If Celsus willingly accepts the fabulous and wonderful in Greek thought, why could he not more readily accept the miraculous among the Jews and Christians, and see that the latter established a system of thought more moral and that the power of Jesus continues to produce conversion and amelioration of life. And when Celsus couches his antimiraculous arguments in the person of a Jewish antagonist, Origen easily points out that the Old Testament contains miracles as well and

---

urative). In others he saw nothing legitimate in the literal meaning at all and so commented only on the "soul" and then "spirit" of the passage. Some passages have a mingling of all of these elements, and only the skillful interpreter can discern the true meaning. Sometimes, according to Origen, the narrative sections of Scripture exclude records of things that did not actually happen: either "what could not have happened, or what could, but did not." Sometimes only a few words appear that will not bear a literal acceptation, and sometimes many. Sometimes the law appears in forms in which it is useful in itself and in its own time; sometimes what is not useful is recorded and sometimes what is impossible. These appear purposefully in this form, inspired by the Spirit of God (both before and after Christ) "for the sake of the more skillful and inquisitive, in order that they may give themselves to the toil of investigating what is written, and thus attain to a becoming conviction of the manner in which a meaning worthy of God must be sought out in such subjects" (*De Principiis* 4:1–15). From this we can see that many conservatives today, of course, would not agree with Origen's methods of interpretation and would think that he sacrifices too much of the historical reality and literal facticity of events recorded in Scripture. It is just as clear, however, that Origen contended these things were never supposed to be understood in that way. He does not see the writer as having assumed a primitive world-view and written things erroneously, from which we are to salvage some theological message. He contends that the meaning from the very beginning was spiritual. It is one thing to say "There is real error, but we can still find truth"; it is another to say "The Bible is inspired and cannot err—therefore, the meaning of this passage is allegorical." Had Origen been convinced the writers intended a passage to be taken literally, he would have done so with no question and not have felt his intelligence offended at all. His self-emasculation bears eloquent, though sad, testimony to this.

says, "I who am a Christian [am] . . . not disbelieving . . . Ezekiel and Isaiah." Celsus certainly showed naivete in his approach, and Origen determined to demonstrate that "Celsus showed no sound judgment in representing a few as disbelieving on such grounds [i.e., the miraculous], a fact which has greater probability in its favour than many events in which he firmly reposes confidence."[12]

Thus we see that even as early as Origen the question of the historical truthfulness of the gospel narratives was of great concern to Christian apologists. For they perceived, even as their pagan opponents did, that if historical falsehood were demonstrated within the gospel accounts, it would severely compromise the assertion that Christianity was of God. Contemporary theologians should be as enlightened as second-century pagans.

The Reformation Period

While it is true that the Patristic period affirmed the inerrancy of Scripture and dealt with the particular problems outlined here, the clear and decisive delineation of Scripture as the *sole* authority awaited Reformation times. Some of the Fathers were quite confident that the *logos* had revealed himself savingly through other means. Justin Martyr concluded that Socrates and Heraclitus might very well have been Christians because of the activity of the *logos* in them. Clement of Alexandria and Origen would have been receptive to that idea also. Even Tertullian, whose zeal for revelation above philosophy finds expression in his question, What has Athens to do with Jerusalem? became susceptible to the error of postcanonical revelation, as shown by his temporary union with the Montanist movement and their immediate inspirationism. Even in regarding these factors, we must still affirm that the early church was very careful in its understanding of the canonicity of written works. The Muratorian Fragment confirms this by saying some writings would never be placed among the prophets or among the apostles "to the end of time," and clearly maintained that "it is not fitting that gall be mingled with honey."

Doctrinal developments during the Middle Ages show, how-

12. Ibid. 4:415.

ever, that a well-developed teaching of the sole authority of Scripture would be a help to the church. Reformation doctrine left much medieval tradition stripped and bleeding. Roman Catholicism raised a bastion of defense, however, by affirming at the Council of Trent that a continuing teaching ministry of the Holy Spirit existed in the magisterium of the church. The "unwritten traditions" were declared of equal authority with Scripture. The church gave authority to Scripture, they said, and in the person of the pope, new dogma could be presented. To this Calvin commented, "Oxen usurp the reins, and asses play the lyre."[13] The Reformers insisted that a viable doctrine of Scripture must affirm that Scripture, and Scripture alone, is the final authority in matters of faith and practice. Furthermore, given only one authority, with neither human reason nor church tradition above it (as an authority, that is, but certainly informing the process of interpretation), that authority by definition is without error.

Roman Catholicism, however, was not the only group against which this doctrine was clearly delineated. Another more subtle, and perhaps even more destructive, influence drew the attention of both Luther and Calvin. The Inspirationists, or Spiritualists, a radical group during the Reformation who believed that God immediately revealed new truth to them or inspired interpretations of Scripture disconnected from its grammatical-historical meaning, caused the Reformers some concern. Calvin dealt with this problem in both his *Institutes of the Christian Religion* and in special tracts designed to refute the radicals. These radicals fit in well with what J. I. Packer has described as Illuminists. These, according to Packer, hold that "the Holy Spirit in our consciences uses the human material of Scripture to trigger real theological and spiritual insight that they may have only a loose, nonlogical link with what the human writer meant the text originally to convey. That position agrees in principle with historic Quakerism, which trusts the inner light; it is a stance of various sorts of contemporary liberals and existentialists."[14] Packer goes on to say that Calvin did not have to deal with that

13. John Calvin, *Calvin's Selected Works: Tracts and Letters,* ed. Henry Beveridge and Jules Bonnet, 7 vols. (Grand Rapids: Baker, 1983), 3:75.

14. J. I. Packer, "John Calvin and the Inerrancy of Holy Scripture," in *Inerrancy and the Church,* ed. John D. Hannah (Chicago: Moody, 1984), 147.

sort of a person, but Packer has overlooked the Spiritualists. Calvin's controversy with the Spiritualists can be understood only in the context of his view of Scripture.

Calvin's understanding of original sin, which he adopted from Augustine and clarified, served as a basis for his affirming the necessity of inerrant revelation. Since man's disposition against God causes him to reject the revelation of God that is in nature and in conscience, Scripture is necessary to show us the true God clearly. In Scripture, God "employs not dumb teachers merely, but opens his own sacred mouth."[15] In the Word he has given us "a surer and more direct means of discovering himself."[16] Therefore, according to Calvin, it is "necessary to apply to Scripture, in order to learn the sure marks which distinguish God, as the creator of the world, from the whole herd of fictitious gods."[17] Indeed, "God, the maker of the world, is manifested to us in Scripture, and his true character expounded, so as to save us from wandering up and down, as in a labyrinth, in search of some doubtful deity."[18]

Calvin is so sure of the necessity of Scripture that he repeats these same affirmations in many ways with slightly different applications. "If true religion is to beam upon us," says Calvin, "our principle must be, that it is necessary to begin with heavenly teaching, and that it is impossible for any man to obtain, even the minutest portion of right and sound doctrine without being a disciple of Scripture."[19] This proneness of man to lapse into error apart from specific guidance is that which not only called forth a revelation from God in words (so God would hedge us in by a clear statement, which we could not evade) but necessitated that this revelation be without error. "For if we reflect how prone the human mind is to lapse into forgetfulness of God," Calvin continues, "how readily inclined to every kind of error, how bent every now and then on devising new and fictitious religions, it will be easy to understand how necessary it was to make such a depository of doctrine as would secure it from either per-

---

15. John Calvin, *The Institutes of the Christian Religion*, trans. Henry Beveridge (Grand Rapids: Eerdmans, 1964), 1:6.1
16. Ibid.
17. Ibid.
18. Ibid.
19. Ibid. 1:6.2.

ishing by the neglect, vanishing away amid the errors, or being corrupted by the presumptuous audacity of men."[20] Scripture, therefore, in order to avoid the common malady of man, must be preserved from error.

The Spirit of God forwards the authority of Scripture in two ways. First, the Spirit reveals Scripture so that it comes to us with the infallible authority of God behind it. Second, the Spirit, in convincing men of sin and granting them repentance, convinces men that God has deposited an inerrant revelation in Scripture. Calvin applies the doctrine of effectual calling to the doctrine of Scripture at this point, so that no one will ever be absolutely convinced of the inerrant nature of Scripture apart from the radical change of heart that is brought only by the sovereign activity of God upon regenerate man. So first, those "whom he has ever been pleased to instruct effectually" have been given Scripture. Second, they have had their minds changed by the Spirit of God. Calvin affirms that "this singular privilege God bestows on his elect only, whom he separates from the rest of mankind."[21]

No matter how much evidence we may present for the inspiration and divine authority of Scripture, and no matter how forcibly we may refute the objections of gainsayers, "it does not follow that we shall forthwith implant the certainty which faith requires in their hearts."[22] We are finally convinced of the inerrancy of Scripture, therefore, by the persuasion of the Holy Spirit. It is from his work that we are saved from being driven about "in a whirl of uncertainty, from wavering, and even stumbling at the smallest obstacle."[23] Thus, the secret testimony of the Spirit is Calvin's application of the doctrine of effectual calling to the epistemology of the Christian.

The strength with which Calvin sets forth this doctrine of the secret, or internal, testimony of the Spirit should not lead us to believe that he rejected the use of evidences or that he thought that Scripture could not be defended with objective, verifiable proofs. Calvin himself confesses, "True, were I called to contend with the craftiest despisers of God, I trust, though I am not pos-

---

20. Ibid. 1:6.3.
21. Ibid. 1:7.5.
22. Ibid. 1:7.4.
23. Ibid.

sessed of the highest ability or eloquence, I should not find it difficult to stop their obstreperous mouths; I could, without much ado, put down the boastings which they mutter in corners, were anything to be gained by refuting their cavils."[24]

Calvin, however, did not see evidences as convincing the unbeliever, but as comfort for the believer. For that reason, he devotes a full chapter in the *Institutes* to showing how all reasonable doubt of the inspiration of Scripture can be removed by argument. Calvin argues from the dignity of Scripture, the simplicity of Scripture, the efficacy of Scripture, the antiquity of the Books of Moses, the majesty and freedom from cultural curiosities in the writings of Moses, and the fulfillment of prophecies (including prophecies in Isaiah, Jeremiah, and Daniel).[25] He presents similar evidences from the New Testament that show the harmony of the writers, the character of the writers, the nature of the doctrines they set forth, and the change that came over such unlikely candidates for godliness.[26] He also affirms that the testimony of the church in all ages has been to the inspiration and authority of Scripture.[27]

In addition, the miraculous preservation of Scripture through the most difficult times of persecution is an evidence of its divinity, and especially that men were willing to guard it and maintain its safety, even at the threat of death. But even with all the evidence, Calvin comes back to affirm the following: "These, however, cannot of themselves produce a firm faith in the Scripture until our Heavenly Father manifests his presence in it, and thereby secure implicit reverence for it. Then, only, therefore, does Scripture suffice to give a saving knowledge of God when its certainty is founded on the inward persuasion of the Holy Spirit. Still, the human testimonies which go to confirm it will not be without effect, if they are used in subordination to that chief and highest good, as secondary helps to our weakness. But it is foolish to attempt to prove to infidels that the Scripture is the Word of God. This it cannot be known to be, except by faith. Justly, therefore, does Augustine remind us, that every man who would

24. Ibid.
25. Ibid. 1:8.1–10.
26. Ibid. 1:8.11.
27. Ibid. 1:8.12–13.

have any understanding in such high matters must previously possess piety and mental peace."[28]

For Calvin, the mind follows and affirms what faith has discovered and implicitly believes. Faith, however, is not mindless or, in the wider philosophical sense, simply "fidestic." If that were Calvin's position, he would not have presented a chapter discussing evidences of the divine origin of Scripture. Should evidence absolutely contradict inner belief, then belief must fall or change. Scripture, however, so reads us that the believer can never escape the searching profundity of its words, and it always stands as the canon against which our ideas are judged. Scripture becomes the major evidence for or against any belief and the hardware that shapes and transforms the mind to reflect the character of Christ.

The greatest change in the mind of man is moral. He must be subdued from his rage as a rebellious creature against the law of his sovereign Creator and Judge, not merely come to be convinced of the intellectual viability of the biblical world-view or the rationality of redemption. Moral subjection is the greater; intellectual conviction is the lesser. Accomplishing the lesser and missing the greater is useless and tragic. Accomplishing the greater makes the lesser follow. The inward testimony of the Holy Spirit is absolutely essential in one's doctrine and understanding of Scripture.

How does this relate to the Spiritualists? Calvin is first of all a theologian of the Holy Spirit. Not for one instant does he seek to diminish the necessity of the Spirit for divine revelation, regeneration, or illumination. This emphasis on the Spirit, however, should not lead us to think that the Spirit works independently of Scripture. The secret working of the Spirit in the present-day believer does not result in the giving of revelation or even hidden interpretations of Scripture. Instead, the Spirit produces a conviction of the truth of the words of Scripture, teaches the human mind to love and understand Scripture, and produces the desire for godliness arising from confrontation with the Scripture.

In opposition to the Inspirationists, Calvin affirms that "the office of the Spirit promised to us, is not to form new and unheard of revelations, or to coin a new form of doctrine, by which we may

28. Ibid. 1:8.13.

be led away from the received doctrine of the gospel, but to seal on our minds the very doctrine which the gospel recommends."[29] Since there are so many false teachings around, and Satan is so intent upon perverting the pure doctrine of the gospel, we must ask ourselves, "What authority can the Spirit have with us if he be not ascertained by an infallible mark?"[30] In response, Calvin affirms the necessity that the words of Scripture taken in their proper literal meaning provide us with an infallible revelation of God. Some may say, though, that it is insulting to subject the Spirit to such a narrow compass as the words written in a book. "How can it be disgraceful to the Holy Spirit," Calvin answers, "if he maintains perfect resemblance [consistency] throughout and be in all respects without variation consistent with himself? True, if he were subjected to a human, an angelic, or to any foreign standard, it might be thought he was . . . brought into bondage; but so long as he is compared with himself [that is, with the very words he has delivered in Scripture], how can it be said that he is thereby injured?"[31] For indeed, Calvin continues: "The author of the Scriptures cannot vary, and change his likeness. Such has he there appeared at first, such he will perpetually remain. There is nothing contumelious to him in this, unless we are to think it would be honorable for him to degenerate, and revolt against himself."[32]

So attached is the work of the Spirit to Scripture that Calvin can say, "The Holy Spirit so cleaves to his own truth, as he has expressed it in Scripture, that he then only exerts and puts forth his strength when the Word is received with due honor and respect."[33] Thus Calvin would justify the energy with which he decries all who detract from the Word of God as the only authority in our understanding of God and his ways with the world and with men. He rails against "those swelling enthusiasts in whose idea the only true illumination consists in carelessly laying aside and bidding adieu to the Word of God while . . . they fasten upon any dreaming notion which may have casually sprung up in their minds."[34]

29. Ibid. 1:9.1.
30. Ibid. 1:9.2.
31. Ibid.
32. Ibid.
33. Ibid. 1:9.3.
34. Ibid.

Such flippancy regarding the Word of God is not characteristic of true children of God, according to Calvin; rather, "as they feel that without the Spirit of God they are utterly devoid of the light of truth, so they are not ignorant that the Word is the instrument by which the illumination of the Spirit is dispensed. They know of no other Spirit than the one who dwelt and spake in the apostles—the Spirit by whose oracles they are daily invited to the hearing of the Word."[35] In his treatises against the Anabaptists and the libertines, Calvin again affirms the same congeniality between the Spirit and the Word. The severity of Calvin's feeling is seen in some of the language that he uses about those who would seek to place the Spirit above the Word. For example, he says: "In fact, the swine Quintin assigned insulting nicknames to each of the apostles, in order to make them contemptible. . . . This is how this disgusting wretch dared to blaspheme with his own foul mouth."[36]

Calvin saw a common principle uniting the Inspirationists and the Papists: They sought revelation outside of Scripture. "Though this sect is certainly different from the Papists, inasmuch as it is a hundred times worse and more pernicious," writes Calvin, "nevertheless both of them together hold this principle in common: to change Scripture into allegories and to long for a better and more perfect wisdom than we find in it."[37] These Inspirationists would cause us to err if they led us beyond the limits of Scripture. God did not promise the Spirit for the purpose of forsaking Scripture, but in order that we might "gain its true meaning and thus be satisfied."[38]

When Jesus opened the minds of the two disciples on the Emmaus Road, he did not inspire them with subjects not found in Scripture but helped them understand Scripture itself. Indeed, the apostles themselves were not led by the Spirit to lay aside Scripture or to create in them mistrust for it, "but on the contrary we see that the Scripture became the focus of their entire study and obedience. And we hold to the same obedience."[39]

35. Ibid.
36. John Calvin, *Treatises Against the Anabaptists and Against the Libertines*, trans. and ed. Benjamin Wirt Farley (Grand Rapids: Baker, 1982), 221.
37. Ibid., 222.
38. Ibid., 224.
39. Ibid.

Thus, we see that the concept of finding a canon within the canon, or of discerning the theological truth from the historical trappings, was not at all foreign to Calvin and his reforming contemporaries. Both the Spiritualists and the Papists adhered to a principle alien to Scripture by which its teachings were augmented (immediate inspiration or unwritten tradition) or diminished ("fleshly" parts). Much modern scholarship assumes an ability of the Christian consciousness to distinguish theological and ethical truth from the morass of its historical trappings. While this places Scripture on a procrustean bed, on the one hand similar to Marcionism, it assumes a sort of private revelation and inspiration on the other. William Hall, in his controversial article, "Shall We Call the Bible Infallible?" stated this position as candidly as possible when he said, "Distinguishing between the human and the divine in the Bible may be a tedious process, but it is absolutely essential if the fundamental difference between God as perfect and man as imperfect is to be maintained."

Since when did dualism rather than confluence characterize the biblical doctrine of inspiration? If "all Scripture" (2 Tim. 3:16) is not inspired, and if Scripture did not arise from holy men being carried along by the Holy Spirit as they spoke (2 Pet. 1:20–21), then by what means may one discern the human from the divine? Certainly not by purely human means, or the biblical writers could themselves have eliminated the errors (unless we feel that we are of a different nature than they). Only by a separate "inspiration" could such a discernment be made.

The efforts of many modern critical scholars to make this very discernment (unless inspiration of Scripture is denied entirely), as well as to reconstruct Scripture to reflect hypothetical *proto* documents and sources, are reminiscent of the pure subjectivism of the Spiritualists. Calvin would reject the attempts as profane and faithless.

Post-Reformation Issues
Related to Scripture

The doctrine of *sola scriptura* raises legitimate questions about the location of the authoritative text. Catholics at the Council of Trent located it in the Latin Vulgate. The first decree of the fourth session stated, "Whosoever shall not receive these entire Books with all their parts, as they are accustomed to be read in the Catholic Church, and are contained in the Old Vulgate Latin edition, as sacred and canonical, and shall knowingly and intentionally despise the foresaid traditions, let him be anathema."

Protestants rejected this. It appears clear to me that when the reality of this decree dawned upon the Reformers, their understanding of the inerrancy of Scripture related to the original manuscripts. Calvin comments clearly and forcefully about this: "But as the Hebrew or Greek original often serves to expose their ignorance in quoting Scripture, to check their presumption, and so keep down their thrasonic boasting, they ingeniously meet this difficulty also by determining that the Vulgate translation only is to be held authentic. Farewell, then, to those who have spent much time and labour in the study of languages, that they might search for the genuine sense of Scripture at the fountainhead!"[40]

Calvin continues his show of utter disgust with the Romish decision in his exposition of other elements of the decree. "In condemning all translations except the Vulgate, as the error is more gross, so the edict is more barbarous. The sacred oracles of God were delivered by Moses and the Prophets in Hebrew, and by the Apostles in Greek. . . . No man possessed of common sense ever presumed to deprive the Church of God of the benefit of learning. The ancients, though unacquainted with the languages, especially with Hebrew, always candidly acknowledged that nothing is better than to consult the original, in order to obtain the true and genuine meaning. . . . The Council, however, insists that we shall shut our eyes against the light that we may spontaneously go astray."[41]

Such affirmations clearly imply infallibility in the autographs, or original manuscripts, of Scripture. To conclude otherwise would fly in the face of the normal use of language. And it was not held naively, for Calvin and other Reformers were quite aware of and engaged in the practice of textual criticism. Calvin even mentions the work of Erasmus and Lorenzo Valla in *Anti-*

---

40. *Selected Works* 3:68.
41. Ibid. 3:71.

dote to the Decrees of the Council of Trent. Any study of Calvin's commentaries will demonstrate his strong linguistic studies and his awareness of these various manuscripts. We also see him seeking to establish what he feels is the clearest, purest text, and when he refers (as he seldom does) to errors, he is referring to errors of transmission, not errors in the inspired volume.

The contributions of Theodore Beza to biblical science can hardly be called into question. He personally owned one of the most significant of the early codices, the Codex Bezae, which he presented personally to the University of Cambridge.[42] Thus, the Reformation appeal to *sola scriptura* involved an informed commitment to the original languages of Scripture with an accompanying discipline to determine the original text. So, in 1607, when the Baptist John Smyth affirms that "the Holy Scriptures, viz., the originals, Hebrew and Greek, are given by divine inspiration and in their first donation were without error," and when John Gill, the major Baptist theologian of the eighteenth century, says the Vulgate abounds with innumerable errors and mistakes but affirms that the Scriptures in their "original exemplar" are inspired of God, and thus infallible, they are only reflecting what had been clearly set forth by the Reformers and, in English life, by the Cambridge Puritans during the last part of the sixteenth and early part of the seventeenth centuries.

William Whitaker, a Cambridge man during the reign of Queen Elizabeth I, had solidly affirmed the inerrancy of Scripture and had made it clear that he was speaking of the original manuscripts of Scripture. The same was believed and taught by William Ames and a host of other Puritans, even before the Westminster Assembly's highly influential Statement of Faith, which says: "The Old Testament in Hebrew and the New Testament in Greek, being immediately inspired by God, and by his singular care and providence kept pure in all ages, are therefore authentical; so as in all controversies of religion the Church is finally to appeal unto them."

42. S. L. Greenslade discusses the whirl of scholarly linguistic activity in Geneva during the days of the Marian exile especially around 1557–1560. The development of the Geneva Bible shows the open interaction Reformers had with textual variants in the production of translations. Cf. S. L. Greenslade, ed., *The Cambridge History of the Bible: The West from the Reformation to the Present Day* (Cambridge: Cambridge University Press, 1963), 155–61.

But if we say the Bible is inerrant in the original manuscripts, what do we mean by inerrant? Does this extend even to matters of history and other matters of fact? Some would insist that modern evangelicals who extend inerrancy even to nontheological issues engage in a novel enterprise. But history shows clearly that a plenary inerrancy is not the invention of the last 100 years.

The contention that Scripture is infallible only in spiritual matters had already been brought up in the eighteenth century by Deists and had been rejected by orthodox believers. Among the Baptists, Andrew Fuller was one of the staunchest defenders of this thorough inerrancy of Scripture. Andrew Fuller affirmed against deism that the inspiration of the Scriptures demonstrated the truth of the Christian faith and that the inspiration of Scriptures could be maintained only if it were affirmed that they were true in all their parts. He said that if the Scriptures can be proved to harmonize with historic fact, with truth, with themselves, and with sober reason, they must (considering what they profess) be divinely inspired and Christianity must be of God. To Thomas Paine's accusation that the prophecies of Scripture were false, Fuller replied: "Mr. Paine says the Scripture prophecies are a book of falsehoods. Let us examine this charge. Isaiah, above 100 years before the captivity, predicted the destruction of the Babylonish Empire by the Meads and Persians and Judah's consequent deliverance. 'The plunderer is plundered, and the destroyer is destroyed. Go up, O Elam, besiege, O Media. All the crying thereof have I made to cease.' Ask Herodotus and Xenophon: 'Was this a falsehood?' "[43] And this same book that contains true prophecies that have already been fulfilled says that judgment will eventually come upon the unbeliever. Fuller asks the sobering question, "Let Mr. Paine and other infidels consider well the above picture and ask their own consciences: 'Is this a falsehood?' "[44]

Fuller claimed the Scriptures are consistent with an enlightened conscience and consistent with the truth we observe about human society at large. When Paine said the Bible was filled with bombasts beneath the genius of a schoolboy, Fuller rejected

---

43. Andrew Fuller, *The Gospel: Its Own Witness of the Holy Nature and Divine Harmony of the Christian Religion* (Clipstone: J. W. Norris, 1799), 184–85.

44. Ibid., 195–96.

the appropriateness of the charge. Bombast occurs only where exaggerated words are used to support inferior ideas. Such is not the case with Scripture. The themes discussed are not small, and if any inadequacy exists, it exists only because the words are too reserved rather than too embellished. Even Jean-Jacques Rousseau praised the dignity of Scripture as "so simple and sublime as to render the works of other men as mean and contemptible."[45]

The very claims that Scripture makes for itself, Fuller says, impose a great obligation upon anyone drawing a conclusion about the nature of Scripture. Either it must be a revelation from God, or we must consider the Scriptures as mere imposture. It is absurd to pretend that their authentic records are productive of enlightened morality and at the same time reject their inspiration. There is no consistent medium between faith and unbelief. Inspiration, therefore, demands that every matter recorded in Scripture be true, and even in matters that were common phenomena observed by the writers, inspiration would preserve them from error and from other defects and faults to which ordinary historians are subject. Sometimes a higher degree of inspiration may accompany the writings of things not observable by the writer and things concerning the nature of God and salvation, but in whatever degree inspiration occurred, "it requires that a book professing to be a revelation from God should contain truth, and nothing but truth. Such, particularly, must be its history, its prophecies, its miracles, and its doctrines."[46]

Joseph Priestly, a leading Unitarian of his day, considered that the Bible must have error in it because it was written by men. Fuller saw clearly the premise from which Priestly worked, that is, it is impossible for God himself so to inspire a man as to preserve him from error without destroying his nature. Fuller showed Priestly's argument to be absurd. Nevertheless, he entered a somewhat satirical plea with Priestly to publish a Bible with all the error removed. "In short," Fuller responded, "if we must never quote Scripture except according to the rules imposed upon us by Socinian writers, we must not quote it at all, not at least until they shall have indulged us with a Bible of their

45. Ibid., 214–19.

46. Andrew Fuller, *The Complete Works of the Rev. Andrew Fuller*, ed. Joseph Belcher, 3 vols. (Philadelphia: American Baptist, 1845), 1:699.

own that shall leave out everything on which we are to place no dependence. A publication of this sort would, doubtless, be an acceptable present to the Christian world, would be comprised in a very small compass, and be of infinite service in cutting short a great deal of unnecessary controversy, into which, for want of such a criterion, we shall always be in danger of wandering."[47]

Myriads of defenders of inerrancy could be garnered for our investigation, but I purposefully pass over discussion of Archibald Alexander, Charles Hodge, Robert Dabney, A. A. Hodge, B. B. Warfield, John L. Dagg, J. P. Boyce, and others; however, I must now ask, What is old and what is new in the present debate?

Something Old, Something New

First, the assertion that the reality of the Christian faith depends upon whether the Bible is actually true in all its affirmations is old. That is so obviously true that it has been asserted and defended in every age. The negative of this also is old. S. D. F. Salmond's introductory essay to Augustine's *Harmony* in *The Nicene and Post-Nicene Fathers* states: "Paganism, having tried persecution as its first weapon, and seen it fail, attempted next to discredit the new faith by slandering its doctrine, impeaching its history, and attacking with special persistency the veracity of the Gospel writers. . . . And it was a favorite method of argumentation, adopted both by heathen and by Manichaean adversaries, to urge that the evangelical historians contradicted each other."[48] The Socinians and Deists did the same.

Second, that the Bible in its original manuscripts is the particular document being defended when the claim for inerrancy is made is not a new claim, but extends at least as far back as the Reformation. This position is not only unjustly caricatured but irrationally resisted. No one can seriously believe that original manuscripts never existed (nor blame inerrantists for limiting this position on inerrancy to those autographs). The autograph position does not remove the challenge of proper interpretation, nor is it an idolatrous grasp for exhaustive knowledge, similar to Eve's quest for divine knowledge in Eden.

---

47. Ibid. 2:205.
48. S. D. F. Salmond, "Translator's Introductory Notice," in *The Nicene and Post-Nicene Fathers,* 1st series, 14 vols. (Grand Rapids: Eerdmans, 1956), 6:79.

Gossip is a game often played at children's parties. One child at the head of a line of children whispers a sentence to the next child. This process is repeated until the last child has had the sentence whispered in his ear. One rule, however, is that the sentence may not be repeated between partners. One cannot check the accuracy of his understanding. By the time the last child reports aloud what he heard, it hardly resembles at all what was said in the beginning. God has not played "gossip" with us. We can check with great confidence the accuracy of our understanding of what God said.

Third, that Christians have claimed the Bible to be completely consistent internally and thus have engaged in attempts at harmonization is not new. From the ante-Nicene period (A.D. 170) to the present, this has been done. Perhaps not all apparent discrepancies have been harmonized; some have been harmonized rather awkwardly. But such persistence in the attempts witnesses to the innate necessity we have for affirming that two statements both deemed as true cannot be in contradiction. That John Broadus, a significant New Testament scholar, would attempt to construct a harmony at a time when theories from Tübingen had denied the possibility of harmony stands as startling testimony to this conviction. We may confess that in any particular case all the information is not yet in or that our understanding is slow, but we cannot believe that one *truth* contradicts another *truth*. That is an absurdity.

What is new in the present debate? It is that all the attacks once used by pagans are now used by supposed Christians. Christians are now defending the inspiration and full truthfulness of Holy Scripture from others who claim to be Christians. One is tempted to treat this in the way that J. Gresham Machen did in *Christianity and Liberalism*. "Liberalism is totally different from Christianity, for the foundation is different. Christianity is founded upon the Bible. It bases upon the Bible both its thinking and life. Liberalism, on the other hand, is founded upon the shifting emotions of sinful men."[49] For example, when an interpreter says that Jesus made an error in his predictions in Mark 13 concerning the consummation of the age,[50] he sounds

---

49. J. Gresham Machen, *Christianity and Liberalism* (Grand Rapids: Eerdmans, 1956), 79.

50. E. Glenn Hinson, *Jesus Christ* (Wilmington, N.C.: Consortium, 1977), 76.

not like the Christian apologist but like the pagan Julian, who sought to disprove the predictions of Jesus and of Daniel about the destruction of the temple by rebuilding the temple. (An earthquake destroyed his efforts.) If Jesus made a mistake in his prediction, he is certainly not a true prophet and, therefore, can hardly claim our allegiance as Prophet, Priest, and King. In Old Testament Israel, he would have been stoned.

When an interpreter says "Jesus himself had no conscious-ness of 'divinity'"[51] and represents the biblical writers as enlarg-ing Jesus' messianic consciousness when they recorded the confession at Caesarea Philippi in Matthew 16, he plays the part of a second-century pagan or an eighteenth-century Socinian more than a Christian. To state concerning the gospel writers that "some embellishments undoubtedly occurred"[52] does not sound like a Christian writer, but like Porphyry the pagan. Yet, all of these statements come from one who claims to be defending a piestistic tradition of Christianity.

Perhaps one of the newest twists of an old attempt to discredit inerrancy comes from Charles H. Talbert, a professor at Wake Forest University. "When inerrantists argue that when Christ speaks, even about matters of fact, it is God talking," contends Talbert, "we are to recognize it for what it is, Apollinarian heresy at worst, Monophysite error at best. If Christ's humanity is not to be seen in his being a man of his own times in the area of matters of fact, then I fail to see where his humanity is to be found insofar as his human mind is concerned."[53]

He draws upon orthodox Christology in an attempt to argue for an errant Bible and reasons that since Christ was a human and therefore a man of his own times, he made the same mis-takes concerning the authorship of the Pentateuch, the existence of Noah, the existence of Abel, and the unity of Isaiah as his con-temporaries did. "To draw upon Jesus' view of Scripture as evi-dence for inerrancy is a denial of his true humanity and therefore heresy" is the argument. I will pass by the epistemological diffi-culty of believing Chalcedon without believing Scripture, the implicit Nestorianism of his Christology, and the insurmount-

51. Ibid., 83–84.
52. Ibid., 66.
53. Charles Talbert, "Inerrancy: The Central Question," in *Southern Baptist Convention Today*, Feb. 1986, 14.

able inconsistencies confronted if he contends that Jesus used his "human faculties" to teach religious truth. I will only remind the reader of the insight of Andrew Fuller, mentioned earlier, who pointed to a fundamental flaw in the system of the Unitarian Joseph Priestly. Priestly believed that God could not so inspire a man so as to preserve him from error without destroying his essential human nature. Fuller points out that the idea that human nature necessarily involves factual error, or even that the doctrine of total depravity necessitates factual error, is not true. Wise humans will not speak where they do not know, and in areas of life and death they will speak as carefully and truthfully as possible. Jesus could certainly partake of the culture of his day without absorbing its errors (abundant evidence exists for this) and could certainly epitomize wisdom and truthfulness without becoming nonhuman.

I will close with sentiments expressed by two important Baptists who lived in daily intimacy with the Bible and dealt thoroughly with every conceivable attack on its absolute truthfulness in every area. Adoniram Judson, the revered Baptist missionary of the nineteenth century, said:

> The Word of God is the golden lamp hung out of heaven, to enlighten the nations that sit in darkness, and to show them the path that leads from the confines of hell to the gates of paradise. The Bible, in the original tongues, comprises all the revelation now extant which God has given to this world. It is, in all its contents, and parts, and appendages, just the book, the one book, which infinite wisdom saw best adapted to answer the end of a written revelation. It may not be reducible to the rules of human philosophy or logic, for it transcends them all. It is just as clear and obscure, just as copious and scanty, has just as many difficulties and apparent contradictions, as infinite wisdom saw necessary, in order to make it, like all the works of God, perfect and unique. This one perfect book is the sacred deposit in the hands of the church. It has been deposited with the injunction, "Freely ye have received, freely give." Woe be to that man who withholds the treasure from his neighbor. Woe be to him who attempts to obscure the light of the lamp of heaven.[54]

54. Adoniram Judson, *A Memoir of the Life and Labours of Adoniram Judson,* ed. Francis Wayland, 2 vols. (Boston: Phillips, Sampson and Co., 1853), 2:236–37.

Finally, John L. Dagg, the first writing Baptist systematic theologian in the United States and greatly loved for his godliness and perseverance in overcoming personal obstacles, said:

> For myself I realize that I am standing on the shore of the boundless ocean, with but an inch of crumbling sand remaining. I hear the shrieks of the dying infidel at my side, to whose view all is covered with impenetrable darkness. He, too, has come to the brink, and would gladly refuse to proceed, but he cannot. Perplexed, terrified, shuddering he plunges in and sinks, he knows not whither. How cheering this Light from heaven! Before it I see the shades retiring. The Bible lifts its torch—nay, not a feeble torch, such as reason may raise, to shine on the darkness and render it visible; the Bible sheds the light of the noonday sun on the vast prospect before me, and enables me, tranquil and joyful, to launch into eternity with the full assurance of hope. Mortals hastening to the retributions of eternity, be wise; receive the revelation from heaven presented to you in the Bible; attend diligently to its instructions and reverence its authority as the word of the final Judge before whom you will soon appear.[55]

But we must go much further back than either Judson or Dagg, and much further back than even Augustine or Origen. We must recapture the faith of our father Abraham.

55. John L. Dagg, *Origin and Authority of the Bible* (Charleston: Southern Baptist, 1853), 31.

PART 2

Some Practical Implications

6

Biblical Authority and Homiletics
David Allen and Jerry Vines

John W. Montgomery described his impressions of the Barth Lectures of 1962 at the University of Chicago Divinity School by noting that much of Barth's preaching appeared to be vitiated by his long-standing disregard for adequate epistemological foundations for theology.[1] During the lectures, Edward J. Carnell directed a question to Barth regarding his refusal to assert the ontological existence of the devil. Barth countered by saying that the attitudes of Jesus and the gospel writers to the existence of Satan cannot be considered sufficient reason for affirming it.

Later in the same session Barth gave a detailed analysis of the meaning of *hupotassō* ("submit") in Romans 13:5 and indicated that the Christian is bound to be involved in society by this verse. Montgomery summed up the problem revealed by the above statements when he concluded, "But why bother to milk

1. John W. Montgomery, *The Suicide of Christian Theology* (Minneapolis: Bethany, 1970), 192.

any New Testament word for its full theological import if the unwavering position of the Gospels with regard to the ontology of the demonic can be discounted?"[2]

This scenario is both analogous to and illustrative of the situation in the current theological debate about biblical authority and its impact upon homiletics. We may rephrase Montgomery's query to read, Does not a position of biblical errancy erode the necessary epistemological foundation for homiletics? Put in a positive way we may ask, Does not a position of biblical inerrancy provide one with the necessary epistemological foundation upon which preaching rests? The thesis of this chapter is that the answer to both of these questions is a resounding yes.

In the Patristic age the crucial theological debate centered around Christology. In the Medieval and Reformation periods the emphasis was upon soteriology. From the Enlightenment until the modern period there can be little doubt that the crucial theological debate has centered around epistomology and specifically the nature of biblical authority. Throughout the debates about the inerrancy of Scripture that have continued until the present time, there is an area of concern that has received little attention in theological or homiletical circles: In what way does one's view of biblical authority inform one's approach to preaching? It is our belief that the doctrine of inerrancy serves as a foundation for homiletics in a twofold way: epistemologically and methodologically. This chapter treats the issue of inerrancy under these two rubrics.

Epistemology

There is irrefutable evidence that Baptists have historically held to the doctrine of the inerrancy of Scripture. Clark Pinnock, noted Baptist theologian and author, writes: "There is an historic view of the Bible, and Baptists have held to it. The conservative doctrine of inspiration has history on its side. It is a mistake often made by progressive theologians to suppose that belief in Biblical infallibility is a recent aberration of fundamentalist thought. As a matter of fact it is not. It has been the position of all Christian churches for eighteen hundred years."[3] L. Russ Bush

2. Ibid.
3. Clark Pinnock, "Baptists and Biblical Authority," *Journal of the Evangelical Theological Society*" 17 (1974): 197.

and Thomas J. Nettles have clearly shown in their comprehensive work, *Baptists and the Bible,* that Baptists have historically believed in the inerrancy of Scripture.[4] After a careful analysis of the major Baptist theologians from John Smyth to the present day, and an analysis of Baptist confessions of faith through 1963, Bush and Nettles conclude that the words *infallible* and *without error* have been invoked by Baptists to describe their understanding of biblical inspiration. It is further pointed out that there is no appreciable difference in the meaning of these terms. Article 1 of the 1963 *Baptist Faith and Message* statement is quite clear when it affirms that the Bible "has God for its author, salvation for its end, and truth, without any mixture of error, for its matter."[5]

John Broadus expresses the same historical conviction about the Scriptures when he says that the biblical writers "were preserved by the Holy Spirit from error. . . . There is no proof that the inspired writers made any mistake of any kind."[6]

Two questions must be asked and answered at this point. Has there been a departure from the historic Baptist position of biblical inerrancy by Baptist theologians today? If so, then we must ask, Has such a departure affected biblical preaching in Baptist pulpits?

There is no doubt that there has been a departure from the historic Baptist position of biblical inerrancy. Bush and Nettles have documented not only the historic Baptist view but also the modern shift away from that view to a position of scriptural errancy on the part of many Baptist theologians. The contemporary debate in the Southern Baptist Convention over the issue of biblical authority clearly witnesses to the fact that there has been a departure from biblical inerrancy. Clark Pinnock confirms the defection from the historic Baptist position: "To what extent did Baptists share in the great defection from belief in the infallible Scriptures? The answer has to be, at least in reference to the writing theologians of stature, to a large extent. This can be seen negatively from the almost complete silence of recent

4. L. Russ Bush and Thomas J. Nettles, *Baptists and the Bible* (Chicago: Moody, 1980).

5. Ibid., 371–92.

6. John Broadus, *A Catechism of Bible Teaching* (Philadelphia: American Baptist, 1892), sec. 3, part 2, lines c, f.

Baptist theologians to come out in defense of Biblical infallibility in the face of the blistering attack on it."[7]

Pinnock surely penetrates to the heart of the issue when he
declares that what is at stake in the debate about the nature of
the Scriptures is nothing less than the possibility of normative
theology, and with it the possibility of clear, bold preaching. "The
crisis of the Scripture principle for theology," continues Pinnock,
"is simply the fact that, if the new view of the Bible is correct, we
do not know what constitutes revelational data and, not knowing
that, cannot speak confidently about the truth of God."[8]

Of course Baptists are not the only major Protestant denomination to see many of its theologians adopt a non-inerrantist
view of biblical authority. With the rise of higher criticism during the Enlightenment, every major Protestant denomination
has seen a shift away from the historic doctrine of scriptural
inerrancy.

Bernard Ramm's book *After Fundamentalism* attempts to
support the thesis that Karl Barth's theology offers to evangelicals a paradigm of how best to come to terms with the Enlightenment especially in relation to the doctrine of biblical authority.
Our specific interest with Ramm at this point is twofold. First,
he serves as an example of a Baptist theologian whose theology
of biblical authority has shifted from a position of inerrancy as
reflected in *Protestant Biblical Interpretation* (1970) to one of
scriptural errancy in *After Fundamentalism* (1983).[9] Second, he
illustrates the fact that it is Barth's theological position that informs his own understanding of biblical authority.

Ramm is convinced that the theology of Karl Barth best
presents us with a correct understanding of the doctrine of biblical revelation.[10] The importance of this for Baptists is that it represents what has been taking place in the thinking of many of

7. Clark Pinnock, "Baptists and Biblical Authority," 199.

8. Ibid., 202.

9. Bernard Ramm, *Protestant Biblical Interpretation*, 3d rev. ed. (Grand
Rapids: Baker, 1970); *After Fundamentalism* (San Francisco: Harper and Row,
1983). It should also be noted that Clark Pinnock has shifted somewhat to the left
of his earlier position on the inerrancy of Scripture as can be seen from comparing his *Biblical Revelation* (Chicago: Moody, 1971) with some of his more recent
writings.

10. Ramm, *After Fundamentalism*, vii.

our theologians on this particular issue. We are convinced that a latent neoorthodox influence is responsible for the shift in Baptist theology away from a position of biblical inerrancy.

In describing Barth's view of how Scripture can be described as God's Word, Ramm uses the words *diastasis* and *diffraction*. By *diastasis* Ramm means that there is an "interval" between the Word of God and the Scriptures.[11] This interval allows historical and literary criticism of the text without surrendering the theological integrity of the text. What Ramm does not mention is that such a *diastasis* can surrender the historical and scientific integrity of the text to the historical and literary critic and furthermore many push the *diastasis* to such an extreme that oftentimes the theological integrity of the text is sacrificed as well. This is indeed the result with Barth. His *diastasis* causes him to allow theological error in the text of Scripture.

By diffraction Ramm posits that when the Word of God enters the language of the Bible, it is no longer perfectly reflected.[12] In spite of all this, Barth (and Ramm) maintain that the Word of God is still to be found in the Scriptures. But this is precisely the point at issue. If we grant the notion of *diastasis* and diffraction as Ramm defines it, we are left in an epistemological quandary. Who or what will tell us what is and what is not to be considered as God's word in the written Word? As noted earlier, Barth may consider the biblical idea of Satan to be false while we may consider it to be an accurate reflection of the Word of God in the written words of Scripture. Who arbitrates such a dispute? In Barth's theology there is no one to arbitrate; the epistemological foundations of an inerrant text have been undercut.

In this vein consider the title of Eric C. Rust's book on the subject of a theology of preaching: *The Word and Words*. His presentation is clearly informed by a neoorthodox outlook as he develops the thesis that God's Word comes to us through the clearly fallible and errant words of Scripture. He clearly states that Scripture contains both historical and theological errors when he says: "Indeed, the Old Testament is the Word of God in promise. . . . That does not mean that we use words like *inerrancy,* for historically it is not inerrant. Furthermore, theologically it is

11. Ibid., 89.
12. Ibid., 90.

not inerrant. . . . The inerrancy lies in the promise of redemption."[13]

Likewise, Clyde Fant, considered by many to be the dean of Southern Baptist homileticians, reflects his dependence upon a neoorthodox framework in *Preaching for Today*. Fant suggests that an extreme emphasis on the original language of the text has resulted in the various dictation theories of inspiration. "Because the human element is so feared," says Fant, "these mechanical theories had to be concocted in order to protect the transmission of the word from human instrumentality. This is the reason that the expression 'inspired in the autographs' is so popular among some groups, and also why the most extremely conservative theological seminaries devote such a preponderance of the curriculum to original language studies."[14]

We presume that Fant is here alluding to the doctrine of inerrancy as an example of a so-called dictation theory of inspiration[15] and that he therefore does not accept the inerrancy of the Scriptures. "This slide-rule method of solving all questions of interpretation," continues Fant, "attempts to achieve an impersonal, objective—and therefore infallible—statement of the meaning of the Bible."[16]

Surely those of us who practice biblical hermeneutics from an inerrancy perspective can do so with a recognition of the personal, subjective, and fallible features that an interpreter brings to the text. The inerrancy of the text does not in any way suggest the infallibility of the exegete or guarantee the infallibility of all of his interpretations. The fallibility of the exegete, yes; the fallibility of the text, no.

Fant appears to accept the neoorthodox understanding of revelation and biblical authority in so far as he advocates the Word of God behind the words of the Bible.[17] This nebulous concept of the Word of God behind the words of the Bible results in the preacher opposing the notion of gospel, or kerygma, with written

13. Eric C. Rust, *The Word and Words* (Macon: Mercer University Press, 1982), 7–8.

14. Clyde Fant, *Preaching for Today* (New York: Harper and Row, 1975), 33–34.

15. Cf. chapter 1 in this volume for a discussion of the various theories of inspiration and especially comments about the dictation theory.

16. Fant, *Preaching for Today,* 34.

17. Ibid., 33.

Scripture. When attempts are made to peel away the skin to get to the essential kerygma, the result is a net loss of biblical truth and authority.[18]

The neoorthodox view of revelation may be summarized in the following way. The Bible is not the Word of God directly but is rather a record and a witness to the Word of God. The Bible contains the normative witness of revelation to the past and the promise of revelation in the future. It is a trustworthy, but fallible, witness to God's revelation. The key point to note in the neoorthodox position is that one is forever looking for the Word of God behind the words of the Bible, and this bifurcation is foreign to the Scriptures themselves.

When such an approach to biblical authority is carried into homiletics, the Bible begins to be described as a *model* for preaching rather than the *content* of preaching. Preaching begins to be described in such terms as *relational, witness,* or *model,* rather than *content* or *exposition.* We are not denying that words such as *relational* can be used of preaching; rather we are noting the shift in perspective, approach, and vocabulary of those who accept a view of biblical authority that is informed by neoorthodoxy.

Given the fact that Baptists have traditionally held to the inerrancy of Scripture, why would some Baptist theologians adopt an essentially neoorthodox view of biblical authority? Clark Pinnock offers an answer to this question, though possibly he overstates the case. He suggests that Baptists have a strong tendency to locate truth in the saving encounter with Christ rather than in objective truth outside themselves. He attributes this to the effects of revivalism upon Baptists and suggests that this has opened the way for Baptists to be infiltrated by liberal and neoorthodox theology. The reason for this is that both liberalism and neoorthodoxy ground doctrine in personal religious experience and not in an external authority. Pinnock points out that to the "extent to which Baptists make their subjective experience of salvation, rather than the objective Word of God, the main weapon in their defense of the truth, is the same measure they are vulnerable to theological compromise."[19]

The results of such a theological compromise of biblical au-

18. Richard Lischer, *A Theology of Preaching* (Nashville: Abingdon, 1981), 77.
19. Pinnock, "Baptists and Biblical Authority," 203.

thority for the homiletical task should be evident. The preacher, armed with improper historical and literary critical presuppositions, may so edit the text that certain features (like the existence of Satan) are said to be examples of cultural conditioning. Thus, when confronted with preaching on such a text, he must interpret it to mean something other than what it overtly says regarding the ontological existence of the devil. The result is nothing short of a twisting of the Scriptures, and the preacher is left with "no sure word of prophecy."

If it be argued that such a twisting of Scripture is not a necessary result of the neoorthodox approach, we must reply that even with Barth (as has been shown above) and with many of his followers, such a result does occur. Whether it is a necessary concomitant or not is a moot point. The fact is that the result of such an approach ladens the interpreter with the awesome responsibility of determining what is and what is not the Word of God in the written words of Scripture.

The crucial point to notice about this approach is the fact that the Word of God is not identified with the words of the Bible, and hence the Bible is not the revelation of God to man but the record of God's revelation to man. It contains outmoded language, legends, and myths, which must be cast off or reinterpreted by the modern preacher in the attempt to communicate the Word of God in the words of men. Such a damaging bifurcation in preaching rests upon the foundation of neoorthodoxy provided by Barth and robs the preacher of a solid epistemological foundation.

The major problem here is the fact that if, as most neoorthodox theologians concede, the Scriptures contain both historical and theological errors, who will disentangle that which is accurate from that which is inaccurate for us in the Scriptures? One person may argue that a given saying of Jesus is inauthentic; the next, that it is authentic. How is such a problem arbitrated under the model of biblical authority advocated by Rust, Fant, Ramm, or Barth? Furthermore, as Schubert Ogden has shown of Rudolf Bultmann's approach, why demythologize everything except the Christ-event?[20] What sanctions the Christ-event and places it beyond demythologization? Only Bultmann's inconsistency in his program of demythologization provides such sanctions. If the

20. Schubert Ogden, *Christ Without Myth* (New York: Harper and Brothers, 1961), 105–26.

Scriptures are so tainted with human fallibility, how do we know that the description of the Christ-event is not also an inaccurate picture of the way things really are? Take away the epistemological foundation of inerrancy and add historical and literary critical presuppositions about the text and the preacher is left with no sure word from the Lord.

Merrill F. Unger is one of the few writers on the subject to discuss the relationship one's view of inspiration has upon his preaching. "Wholesale rejection of the doctrine of verbal plenary inspiration of the Scriptures in critical circles," he writes, "with insistence that the Bible is subject to errancy and human limitation, has resulted in an inevitable reduction of its authority and a sharp decline in preaching it. If the Bible is considered merely to contain the Word of God, rather than actually to be *in toto* the Word of God, there is naturally a decreased sense of responsibility to study its text minutely, or to systematize its theology, or authoritatively to declare its message."[21]

Unger goes on to note that some seminaries have abandoned the synthetic and analytic study of the Scriptures by relegating this task to the Bible institute. The biblical languages are taught mainly to meet the needs of the critical scholar rather than to aid the preacher in biblical exposition. Unger suggests that many young preachers leave the seminary unprepared for the supreme task of declaring the Word of God and expounding the Scriptures as a coherent body of revealed truth.[22]

We may note several examples of the epistemological effect that this damaging bifurcation between the Word of God and the words of Scripture has upon preaching. In *The Word and Words* Rust suggests that preaching today must deal with the political, social, environmental, and technological problems of mankind. He fails to recognize that preaching the Scriptures as we have them will speak to these problems without the preacher having to turn his gospel into a social gospel to which Rust's approach appears susceptible. As noted above, Rust's distinction between the words of the Bible and the Word of God provides the springboard for the preacher to begin with any text and move into a discourse on contemporary problems, which the text itself may not

21. Merrill F. Unger, *Principles of Expository Preaching* (Grand Rapids: Zondervan, 1955), 18.
22. Ibid., 19.

justify at all. This is not to say that Scripture does not speak to
social ills, for indeed it does. We are simply saying that the door
is now open for a preaching ministry that amounts to little more
than some form of the social gospel.

Eric C. Rust and James Cox contributed a chapter to *Biblical
Preaching* entitled "The History of the Exodus Wanderings and
the Settlement." They suggest that the notion of holy war found
in Joshua and Judges is "repugnant" to us today, and they find it
difficult to believe that God had anything to do with the campaigns, in spite of the fact that the text clearly claims that God
directed their actions. Their own conclusion is illuminating
when they point out that these factors make sections of Joshua
and Judges difficult preaching material for the homiletician.[23]
Here is a clear example of how one's view of biblical authority
affects one's approach to preaching. Rust and Cox conclude that
God never told Joshua to kill people during the campaigns to
take over the land. In other words, the texts as we have them are
simply in error and the preacher cannot preach them as they are.
He must go behind the text to say to his people today what God
apparently intended. The result is clearly a loss of biblical authority in preaching.

Often an appeal is made to the spirit of Jesus as the final
guide for what is true or false in the biblical accounts, as Rust
does. "The Bible is authoritative for us," says Rust, "but it is derived authority. It is authoritative for us only as it points to him.
. . . The Christ towers above its testimony and lights up its words
with new and vital meaning. Many of its limited insights stand
condemned in the light of God's grace in him."[24]

If it be argued that the kerygma itself or the spirit of Jesus
himself becomes the final authority for mediating between truth
and error, then it must be understood that our knowledge of both
the kerygma and the life of Christ are both conditioned by inscripturation and are thus not able to escape the possibility of
error, according to this particular model of biblical authority.[25]

---

23. Eric C. Rust and James Cox, "The History of the Exodus Wanderings and
the Settlement" in *Biblical Preaching,* ed. James Cox (Philadelphia: Westminster, 1983), 61.

24. Rust, *The Word and Words,* 9.

25. Robert Dunzweiler, "Inspiration, 'Inspiredness,' and the Proclamation of
God's Word Today," in *Interpretation and History,* ed. Laird Harris, Swee-Hwa
Quek, and J. Robert Vannoy (Singapore: Christian Life, 1986), 193.

Elsewhere in *Biblical Preaching,* William P. Tuck argues that
the Book of Daniel was written in the second century B.C., and
that the writer took the name Daniel and set the story in the
sixth century B.C.[26] The result of this for the preacher is that the
prophetic character of the book is lost. Daniel purports to be a
book of prophecy, but Tuck has not allowed it to stand on its own.
Having accepted historical-critical presuppositions regarding it,
he relegates the book to a second-century date of writing. The
man Daniel really did not receive a prophetic vision from God in
the sixth century, but rather a second-century writer placed
these events in the time of the sixth century to give the appearance of prophecy. Again, one's view of inspiration and the nature
of biblical authority invariably affects the way the text is
preached, and the result in Tuck's case, again, is a loss of biblical
authority.

Tuck goes on to argue that in the case of Esther and Ruth, the
stories are based upon a nucleus of historical truth, but fictional
dimensions are probably employed in the books much like a historical novel today.[27] Again the problem is who determines what
is fictional and what is not.

Clyde T. Francisco contributed a chapter to *Biblical Preaching* entitled "Preaching from the Primeval Narratives of Genesis." In this chapter he suggests that Matthew 5:17–20 probably
does not contain the *ipsissima verba* of Jesus but is rather Matthew's own understanding of what Jesus meant by what he said.
He further suggests that as such, this may simply be one man's
opinion! But we are allowed to trust this opinion, according to
Francisco, because Matthew is a part of the canon and the witness of the church is that he understood the words of Jesus correctly.[28] But we must ask at this point, What sanctions the
church as an infallible norm for determining whether Jesus'
words have been understood correctly or not? If God is not the one
who guarantees the truthfulness of the words via inspiration
and the resultant inerrancy of the text, then again, we are left
with no sure word of prophecy.

26. William P. Tuck, "Daniel, Ruth, Esther, and the Song of Songs," in *Biblical Preaching,* ed. James Cox, 152.

27. Ibid., 157.

28. Clyde T. Francisco, "Preaching from the Primeval Narratives of Genesis," in *Biblical Preaching,* ed. James Cox, 23.

Francisco argues that regardless of the historical or scientific inaccuracies in the text, the basic thrust of the text is from God and can be preached with authority. Yet how can this be so if the text is also fraught with theological errors as Rust claims? The problem here is that if the texts are presented in mythological language, and if there is scientific, historical, or theological error in the text, by what authority do we determine their basic truthfulness?

In an interview with *Faith and Thought,* Clark Pinnock responded to the question of whether legend was a literary genre found in the Scriptures. His answer pinpoints the problem for contemporary preaching that faces those who, denying the inerrancy of Scripture, accept "inaccurate historical accounts" under the guise of a certain literary genre such as legend. "The difficulty I have with it," answers Pinnock, "is of course one of consistency. If I say the story of the axe head floating is a legend, is this not demythologizing a biblical miracle, and where will that stop now? It puts a lot of weight on our ability to identify the genre legend literarily. If the axe head floating looks like a legend to me, the virgin birth looks like a legend to the liberals. So while in principle I have no problem admitting legend in the Bible, in practice I do."[29]

These examples are sufficient to illustrate the loss of biblical authority and the concomitant problems for preaching that are evident when one rejects the notion of the inerrancy of Scripture. John R. W. Stott is surely correct when he makes the insightful statement that the essential secret of preaching is not "mastering certain techniques but being mastered by certain convictions."[30] He argues that if our theology is right, then we have all the basic insights we need for preaching, as well as the basic motivation to induce us to do it faithfully.

Since Scripture is the Word of God written in the words of men, preaching rests upon certain convictions about the nature of God and the nature of the Scriptures. The biblical writers neither invented nor distorted what they have written, but have faithfully written what God wanted written. Furthermore, God

29. "An Interview with Clark H. Pinnock," *Faith and Thought* 2 (Fall 1984): 56.

30. John R. W. Stott, *Between Two Worlds* (Grand Rapids: Eerdmans, 1982), 92.

still speaks through what he has spoken. This is evidenced by the alternate uses of *gegraptai* ("it is written") and *legei* ("he says") as introductory citation formulas for Old Testament quotations in the New. In the perfect tense *gegraptai* emphasizes the written character of God's Word, while in the present tense *legei* emphasizes the fact that God's Word continues to speak today. The Book of Hebrews, perhaps more than any other New Testament book, brings out the fact that what Scripture says, God says, by its consistent use of some form of *legō* as a citation formula. These two concepts are necessarily interrelated. Overemphasis on one at the expense of the other leads to theological error.

When the preacher stands in the pulpit, what exactly is the source of his authority? Of course, the Triune God furnishes the preacher his authority to speak God's Word. But where is it that the preacher receives God's Word? Is it through direct divine revelation as with the prophets of old? No, the Word of God comes to the preacher through the Scriptures and is in fact for the preacher the Scriptures themselves. Apart from the Bible, the revealed Word of God, the preacher has no kerygma, no didache, no message to proclaim. His source of authority is the text of Scripture itself.

In his recent work entitled *Preaching,* James Cox lists six sources of authority for the preacher: divine call, ordination, education, experience, character, and the biblical text.[31] He then, under the heading "Special Authority," discusses the role of the Holy Spirit in preaching. Certainly he is right about the role of the Holy Spirit. Our problem here is that Cox does not seem to give enough emphasis to the biblical text as the preacher's primary authority, and he does not discuss the impact of one's view of inspiration on preaching. Although he does not state it overtly, the implication is left in the mind of the reader that the text of Scripture lies on the same plane of authority as these other five sources. If it is the Bible itself that furnishes the preacher with his authority, then one's view of biblical authority will greatly affect his preaching ministry.

In conclusion, the unscriptural and philosophically untenable bifurcation between a reliable and infallible gospel and a somewhat unreliable and fallible Bible is theologically intolerable.

---

31. James Cox, *Preaching* (San Fransciso: Harper and Row, 1985), 19–24.

The result of such a theological stance is a weakened epistemological foundation for homiletics. We maintain that the doctrine
of scriptural inerrancy is foundational to homiletics. Since other
chapters in this volume discuss and define inerrancy, we have
not done so here. Our purpose has simply been to illustrate how
inerrancy as a theological construct informs the homiletical task
of today's preacher, and how a denial of inerrancy greatly weak-
ens the epistemological foundation upon which homiletics rests.

Methodology

Does one's acceptance of inerrancy as a theological construct
for biblical authority affect homiletics from a methodological
standpoint? Indeed it does. In this section we offer the thesis that
inerrancy provides the methodological foundation for expository
preaching.

James Barr, in his influential book *The Bible in the Modern
World,* states that he doubts whether the Bible itself, regardless
of one's view of inspiration, can furnish the preacher with a
model for the form and content of sermons that could be taken as
normative.[32] While some who hold to the same view of biblical
authority as Barr would disagree with his statement, the fact
remains that a low view of biblical inspiration ultimately un-
dercuts the homiletical task both epistemologically and methodologically.

Many today consider expository preaching to be one method of
preaching among many other methods (e.g., topical or textual
preaching). It is our contention that expository preaching must
be defined in broader and more comprehensive terms than just
a method among other methods. As a matter of fact, we contend
that all preaching, regardless of form, should be expositional in
nature, regardless of which homiletical method is employed.[33]

Unger's definition of expository preaching suggests the fact
that this type of preaching is more than just a method among
methods, but is really the foundation of all methods. "It is not the
length of the portion treated," Unger explains, ". . . but the manner of treatment. No matter what the length of the portion ex-

---

32. James Barr, *The Bible in the Modern World* (London: SCM, 1973), 139.
33. Jerry Vines, *A Practical Guide to Sermon Preparation* (Chicago: Moody,
1985), 11–18.

plained may be, if it is handled in such a way that its real and essential meaning as it existed in the light of the over-all context of Scripture is made plain and applied to the present-day needs of the hearers, it may properly be said to be expository preaching."[34]

James Daane suggests that in the strict sense of the term, authentic preaching is expository preaching. Expository preaching represents the assertions of a given text in the form of a sermon. The word *homiletics* has its etymology in the Greek words *homo* ("same") and *legō* ("speak"). Homiletics, therefore, is the technique which constructs a sermon that says the same thing as the text says.[35]

Haddon Robinson offers this definition of expository preaching: "Expository preaching is the communication of a biblical concept, derived from and transmitted through a historical, grammatical, and literary study of a passage in its context, which the Holy Spirit first applies to the personality and experience of the preacher, then through him to his hearers."[36]

Since our preaching must be based upon the Scriptures, Robinson argues that expository preaching emerges not merely as a type of sermon, but rather as the theological outgrowth of one's view of scriptural inerrancy. Practically speaking, the concepts set forth in the sermon must be based upon and have their source in the Scriptures. For him, expository preaching originates as a philosophy rather than a method.[37]

John MacArthur expresses the same sentiment when he comments that expository preaching is the declarative genre in which inerrancy finds its logical expression.[38] Likewise, he argues that inerrancy demands exposition as the only method of preaching that preserves the purity of God's Word and accomplishes the purpose for which God gave it.[39] He makes it clear

34. Unger, *Principles of Expository Preaching,* 33.

35. James Daane, *Preaching with Confidence* (Grand Rapids: Eerdmans, 1980), 49.

36. Haddon Robinson, *Biblical Preaching* (Grand Rapids: Baker, 1980), 20.

37. Haddon Robinson, "Homiletics and Hermeneutics" in *Hermeneutics, Inerrancy, and the Bible,* ed. Earl D. Radmacher and Robert D. Preus (Grand Rapids: Zondervan, 1984), 803.

38. John MacArthur, "A Response to Homiletics and Hermeneutics," in *Hermeneutics, Inerrancy, and the Bible,* ed. Earl D. Radmacher and Robert D. Preus, 820.

39. Ibid., 821.

that he believes expository preaching is really exegetical preaching and not so much the homiletical form of the message.

Walter Liefeld argues that exposition is a basic concept in preaching, the essence of which is explanation. The essential nature of expository preaching is that it explains a passage so that it leads the congregation to a true and practical application of that passage.[40]

He argues for the primacy of expository preaching because it forces the preacher to stay close to the text of Scripture, which is the revealed Word of God. Further, expository preaching is more likely to impress upon the congregation the fact that God's Word is their ultimate source of authority, not the preacher. However, it needs to be stated that much of what goes on in pulpits today under the name of expository preaching is really not true exposition by these definitions given above. Many who are inerrantists do not follow the logical conclusion of their theological convictions in their pulpit ministries. Thus, sometimes a preacher who is known to be an inerrantist is guilty of spiritualizing an Old Testament text in order to provide sermon material. Such spiritualizing or allegorizing is an unwarranted practice among some preachers, given their theological convictions about biblical authority. We often accuse the liberal of not being faithful to the text of Scripture and then we hermeneutically violate that same text of Scripture through allegorizing. True expository preaching demands both attention to the text in context and carefully distinguishing between the meaning of the text and its multifaceted significances or applications.

Furthermore, not all who hold to the inerrancy of Scripture preach in an expository fashion, and not all who preach in an expository fashion hold to the inerrancy of Scripture. But by and large we believe it can be clearly shown that the logical outcome of an inerrantist perspective is an expository preaching ministry. If the very words of the Bible are inspired as 2 Timothy 3:16 teaches, then the homiletician will want to take great pains to faithfully convey the meaning of these very words in the sermon. C. H. Spurgeon, that prince of Baptist preachers, declares that the sermon comes with far greater power to the minds and hearts

40. Walter Liefeld, *New Testament Exposition: From Text to Sermon* (Grand Rapids: Zondervan, 1984), 6.

of its hearers when it is not a lecture about Scripture, but Scripture itself opened up and taught. He recommends that preachers preach the *ipsissima verba*, the very words of the Holy Spirit, for it is these sermons that best convey to the people the Word of God.[41]

An expository sermon, therefore, will be the fruit of exegetical and hermeneutical tasks performed previously in a diligent study of the text upon which one plans to preach. The sermon form will be guided by the text itself, so that the preacher is careful to convey the meaning of the text and not his own thoughts about a particular subject.

Indeed, it is at this point that the difference between topical preaching, which is largely the type of preaching practiced in America today,[42] and expositional preaching can be clearly seen. Topical preaching conveys the preacher's thoughts about the Bible or some topic, which employs a text or texts as a peg upon which to hang the sermon. The expository preacher preaches the actual words of the Bible itself so that the people hear God's Word expounded. If what Scripture says, God says (and we believe this to be exactly what Scripture claims for itself), then the best method of communicating God's truth to his people is through expository preaching. Expository preaching is the natural result of both a high view of Scripture and a proper exegetical process.

In Paul's correspondence with Timothy, it is no accident that we find a strong statement regarding the full inspiration of the Scriptures in 2 Timothy 3:16–17 and then the charge in 2 Timothy 4:2 that Timothy is to "preach the Word." There can be little doubt that the Word here is identified with the inspired Scripture of 3:16. Preaching the Word cannot be done authoritatively without the necessary epistemological foundations of an inerrant text and a philosophy of preaching that is built upon true exposition. The dearth of true biblical preaching in America today evinces the theological shift away from an inerrant Scripture. This is a weighty matter, for nothing less than the authority of God's message and God's messenger is on the line.

41. C. H. Spurgeon, *Lectures to My Students* (Grand Rapids: Zondervan, 1972), 73.

42. J. I. Packer, "Why Preach," in *The Preacher and Preaching*, ed. Samuel T. Logan (Phillipsburg, N.J.: Presbyterian and Reformed, 1986), 4.

7

Biblical Authority and the Christian Mission
William Wagner

Dramatic reports of revivals, awakenings, renewals, and unprecedented church growth in countries in most parts of the world give rise to a new sense of optimism for the church of Jesus Christ. This is not to say that missions prior to the last few decades has been unsuccessful. On the contrary, we have observed a steady move forward for several centuries. Arthur Johnston called the period from 1800 to 1914 the "Great Century of World Missions,"[1] while John E. Kyle states "some thoughtful missiologists have suggested that we are entering a new era of World Missions."[2] The successes of the past, coupled with the opportunities and challenges of the future, may combine to give the church its greatest period of expansion in the last fifteen centuries, even rivaling the rapid growth of the New Testament church, which influenced the civilized world in an unprecedented manner.

1. Arthur Johnston, *The Battle for World Evangelism* (Wheaton: Tyndale, 1978), 34.
2. Samuel Wilson, ed., *Mission Handbook,* 12th ed. (Monrovia, Calif.: MARC, 1979), 16.

Even though optimism reigns, we are constantly reminded that there remain over three billion people who have not accepted Jesus Christ as their Savior. This makes the task great. Large blocks of tribal, Muslim, Hindu, and Chinese peoples remain untouched by the message of love and salvation as given by Jesus Christ. Islam, as well as some of the Eastern religions, is now in a resurgent phase and, having learned missionary methods from Christians, is creating large and sometimes effective missionary endeavors that compete with the efforts of Christians.

As the lines of future conflict for the souls of men begin to take shape, it is essential for us to be aware of two facts: who the enemy is, and whence cometh our help. At a recent conference on missions to Muslims, the speaker mentioned that he had no fear of other religions, no matter how advanced or sophisticated their theology, since the Bible has promised spiritual power to the church. Rather, he feared the enemy within who might cause us to face the danger of approaching the battle with blunted swords and in total disarray. This chapter will focus on the internal threat to the worldwide missionary endeavor from the sedating effect of the doubt syndrome increasingly dominant in many churches in the West.

Tracing the Problem Historically

It is difficult to pinpoint the beginning of the modern missionary movement. Some would say that it began with the work of Nicolaus Ludwig von Zinzendorf (1700–1760), while others would point to William Carey (1761–1834), the Baptist shoemaker and lay preacher. He proposed the convening of the World Missionary Conference, which he had hoped to hold in the year 1810—a hope that was realized exactly 100 years later at the conference in Edinburgh. Others might suggest even other names for the honor of founding the missionary work now taking place. It is not important that we determine exactly when this began; it will be sufficient to identify some of the changes that took place in the theological world and to show how they affected missionaries involved in the greatest task on earth.

Wayne A. Detzler, in attempting to pinpoint the beginning of the triumph of secularism within the Christian church, writes,

"Since 1960, the Church in Europe has been plunged more deeply into the deep freeze of secularism, which had its beginning between 1870 and 1940, when the academic and labor world turned away from the Church."[3] Those alive at that time were not aware of a radical change, but as the historian looks back into the history of the Christian movement, he can see that in some Western nations, especially Germany, new thought forms including socialism, rationalism, Marxism, and Darwin's evolutionism arose. Some theologians began to apply new scientific principles to their understanding of the Bible. They sought a more complete comprehension of Scripture and in doing so developed new methods, such as literary and historical criticism. Many began to have real questions about the accuracy of certain sections of the Bible, particularly the first eleven chapters of Genesis, as well as the authorship of many of the Old and New Testament books. Those who were involved in this study were often brilliant individuals seeking a better understanding of God's Word, but in time, the development of this new scientific understanding of the Bible tended to vitiate the prevalent concept of the inerrancy of the Scriptures.

During the earlier years of this process, there was little real negative influence on the Western church and its missionary zeal, since faith in God's Word was strong. In his book *The Battle for World Evangelism,* Arthur Johnston states: "No one questions seriously the evangelical stance of the missionary movement of the nineteenth century. It was known to be biblical in doctrine, godly in conduct, emphasizing personal reconciliation with God and concern for human and national welfare."[4] During the latter part of the nineteenth century and the early twentieth century, the influence of the new form of theology was negligible as far as the Christian masses were concerned. This was partly because communications during this period were both slow and expensive. Nevertheless, inroads were being made. The foundations of what is now known as modernism, or liberalism, though it was limited in its earlier stages, began to have an influence on a wider range of individuals. One of the reasons for this has been

3. Wayne A. Detzler, *The Changing Church in Europe* (Grand Rapids: Zondervan, 1979), 9.

4. Johnston, *The Battle for World Evangelism,* 33.

given to us by Dr. Peter Beyerhaus in his excellent book *Shaken Foundations*. He traces the inroads made by the historical-critical approach into the churches of the Western world. The new converts to liberalism, after having spent three to five years studying theology under those who expressed their doubts as to the inerrancy of the Bible, were now ready to begin work as pastors. But many no longer had a desire to go into this field. Instead, they tended to choose one of three other types of ministry: (1) teaching religion in lower schools, (2) teaching seminary-level theology, or (3) administrating churches. It was a slow process, but by 1948 it became apparent that the critical approach to biblical interpretation had successfully infiltrated a large segment of the Christian church.

By 1900 there was sign of some inroads by liberalism into the missionary movement. John Yoder contends that since 1890, the major churches in the United States have had a strong infusion of biblical criticism and the social gospel.[5] Johnston even feels that the highly praised missionary conference in Edinburgh in 1910 already gave evidence of the decline of belief in the infallibility of the Bible.[6] Others feel that the success of the conference was such that it gave new life to the evangelical message for decades to come. Regardless of how one views Edinburgh, it is evident that the succession of conferences following slowly gave way to the influence of the more liberal wing of the missionary movement. Many attempts have been made to show how the series of missionary conferences beginning in Edinburgh led to the foundation of the World Council of Churches in Amsterdam in 1948. A study of this process is highly recommended to those who are interested in seeing how conservative thought and influence can slowly be transformed into another and opposite form. One is reminded of the old Arab story that speaks about the Arab and his camel, who are sleeping in the desert on a cold night. The man had set up his tent and warmed it with a fire. During the night, he awoke and saw that the camel had his nose in the tent. "What are you doing?" asked the man. "O sire, it's so cold out here. Please let me just put my nose in the tent. It will help me to keep

---

5. John Yoder, *A History of the Ecumenical Movement (1917–1948)*, ed. Stephen Charles Neill and Ruth Rouse (London: SPCK, 1954), 254.

6. Johnston, *The Battle for World Evangelism*, 43.

warm." The man agreed, but soon he awoke again to find that the camel now had his head in the tent. He again asked the camel, "What are you doing?" The camel convinced the man that if he could only keep his head warm, he would be satisfied and once again the man complied. The same thing happened again and again with the front legs, the back, and finally the back legs. The last time the question was asked, the camel replied by telling the man to get out of his tent. The process can be slow, but effective.

From 1910 until 1948 a slow change in the emphasis of missions emerged. The change was affected by the theological climate prevalent during this period. It is somewhat difficult to measure statistically the effect of this change in the understanding of the Bible on missions between 1910 and 1948 because of the unsettled world conditions brought on by two devastating world wars, but a shift of emphasis in missions, which eventually led to the formation of the World Council of Churches, is apparent. Social concern on the mission field was a growing factor and began to become more important than the evangelical position that a person must be born again in order to enter the kingdom. Matthew 28:16–20 began to be replaced by Luke 4:18–19 as the Scripture reference that gave motivation to missions.

In the late 1940s "the Arab began to look for a new tent," and this period saw a new outpouring of God's Spirit that gave rise to new movements and institutions that did hold to scriptural infallibility. Fuller Theological Seminary was founded in 1947 as an apologetic institution based on scriptural truth. The following statement about Scripture was adopted by the faculty and by the Board of Trustees of the seminary: "The books which form the canon of the Old and New Testaments as originally given are plenarily inspired and free from all error in the whole and in the part. These books constitute the written Word of God, the only infallible rule of faith and practice."[7] It is important to note that Fuller's School of World Mission has probably been the most important institution in the evangelical missionary advance in the world during the last forty years.

Also during this time, Billy Graham began his ministry and later was used by God to call into being two very important con-

7. Harold Lindsell, *The Battle for the Bible* (Grand Rapids: Zondervan, 1976), 107.

ferences that were to have a profound effect on world evangelization: The World Congress on Evangelization in Berlin in 1966
and The International Congress on World Evangelization in
Lausanne, Switzerland, in 1974. These two conferences ce-
mented the division of Christian missions into two rather well-
defined movements, which, for lack of more descriptive terms,
are called the ecumenicals and evangelicals. The unity experienced in Edinburgh was no longer visible, and now missiologists
had to take this separation into account when looking at issues
in missions. How does this separation affect the missionary
movement in the last half of the twentieth century? Looking at
the two sides more carefully might give us some insights.

Different Views on Missions

In 1980 two world missionary conferences were held, one in
Melbourne, the other in Pattaya. In an article written for the
magazine *Mission Focus,* David Bosch of South Africa gave a
shorthand understanding of the differences between the ecumenical and evangelical views of missions. No matter how the problem of mission in the 1980s is approached, ultimately there will
be the dichotomy of views seen by these two camps, which also
influences one's view of world missions. Dr. Bosch compared the
two points of view in table 1.[8]

This apparent division within the church has a great effect on
the subject of this paper, for an analysis of the growth or decline
of these two segments of the body of Christ can give us some insights as to the result of particular theological views on the effec-
tiveness of outreach into the world. Everyone is aware of the
dangers of categorizing both denominations and individuals,
due to the large number of exceptions, but there does seem to be
some validity in looking at the broad picture. It is fair to say that
ecumenicals tend to have a lower view of the Bible, while evangelicals tend to have a higher view. Since the ecumenical movement includes a wide range of beliefs, it is certain that many,
though believing in the inspiration of the Bible, have accepted
the validity of the critical method and, thus, come to accept the
presence of errors in the Bible.

8. David J. Bosch, "Evangelism," *Mission Focus* 9 (Dec. 1961): 65–66.

TABLE 1   **Ecumenical and Evangelical Views of Missions**

Melbourne	Pattaya
(Ecumenical View)	*(Evangelical View)*
1. Shows a preference for "Jesus language" of the Gospels	1. Shows a preference for Paul's language in his Epistles
2. Begins with human disorder	2. Begins with God's design
3. Stresses unity (at the expense of truth?)	3. Stresses truth (at the expense of unity?)
4. Believes that God reveals himself through contemporary experience	4. Believes that God reveals himself only through Jesus Christ (and in Scripture and the church)
5. Emphasizes the deed (orthopraxis)	5. Emphasizes the Word (orthodoxy)
6. Regards social involvement as part and parcel (or all?) of the Christian mission	6. Regards social involvement as separate from mission or as a result of conversion
7. Judges societal ethics to be of prime importance	7. Judges personal ethics to be of prime importance
8. Views sin as having a corporate dimension	8. Views sin as exclusively individual
9. Tends to equate mission with humanization or social change	9. Tends to equate mission with a call to conversion or church planting
10. Views proclamation as rendering support to fellowship and service	10. Views proclamation as primary, which gives birth to fellowship and service
11. Emphasizes liberation	11. Emphasizes justification and redemption
12. Hears the cry of the poor and oppressed	12. Hears the cry of the lost
13. Considers humans from the perspective of creation	13. Considers humans from perspective of the fall
14. Judges humanity positively	14. Judges humanity negatively
15. Denies the existence of clear boundaries between the church and the world	15. Affirms the existence of clear boundaries between the church and the world
16. Regards the world as the main area of God's activity	16. Regards the church as the main area of God's activity
17. Underscores the church's credibility	17. Underscores the church's opportunities
18. Is concerned about witnessing where the church is	18. Is concerned about witnessing where the church is not
19. Divides the world into rich and poor, oppressor and oppressed	19. Divides the world into "people groups"
20. Reveals a proclivity toward socialism	20. Reveals a proclivity toward capitalism
21. Heightens Jesus' human nature	21. Heightens Jesus' divine nature
22. Focuses attention on the universality of Christ	22. Focuses on the uniqueness of Christ

Another point can be added to what Bosch has said: ecumenists tend to believe in biblical inspiration, evangelicals, in biblical inerrancy.

In the higher view, the Bible is elevated to a position of great importance (sometimes even leading to a false form of idolatry). This can allow it to become a rallying point for a modern form of pharisaism.

In Jeremiah 23:29 we find the following statement: "Is not my Word like fire . . . and like a hammer that breaks a rock in pieces?" Statements such as this would lead one to believe that the Word of God would be effective, especially for the task given to all Christians to make disciples of all nations. There are numerous testimonies the world over of persons simply reading the Bible and being converted to the Christ of the Bible. In Bangladesh, one method of outreach is to go into a village and just read chapters and books of the Bible and allow God to do his work in the hearts of men through his written Word. The question must then be asked, What effect does a lower view of biblical inspiration have on the outreach ministry of the church? Turning first to the American scene, we refer to an interesting book written by an executive of the World Council of Churches, Dean M. Kelley. His book is entitled *Why Conservative Churches Are Growing,* and in his opening paragraph he states: "In the latter years of the 1960s something remarkable happened in the United States: for the first time in the nation's history most of the major church groups stopped growing and began to shrink . . . at least ten of the largest Christian denominations in the country, whose membership totalled 77,666,233 in 1967, had fewer members the next year and fewer the year after. Most of these denominations had been growing uninterrupted since colonial times . . . and now they have begun to diminish, reversing a trend of two centuries."[9]

A statement made by George M. Winston, formerly the president of the Belgian Bible Institute, could possibly put a finger on the problem. "Preaching that demythologizes the Bible," he says, "also empties the churches."[10]

Kelley then proceeds to show that most of the denominations that are declining are active members of the World Council of

9. Dean M. Kelley, *Why Conservative Churches Are Growing* (New York: Harper and Row, 1972), 10.
10. George M. Winston, "Religious Situation Affects Outreach in Europe," *Evangelical Missions Quarterly* (Jan. 1974): 97.

Churches. Of course, it should be understood that one cannot say that membership with, or even a sympathetic attitude toward, the ecumenical movement will mean a declining church, but there is definitely a relationship between one's theological perspective and one's church. The attitude now prevailing in the leadership of the World Council of Churches both comes from the local churches and flows back into them.

What effect has the ecumenical stance had on missions? With unity being their rallying cry, one should assume that a united church would best be able to bear the banner of Christ in a divided world. It is easy to think that this would be the logical outcome of a super, all-encompassing church, but it seems that the opposite is true. In table 2 Kelley shows what really happened to the missionary force in more liberal churches from 1958 to 1971.[11] The figures for 1980 come from the MARC *Mission Handbook* (12th Ed.).[12]

TABLE 2 **The Overseas Missionary Force of More Liberal Denominations**

	1958	1971	1980
American Baptist Convention	407	290	200
United Presbyterian Church, U.S.A.	1,293	810	359
Presbyterian Church, U.S.A.	504	391	259
United Methodist Church (including EUB)	1,453	1,175	938
Episcopal Church	395	138	69
United Church of Christ	496	356	250
Totals	4,548	3,160	2,075

What are the reasons for the decline in the number of overseas career missionaries among some of the major denominations? Some will say they have changed their philosophy of missions and have progressed to a point of indigenization, while others will say they are adhering to the requested moratorium on sending missionaries to the Third World. Others may say, and possibly rightly so, that they would rather send money to be used in

11. Kelley, *Why Conservative Churches Are Growing*, 10.

12. Wilson, ed., *Mission Handbook*, 12th ed. Statistics taken from reports of each "Missions Report."

social and relief work. In seeking a reason for the decline, Harold Lindsell wrote: "Many factors have contributed to the serious loss of missionaries among the traditional ecumenical denominations. However, it is legitimate to reckon that these figures are a rough index of the depth of conviction about basic Christian doctrine—the nature of the Gospel, the lostness of mankind apart from Christ and the necessity of obeying biblical mandates calling for sacrifice and discipline for the sake of advancing the kingdom of Christ."[13]

This should be compared to another major denomination, which historically has had a more conservative theological position, the Southern Baptist Convention (see table 3[14]). The Foreign Mission Board of the Southern Baptist Convention has a constitution, which has as a basis of belief "The Baptist Faith and Message." In dealing with the Scriptures, it notes that the Bible has " . . . truth, without any mixture of error, for its matter."

TABLE 3 **The Overseas Missionary Force of the Southern Baptist Convention**

Year	No. of Missionaries
1964	1,901
1973	2,507
1976	2,667
1980	2,906

Comparisons of missionary work between those who accept biblical inerrancy and those who reject it is hard to find since there is a differing degree of acceptance by each agency and each missionary. It is possible, however, to see trends. In the twelfth edition of the *Mission Handbook,* comparisons were made between three mission agencies and those who were unaffiliated.[15] The three agencies were these: (1) The Division of Overseas Min-

13. Harold Lindsell, "The Major Denominations Are Jumping Ship," *Christianity Today,* 18 Sept. 1981, 16.

14. Samuel Wilson, ed., *Mission Handbook,* 10th, 11th, and 12th eds. (Monrovia, Calif.: MARC). Statistics taken from report of each "Missions Report."

15. Wilson, ed., *Mission Handbook,* 12th ed., 120.

istries of the National Council of the Churches of Christ in the U.S.A. (DOM), (2) The Evangelical Foreign Missions Association (EFMA), and (3) the Interdenominational Foreign Mission Association (IFMA). The first, DOM, is considered to support the World Council of Churches' concept of missions, and would be considered by most to be more liberal in theology, while the other two, EFMA and IFMA, represent a conservative stance. The fourth group, labeled unaffiliated and including such organizations as Campus Crusade for Christ, Operation Mobilization, and Youth with a Mission, is even more conservative and would consider itself to be in the inerrancy camp.

The relative growth of mission involvement among Southern Baptists (historically a conservative convention) is such that soon it will surpass the total number of missionaries sent out by the twenty-five groups and denominations who are a part of DOM.

At this point we must return to an overall view of missions and not be drawn into the easy solution of equating the World Council of Churches with lack of missionary vision, while we say that biblical inerrancy equals success on the mission field. What has been said is that there is a relationship between one's theological presuppositions and world-view that must include mission, which, in my opinion, is not just a task of the church, but rather the church itself.

The Strange Case of Germany

During the 1960s Dr. J. D. Hughey wrote *Europe: A Mission Field,* in which he attempted to convince the reader of the validity of Europe not only as a sending area but also a receiving area for missionaries. In the past several decades, many voices have been raised, calling upon the established churches, such as the Roman Catholic, Lutheran, Anglican, and Reformed to see the spiritual needs around them. Many writers are now saying that Europe is living in a post-Christian era. Dr. David Barrett estimated that as many as 1.8 million leave the Christian church every year.[16]

An indication of the rather sad state of affairs of the Protestant church of West Germany comes from a recent study that was

16. David Barrett, interview with author, Richmond, Virginia, Jan. 1986.

made by the *Evangelische Kirchen in Deutschland* (Lutheran Church in Germany). This study reports that "... the present decline in membership of Protestant churches in Germany (FRG) will continue into the next century and will likely reach alarming proportions if the prediction is correct ... West German Protestants would lose 12 million members by 2030, bringing their total down from 25 million to 13 million."[17] In the same report, the Lutheran World Federation, which claims nearly seventy million members in the world, predicted that such a drop "could mean a loss of almost one quarter of the world's Lutheran population."

Two suggested reasons for the decline are "a corresponding decrease in the country's population predicted for the same period and the continued defection from the churches by many members who wish to avoid payment of the piggy-bank church tax which the government of West Germany collects on behalf of the church."[18] The population loss from now to 2030 is minimal and the question must be asked, Why would people drop their church affiliation only to escape taxes? I contend that when leaves on a tree begin to die, you do not look for the cause in the leaves, but in the roots. The problem is not the taxes, but rather the theology that no longer meets man's needs.

Even the Baptists of Germany, who experienced steady growth from their beginning in 1834 until 1949, have been declining until the last few years. Baptists have been registering growth in all parts of the world with the exception of Western Europe. What were the forces at play that made the lands of Calvin, Luther, von Zinzendorf, Wesley, Spurgeon, and Onken now an object of missionary endeavor?

At this point we must return to where we left off in the historical section. Those advocating a modern, or liberal, approach to theology came to control both the educational institutions and the administration of the churches. With time it became apparent that a majority of pastors and church leaders in the Lutheran church of Germany no longer accepted the Bible as the ultimate authority for faith. Rather, they saw it only as an authority, a

17. European Baptist Press Service Release (Ruschlikon, Switzerland, 20 Nov. 1986), 1.
18. Ibid.

book to be studied, but not necessarily believed. After the devastation of World War II, the influence of such men as Karl Barth, Emil Brunner, Paul Tillich, and Rudolph Bultmann became immense. Even so, within the writings of each of these men (who held varying views on the credibility of the Bible) statements appear that cast doubt on the authority of the Bible. This same doubt plagued the minds of the laity as well. The results have been empty churches and a static or even dying faith. It is, of course, apparent that growth itself does not justify or prove the correctness of any one form of biblical interpretation. The rapid growth of some Eastern religions, as well as that of the Jehovah Witnesses and the Mormons (which are all growing in Europe) proves this point. But decline does give the impression that something is wrong.

Indeed, the Baptists of Germany did decline from over 120,000 in 1942 to less than 90,000 in 1983.[19] In attempting to analyze this drop in membership, I made an intensive study of the growth rates of the German-speaking Baptists in Europe. After speaking with many Baptist leaders, I arrived at the conclusion that it was difficult to isolate any one cause; rather, there were many. These included immigration, the movement of some to areas where there were no Baptist churches, lack of new missions, and the dropping of Sunday evening services. One German Baptist leader did mention the following two reasons as contributing factors.

First, the post-World War II approach to the Bible caused people to ask, not What does the Bible say? but What does it mean? This introduction of a new hermeneutical priority—the existential situation—proved elusive to the older leaders. They could not cope with its resultant emphasis on the secular.

Second, critical theology entered both the Baptist churches and Hamburg Seminary.[20] To many, the Bible appeared to have lost its uniqueness and authority.

I believe the infiltration of the critical school even into the center of evangelical conservatism in Europe, the Baptist church, though still slight, has been a contributing factor in the numeri-

19. William L. Wagner, *New Move Forward in Europe* (South Pasadena: William Carey, 1978), 141.
20. Ibid., 198.

cal decline of the church. Today the German Baptists have begun to grow again, partly because of the positive influence of the Home Mission Department of the German Baptist Union.

While churches in Europe were declining, it became unpopular to consider that theology had an effect on growth. This was one reason why the Church Growth Movement was slow to take root in German soil.

Dr. Peter Beyerhaus, professor of missions, Tübingen University, mentioned that in Germany today "there is hardly a faster way to ruin one's reputation as a theologian than to speak of the inspiration of the Bible, its inerrancy and the absence of self-contradictions. The authority of Scripture is openly questioned by the younger theological generation and its intellectual leaders."[21] He also quotes a statement produced at a conference of young German ministers: "We cannot naively gauge the way we speak and act from the Bible; rather, we must see orientation from the contemporary social and personal concerns. In contemporary discussion, the Bible meets us as one partner among others."[22]

The result of this partnership is not the creation of a higher form of intellectual achievement but a return to a pre-Christian world-view that rejects the kerygma of the Gospels as being too fanciful to be credible while at the same time accepting the occult. As the traditions of the church, which were rich in ritual and symbolism, began to crumble, they have given way to the rise of an old belief of pre-Christian Europe—spiritism. When a spiritual void occurs in a society, there are plenty of forces poised and ready to rush in. The *International Herald Tribune* reports that "34 percent of West Germans believe in witchcraft," while "in a similar survey in 1956, only 8 percent said that they believed in the existence of witches. . . . A 1973 poll found 23 percent believing in 'persons' with the power to will misfortune and sickness in others."[23]

Not only has the occult grown but secular humanism has also taken root and is rapidly becoming a major religion in Germany. This new message is concerned with civil rights, family life, soci-

---

21. Peter Beyerhaus, *Shaken Foundations* (Grand Rapids: Zondervan, 1972), 3.
22. Ibid., 4.
23. *International Herald Tribune* (Paris), 19 Sept. 1986, 6.

etal life, international peace, and liberation for the oppressed. Sincerity is a trademark of those who proclaim a message of justice, and it is difficult to debate the goals of those involved in such proclamation. The fault lies not in the message, but rather in the means of obtaining the results desired by all. Those who hold to what they often refer to as a holistic approach criticize the evangelical for using weak or erroneous hermeneutics in his search of Scripture, but are themselves unwilling to admit that their approach denies the supernatural aspects of an omnipresent God and his involvement in the affairs of man. The first message emphasizes man doing God's work in the building of the kingdom, while the second emphasizes man as a tool to be used by God so that he can establish his kingdom through us. The goal is the same. Only the starting place differs, and this includes the doctrine of Scripture. Many Germans, while seeking for truth, have chosen to use man's abilities to cure the ills of society.

When we attempt to serve man, we run the risk of creating an organization, but not a living organism. The German Lutheran church was built upon the basics of biblical Christianity, which were hammered out more than four hundred years ago: (1) justification by faith alone, (2) the priesthood of all believers, and (3) the primacy of the Scriptures.

In the past 100 years this church has changed drastically and has become more of a political force than a living faith. Hans M. Wilhelm, a member of this church, states: "Nominal Christianity, better called Christendom in Germany, has substituted organized religion for Jesus Christ as the living Lord. It has become 'a form of godliness, but denies its power'" (2 Tim. 3:5).[24]

It is very difficult for me to understand why theological students and professors alike from both North America and the Third World hold German theological scholarship on such a high pedestal. There is no question that German scholars possess high academic skills and have produced a "science of religion" that has no end of intrigue and speculation, but there seems to be no spiritual substance, no hope in Christ, and no solution to the real heart-felt needs of modern man. The Newman Center of the University of New Mexico invited the famous German Catholic

---

24. Hans M. Wilhelm, "The Problem of Nominality and Church Renewal in Germany" (unpublished paper, 1986).

theologian Hans Kung to give a lecture during early 1986. I attended the lecture and was impressed with the depth of his presentation and with his knowledge of theology. He was truly impressive, as most present would verify. Only at one point did he seem to be at a loss for words, and this was in his reply to a question asked by someone in the audience. The question was, "What effect on your personal life does your belief in Jesus Christ have?"[25] Many mentioned that only at this point did he fail to have a brilliant answer. Dr. Kung seemed to stumble and only uttered a few sentences before asking for another question. There was a missing factor, which was "Christ in you, the hope of glory."

Those considering a change in understanding of the Bible should be required to visit Germany and spend three weeks visiting the churches and talking with their pastors, and then spend three weeks in Korea doing the same. An objective person, especially one who is interested in seeing that the message of Jesus Christ is given to every person in every nation, would see that Germany is in no position to give ideological leadership to the world's missionary movements.

Strange as it may seem, the great Christian continent of Europe is now receiving large numbers of missionaries from previous mission fields. It is no longer unusual to meet messengers of the Lord working in Europe from such countries as Korea, the Philippines, Ghana, Brazil, and Lebanon. During a recent trip to Las Palmas, Canary Islands, it was explained to me that the largest Protestant church was founded by a Korean missionary. This church now has an active outreach ministry not only to its own people but also to the Spanish populace of the island. Speakers such as Paul Yonggi Cho from Korea and Nelson Fanini of Brazil are highly sought because they display a living, exciting faith that is often lacking in the sophisticated, intellectual churches of Europe.

Another example of the position of the present European community could be seen at the two Amsterdam Conferences for Itinerant Evangelists held in 1983 and 1986. On particular Sundays all of the participants were asked to go to the streets and beaches to witness about the saving power of Jesus Christ. It became ap-

25. Lecture given at the University of New Mexico, Nov. 1985.

parent to many that those from the Third World were actively engaged in proclamation, while those from Europe became only observers and evaluators. The dynamism of a living faith was not always present even in those who were considered leaders in evangelism. I was told that even in the selection process there were far too many evangelists wanting to come to the conference from India and some African nations, while it was hard to fill the quota from some of the European countries.

Europe has also become a growing mission field for North American personnel. Table 4 shows the increase both in numbers and percentages of North American missionaries now working in Europe.[26]

TABLE 4 **Distribution of American Missionaries**

	1972	**1975**	**1979**
Africa	7,671 (27%)	7,768 (26.2%)	7,695 (22.2%)
Asia, Mid-East	8,700 (30%)	7,952 (26.8%)	10,628 (30.6%)
Europe & USSR	1,871 (6%)	2,308 (7.8%)	3,525 (10.1%)
Latin America	9,592 (34%)	10,536 (35.5%)	11,535 (33.2%)
Oceania	860 (3%)	1,109 (3.7%)	1,377 (4%)

During the seven-year period of the table, it can be seen that Europe had the greatest growth (6 percent to 10.1 percent), while Africa had the greatest decline (27 percent to 22.2 percent). A further indication of the growth of American mission involvement in Europe can be seen by examining a list of countries with Protestant missions personnel from North America. In 1979 France ranked fourteenth, a 57 percent increase over 1972; West Germany was sixteenth with a 38 percent increase over the same period; and the United Kingdom was twenty-second (just ahead of Guatemala, Haiti, and Argentina) with a 21.8 percent increase in personnel over 1972.

To those of us who live and work in Europe, it is sad to see the large majestic cathedrals and churches empty or at best setting off a small section for worshipers. It is disheartening to hear that when Professor Graham Ashworth of England asked a colleague, "What do you think the function of the church in the fu-

26. Wilson, ed., *Mission Handbook,* 12th ed., 35.

ture will be?" the answer was given, "I think the church's only function in the future will be to take care of the buildings it inherited from the past."[27] Anger comes to the surface every time Muslims purchase a Christian church building and turn it into a mosque. The example is clear and plain for the world to see: The church of Jesus Christ will lose its power and desire to expand when it ceases to accept the Bible as God's infallible Word. Hans Wilhelm, in an article on nominality and church renewal in Germany, wrote concerning the Scriptures: "Essential to the message of renewal is the clear-cut commitment to the Scriptures as God's Word and revelation to man. Without it the message is powerless and cannot produce life or health."[28]

Peter Beyerhaus pleads "for a new understanding of the Bible which relies completely on the interpreting power of the Holy Spirit. . . . It is necessary to do away with an approach to the Bible which sees in it nothing else but a literary collection of contradictory bits of documents reflecting merely the existential self-understanding or the political utopias of past generations in remote cultural surroundings."[29]

If this were the extent of the example, then possibly we could live with it. Of course, we would weep as Jeremiah did for God's people who became disobedient. We would understand Jesus, who cried for his beloved city of Jerusalem. Few would find it difficult to pronounce the words of Paul, "A man reaps what he sows." But the problem goes deeper. The dying church of Europe is actively attempting to export the very theological thought that has left the church spiritually bankrupt. One may well ask, How is this being done? The answer is the same as it was in the early part of this century: through the theological institutions. Allow us to look at the system and see the danger that is before us.

A well-known German evangelical theologian recently visited in my home and explained the problem to me. At least four times, with hands raised for emphasis, he said, "Brother Wagner, our situation in Germany is catastrophic." He was referring to what he called the Babylonian captivity of the theological universities. Before one can be called as a full-time professor in a German Protestant seminary, it is necessary for him to complete

27. Lecture given by Professor Graham Ashworth at the European Baptist Federation Congress, 3 Aug. 1984.

28. Wilhelm, "Nominality and Church Renewal," 8.

29. Beyerhaus, *Shaken Foundations,* 12.

not one, but two steps in postgraduate studies. He must first complete his Ph.D. or Th.D. work and then do another program, which is even more difficult, called the habilitation. It is becoming increasingly difficult for evangelicals to pass the final exams for their doctoral degrees. There are many examples of qualified students who have finished all of their requirements only to be rejected because of a "lack of scientific content" in their dissertations. This actually means that they do not accept or use the critical method of study. In fairness it should be said that not all European universities have taken this stance, and many evangelicals still come to Europe for their graduate studies.

The second step, the habilitation, becomes much more difficult and even impossible for an honest evangelical to reach. In speaking with many in Europe, I am convinced that many Europeans purposely exclude evangelicals from further study, and thus keep them from teaching their belief about the Scriptures. Therefore, those who do the teaching and who have time to write are propagating a theology that is, for the most part, unacceptable to evangelicals. It should be added that the above does not pertain to seminaries sponsored by the free churches, such as the Baptists and Methodists. Since they do not have state recognition, they are free to hire any teacher they please. They have an obligation to set their own standards, which, in Germany, are usually as high as those in the state-supported universities. But what does this have to do with missions, which is the theme of this chapter? Much! Allow me to explain.

There can be no doubt that the Europeans have created an outstanding educational system, and a degree from one of the prestigious universities can open many doors for persons from the rest of the world. Christians, especially from the Third World, look to Europe for educational possibilities when they have completed the best schools in their own countries. Thus, many of the brightest young church leaders come to Europe for their final step before taking leadership positions in their churches and seminaries. This group will influence their churches in the years to come, and this fact is well known by European theologians. Scholarships are available to the brightest and most likely to succeed. The tragedy is that after two years in Europe, they begin to teach what they have been taught, and thus lead the future of the newer, younger churches to the same fate as those in Europe.

Different churches have taken steps to try to counter this influence. Some Pentecostals deride education in general and seminaries in particular. This way they hope to protect their young from thought patterns that might lead to destructive theologies. They prefer to use a discipleship method that allows their older pastors to give on-the-job training to the younger, inexperienced pastors. Success with this approach can be seen by the rapid growth of their number in many parts of the world, but one cannot but see that this is what the Germans call the *Vogelstrauss Politik*. This describes the ostrich who sticks his head in the ground and ignores his problems. The church must face up to its problems and raise up apologists who can give intelligent and convincing reasons for the faith it holds.

Another option adopted by some is the creation and development of theological institutions that remain true to the apostolic faith. Where there are no such institutions, it becomes difficult to create them, since it is not easy to raise the vast sums of money needed for such tasks. Time is also needed for such seminaries to earn the right to be heard. I feel that it is essential that much more time and effort be given to this option, particularly in a Western European context.

A third method is to ignore the problem and accept what is being taught, while recommending that young students attend the seminaries in question. Many fine, dedicated believers have taken this position without really knowing what is taught in the classroom. Just as it is wrong to condemn without the facts, it is equally wrong to approve without the facts. The problem of the church in Germany is that this approach was taken by the majority, and only now is it possible to see the result.

Finally, we can all take a positive step in the area of proclamation. It has been said that the best way to learn how to detect counterfeit currency is to know the genuine. The best solution is to become bold in stating that the Bible is the true and infallible Word of God and proclaim that only in Jesus Christ is salvation to be found. When this message is proclaimed, truth is revealed.

Mission to Muslims

Up to this point, we have been looking primarily at the situation in Western Europe, but now we need to look at another large segment of the world and see if the debate on the infallibility of the Bible has an effect on the church's attempt to work with them.

A sign outside a mosque in Cairo, Egypt, proclaims that Islam now counts one billion persons among its adherents. The correct number is probably more like nine hundred million, but there is no denying the fact that Muslims are making large gains in some areas of the world, such as Africa and India. Understandably, they have turned their eyes to Europe, and now many consider it their number one mission field. One Muslim leader with whom I spoke stated: "If we wish to win the world to our belief, we must first win Europe. To win Europe, we must first win England, and to win England, we must first win London." From all observations, their strategy is now working. They are building new mosques in all the major cities of Europe, including the seat of the Roman Catholic Church—Rome. Rome is where the foundation stone for the new thirty-five-million-dollar mosque was laid on 12 December 1984.[30] It has also been stated that there are now over one thousand mosques and praying centers in Britain to serve the more than 1,500,000 Muslims in that country.[31] In reading their missionary literature, it becomes apparent that they are well versed on modern missionary methods and have borrowed much from Christian missiology. I have been told by two sources (but have failed to find substantial written verification) that one of the World Muslim League's main strategists is a former German Lutheran pastor who has converted to Islam.

From what we in Europe can determine, more European Christians are converting to Islam than those from Islam to Christianity. In attempting to grasp the reasons, I believe it is necessary to understand the rigid and complete faith in the Koran as opposed to the Christian's modern-day acceptance of the Bible as only a book of myth. One Southern Baptist missionary told me about the time he was invited to visit the home of a Muslim Imman he had known for some time. The hospitality of the believer in Allah was first class, and at the end of the day, he was ready to honor the Christian by allowing him to hold his precious Koran. Muslims are often appalled when they see Christians lay-

30. *The Muslim World League Journal* 12 (Feb. 1985): 26.
31. *The Muslim World League Journal* 12 (March 1985): 62.

ing their Bibles on the floor or using them to hold over their heads in rainstorms. They view their book as holy and as coming from God, whereas we increasingly see our book only as a piece of great literature.

In speaking with young Muslims now living and working in Europe, I discover that they are well versed in what many modern Christian theologians are writing. They even have literature with a list of quotes from well-known scholars who deny the historical authenticity of the Bible. They say, "If your own teachers do not believe the Bible, then why should we?" and proceed to explain how the Koran was written in heaven in the language of heaven—Arabic—and dictated to Mohammed word by word. One reason given for the strength of the Islamic faith, even in Europe, is that it does give absolute answers to man's basic needs.

An assumption is often made that the rural populace of the world is given more to an acceptance of a closed conservative theological view, but that those living in a secular, urban society are far more scientific and enlightened in their approach to understanding God. At a recent meeting of Baptist missionaries and leaders in Bordeaux, France, it was observed that the Islamic faith is having more success in the cities than Christianity, even though their faith was born in a nomadic society. Many of the large cities of the world, such as Cairo, Istanbul, Damascus, and Tehran, have been able to retain a large percentage of practicing Muslims, while some Western European cities are doing well to get ten percent of the Christian populace into a church service on a normal Sunday. (Ralph Neighbors estimated that fewer than two percent of the population in that city attended a church during a given week.)[32] I believe that one of the main differences is that most Muslims know the basics of their belief. This is true even if they come from the Sunnite or Shiite branch of the faith. Orthodox Islam requires of its followers the simple confession of faith in one God—Allah—and in Mohammad as his prophet. Devout Muslims pray five times daily, facing Mecca. They fast one month a year during the month of Ramadan, which by tradition was the month the Koran was revealed to Mohammad. They give from two to two and one half percent of

32. Ralph Neighbors, "Study on Brussels, Belgium" (unpublished paper, 1982).

their income to the poor, and perform the hajj, or pilgrimage to Mecca, once in a lifetime. These basic requirements are called the Five Pillars of Islam.

The average Muslim will not question the fact that the Koran comes directly from God, while we in the Christian world have such a wide variety of beliefs that even trained theologians are not sure what is basic. The fact that so many in the Christian church have abandoned the concept of the infallibility of the Word of God has immediately put the church into a defensive posture in its encounter with the masses of Islam. It is no wonder that those with an ecumenical view of missions must emphasize social concern in the Middle East, because they have no foundation for a power encounter with "religion of the desert." They cannot stand and proclaim "Thus said the Lord . . ." but rather must seek to do what Jesus did. Even with all the power that this type of mission work can muster, which often is motivated by a deep love, it simply cannot stand before the onslaught of the Islamic revival. All over North Africa and the Middle East, Christian hospitals and institutions are being closed because the governments are providing these services. In many places, this has left whole areas, and even countries, without a visible witness. Many of those Christians who have survived are now in underground churches and have their Bibles as their greatest source of comfort and power.

In the last several years, I have spoken with leaders of various mission societies that have worked in the Middle East and North Africa. I have also spoken with large numbers of Muslims who have become believers in Jesus Christ and have had a conversion experience. From those discussions, the following six points have been formulated:

1. Despite the resurgence of militant Islam, Christianity is still alive and growing in the area.
2. Those mission societies and missionaries who have a strong belief in the infallibility of the Bible are having more success in their ministry than those who have a weak view of inspiration.
3. There is a growing response to the radio and television ministries and a rapid increase among those who are listening to the gospel.

4. Many of those who have become Christians have done so after having a dream or a vision of the risen Christ. Signs and wonders are no stranger to the church in this part of the world. The concept of myth is.
5. Persecution is on the rise and can be expected to become more severe in the future, especially toward those who have converted from Islam to Christianity.
6. The church in the Middle East and North Africa is alive and well, although small. The Bible is the most important possession for those in these churches and remains the basis of unity for the church.

The area of Europe and the Middle East is faced with militant Islam on one side and a dying Christian church on the other. It is no wonder that many are pessimistic about the church in the twenty-first century. This is why there must be a call for us to return to a strong faith that uses the Word of God as the basis for faith. At this point in history, the Muslim advance can only be stopped by a faith that is not only stronger but also true. This we have in Jesus Christ.

The Future Challenge

Writing history is always much simpler than trying to analyze the present, since factors continue to change and society is in a constant state of upheaval, but futurists are only writing today what historians will report tomorrow. Allow me to play the part of tomorrow's historian. I believe that evangelicals themselves are a little bit amazed at what God has wrought in only four decades. The rapid growth of evangelical missions coupled with the dramatic growth of influence and the rise of influential evangelical individuals and institutions demands that we look upon these as they present a Christian message in our world.

Today there is a revival of unequaled dimensions taking place. Reports from Korea, the Philippines, Brazil, Africa, and even Europe and the Middle East show a resurgence of faith. If we are to meet the needs of a searching world, we must consider the following five points:

First, we must learn to communicate the gospel to all nations in the most effective way possible. There is a need in the communicative process to find dynamic equivalents in each cultural group so that the meaning of the gospel can be grasped and understood. This process, however, must issue forth from a firm foundation in Scripture. If not, varying forms of secularism, humanism, and even Marxism will result. The missionary must develop an incarnational type of ministry that allows for changes in culture, thought patterns, and customs, but not in basic church doctrine. Each missionary faces the danger of a spiritual schizophrenia, which has the believer bouncing back and forth between the Christian message and that of the people to whom he ministers. The valid and honorable desire of the cross-cultural worker to relate to his new people could, and often does, lead to a universalist theology, which allows for an eternal security for all. This conclusion would be acceptable if Christianity were nothing more than a moral code or a set of profound teachings. The result would be that our faith would be brought down to a level equal to other beliefs and movements such as yoga, transcendental meditation, and Amnesty International. This is precisely what has happened in many churches today.

But faith is much more, and Christianity is not one religion among many but is "the one way between God and man." Rather than systematically retreating and giving up our doctrines in the face of pressure from other groups, we must return to the Bible, God's Word for all people for all time. When this is done and when our faith is built on the Word, then all missionaries, home and foreign, will have their house built upon the rock.

Second, we must not allow modern theologians to intimidate us. This seems to have been the fate of some missionaries who sought individual growth while on the mission field. Since their contacts are limited, they search for fellowship with whomever they can find or read books from any and every source. Often the more distinguished the author or the contact, the more influential the source might be. There begins to form a habit of "walking in the counsel of the ungodly." One pastor in a Scandinavian country led me step-by-step through his path of going from a conservative to a liberal and back again to a conservative. His first movement came because of contacts with seminary professors who held reformed Bultmannian views. He was so impressed by their knowledge that he began to change. He read the recommended books and attended the given lectures. During this journey, he ceased to read the Bible, but only read about the Bible. One day he awoke to find that there was neither truth nor power in what he believed. Only through deep, heart-felt searching and days of prayer could he return to his previous views. Later, he learned that the terms *scientific* and *intellectual* need not apply only to modernist theologies but that there are plenty of highly trained academicians who do accept the Bible in its entirety and are willing to proclaim that what it teaches is true. Many Christians have fallen into this trap, and it is time evangelical seminaries begin not only to be on the defensive, but also to go forward unashamedly.

Third, we find ways to make the gospel message relevant to modern man. Especially in the Western world with its multitude of philosophies and its communication glut, the church needs to lead the way in showing the relevancy of Jesus Christ himself to those living at the hectic pace of modern civilization. I am of the opinion that it is not the academic approach to belief that appeals to the masses, but rather the simple, workable truth of the incarnation that scratches where it itches. European missiologists are becoming more and more interested in those who are called the illiterate literates, or those who can read but prefer not to. Their intake of knowledge generally consists of watching television or reading tabloid-style newspapers. Today's conservatives now have the technical means to reach the masses, but the message must be strong and penetrating. This can only be accomplished when we act, not by might or power, but by the Spirit. Some will ask, Is this not the expressed task of all seminaries—making the gospel relevant to today's society?

It would be wrong to say that modern, liberal theologians do not attempt to make their message relevant. Indeed, this very desire could be their downfall, as I. Howard Marshall observes: "While Bultmann's desire to make the Gospel intelligible in the modern world is praiseworthy, it is regrettable that his actual performance is so unsatisfactory. He operates with a very loose and inadequate understanding of 'myth'; he assigns much that should be regarded as historical (e.g., the physical resurrection of Jesus) to the category of 'myth'; he fails to reckon with the fact that our modern world view with its rejection of the supernatural may need to be corrected by the Biblical revelation; and in the course of his 'translation' of the Biblical message into modern terms, a good deal of the original content appears to get lost."[33]

Fourth, we must not allow ourselves to be seen by the world as being negative and legalistic. The liberal theology of the past stressed love and the fatherhood of God to the exclusion of other emphases and, consequently, gave rise to the social gospel, an emphasis on doing good to all, thus bringing in the kingdom of God on earth through societal betterment. As a corrective to the sentimentality of this view, fundamentalism emphasized the severity and justice of God. This emphasis led to a form of pharisaism and a rigid legalism that in practice made minute distinctions concerning right and wrong. Belief in inerrancy became equated with a strange dualistic concept of God—a God of severe judgment and one of compassionate love. It should be clear that we cannot have a distorted image of God and his kingdom, but we must discover the truth of God and his revelation through real and deep study. I am convinced that this will lead to a positive faith built upon orthodox prayers, conventional worship, and conventional doctrine.

Fifth, we must be ready to accept and understand the fact of spiritual warfare. Only persons who can testify how the gospel met their deepest needs and how "the new spirit" from God provided them with the resources needed to overcome Satan and his forces can be "believable witnesses" on the gospel's behalf. In speaking to this matter, Jacob A. Loewen stated, "I have to confess that my experience with so-called animistic peoples in South America and Africa and with Western missionaries who are bringing the Gospel to them, has convinced me that the capacity to believe among animists is far greater than among missionaries who have been conditioned by secularism and materialism and who find it almost impossible to believe in a spiritual world."[34] It is time for those in the work of missions to reevaluate the place of signs and wonders as related to revealed truth and to see if secularism has not left a residue of doubt, even in those who do accept the Bible as God's inerrant Word.

Many will say that some of the statements as well as the recommendations in this chapter are simplistic and do not really

33. John R. W. Stott and Robert Coote, eds., *Down to Earth* (London: Hodder and Stoughton, n.d.), 24.

34. Ibid., 117.

look at the problems as they truly are. Indeed, the biblical message about missions is, after all, a multifaceted one and the world situation is doubly complex, even beyond description. But there seems to be a strange assurance coming from our Creator that tells us that he alone knows both the dangers and opportunities open to us. As we seek a starting point, it is imperative that we begin to build our theologies, philosophies, and practices on the revelation that God has given to man. In Jesus Christ we have a hope that transcends culture, geographical borders, race, and language. The Bible, which is the report of God revealing himself, must be believed if we are to carry out his commission to the church. Jesus made it clear that his followers were "to make disciples" of all nations and "to be his witnesses in Jerusalem, Judea, Samaria, and the uttermost parts of the earth." It has pleased God to reveal his Son to mankind in the human form of Jesus of Nazareth, but the Father's task is not finished until all people are aware of this revelation. Mission is not simply an outgrowth of the gospel message; it is the completion of the divine revelation.

8

Biblical Authority and the Social Crisis
Carl F. H. Henry

The universal problems of poverty, oppression, and crime assault the structures of society and demand a political response that is remedial, ethical, and biblical. It is not enough simply to be eager to do something. If these ills are to be addressed in a comprehensive manner, a framework must be affirmed that both explains the historical process in which human misery exists and provides humanity with appropriate moral imperatives for action. In short, we must know why things are the way they are and what we should do about them. Many secular thinkers have addressed these problems in notably divergent ways.

In ancient times the notion was prevalent that recurring cosmic cycles disallow historical progress, or that human history is declining irreversibly from a primitive golden age, or that human history carries no fixed meaning. Such conceptions offered little hope for a felicitous historical future for mankind in general, let alone for the poor and enslaved. The rise of systematic philosophy encouraged more careful reflection on man's social condition. Plato, for example, felt that humanity's central problem was ignorance, and he projected principles for a state based on knowledge and ruled by philosopher-kings. A more modern viewpoint is the positivism of Comte, which asserts that human misery is due to religion and superstition, and that scientific progress will inevitably lead to the alleviation of social problems. Marxian theory, operating on the basis of a dialectical understanding of history, understands class struggle to be the fundamental fact of human society and promotes proletarian revolution as the solution to social crisis.

For the Christian, however, no man-made answer can either adequately describe the human condition or prescribe the proper course of action to correct it. The Creator's answer, and his alone, can untangle the problems man has incurred. This answer is found in the Bible, but if it is to be significantly invoked, the Bible must be approached with appreciation for its plenary authority. Any interpretation that treats only part of it as normative and the rest as secondary, misguided, or outdated distorts its meaning and arrives at a solution that, while allegedly based on the Bible, merely reflects one's selective preferences.

The Bible approaches the social crisis with the promise of a messianic kingdom. The inspired Old Testament prophets affirmed this end-time kingdom of universal peace and justice not indeed as a human achievement but in terms of supernatural messianic salvation. Yahweh, they insisted, will manifest his power and glory in historical judgment, will inaugurate universal peace and justice, and forcibly vindicate the penitent and righteous. This vision continues to operate throughout the New Testament and has its climactic expression in the hope of an eternal reign of Christ over a new earth.

During the past 150 years, evolutionary conjecture has radically revised this messianic vision. The biblical premise that history will crest in Christ's triumphant righteousness and peace was recast by Hegelian "immanentization of the *eschaton*" into a logical evolution of the Absolute, by post-Darwinian enlistment of biological evolution in tandem with inevitable human progress to utopia, and by Marxian economic determinism, which looked to social revolution rather than to divine intervention to facilitate the coming kingdom.

These theories eclipse Messiah as the millennial catalyst.

They minimize or reject biblical redemption and regeneration and cloud the singular role of the church in the world. They also view utopia as the inevitable outcome of forces already operative in nature and history.

By contrast, the biblical view sets the human drama in the comprehensive context of creation, fall, and redemption. It connects the present condition of human life not with the essential and original character of humanity and the cosmos but with human sin and the willful forfeiture of paradise. Following the fall in Eden, the disruption of society invites divine doom, although after the deluge Yahweh postpones universal judgment until the eschatological end time. Yahweh mercifully enters covenant with a freely chosen people, forgives the sins of the penitent, and places Israel under moral and spiritual obligation as a witness to the world of the blessings of serving the one true God.

The distinctiveness of the human species lies in its creation in the divine image. Moral renewal has as its prime concern not the restoration of human dignity but the vindication of the character of God. Biblical emphasis falls not on horizontal human rights but on transcendent human responsibility: Personal and social duties are subsumed under human duty to God. The Decalogue is the classic summary of God's commandments and stipulates what it means to love God with one's entire being and one's neighbor as one's self. The Old Testament Hebrew theocracy enforced the divine legal code. New Testament believers live in pluralistic societies under diverse forms of government, but these governments too are nonetheless divinely obliged to promote justice and order. It is noteworthy that in summarizing the ideal behavior of godly citizens, the apostle Paul repeats the social commandments of the Law and that in the Book of Revelation, the commandments reappear in the context of final divine judgment.

The biblical view excludes a privatizing or spiritualizing of religion that ignores the plight of fellow humans. It does not view unjust social structures as self-existent and self-sustaining; instead, they are by-products of original sin. In contrast to Hinduism, moreover, biblical theism does not regard human suffering and destitution as a cosmic consequence of one's existence in a previous life. The Bible from the outset (Gen. 4) declares man his brother's keeper. The Hebrews are to respond to the exploited and

oppressed. Concern for the impoverished is a biblical hallmark.
The groan for liberation from death-dealing powers is not a modern phenomenon only. In Romans 8 Paul sets it in widest perspective as an eager longing for deliverance from the futility to which
sin has subjected the whole creation. The project of a new humanity and a society in which justice and peace prevail is by no
means illegitimate. Whoever considers the politico-economic
status quo sacred or normative, or uncritically resigns himself to
it, needs to reread the Bible.

The Bible sets the hope of human liberation from sin and its
consequences in the framework of divine redemption. It espouses
neither liberation for liberation's sake, nor liberation by human
reconstruction of society and reformation of mankind; it champions liberation for the glory and freedom of God by the messianic
Redeemer. Jesus opened his public messianic ministry (Luke
4:18–22) under the banner of Isaiah's reminder (61:1–2) that no
one need accept the crush of evil powers as finally determinative
for human existence. Christ challenges and ultimately will destroy the rebellious forces that exert tyrannical dominion over
humanity.

The plight of the destitute is one facet, but not the only facet,
of the human predicament; one might with good reason say that
even more urgent social concerns exist. The term *poor* is capable,
moreover, of a varying connotation, depending upon whether it
designates existence without the luxuries of life or without the
necessities of life. In the absence of absolute equality of wealth,
which exists nowhere, any and every standard will inevitably
distinguish "haves" from "have nots." In any case the term *poor*
is less precise than *impoverished, indigent, destitute,* or *needy,*
conceptions that carry some insistent demand for relief. In the
developed world many whose living standards are declared sub-
normal would in many Third World countries be considered well
off. Yet both the moral imperatives of the Bible and of our own
century assign special importance to response to the plight of the
poor, exploited, and oppressed.

To be sure, the emphasis that Yahweh has a "special eye" for
the poor must not be distorted to imply that the God of the Bible
declares that the rich are wicked per se or that the poor are exempt from the requirements of justice. The Bible places no pre-
mium either on voluntary poverty or on the acquisition of

wealth. But it does warn against materialistic preoccupation and the deceitfulness of riches, and it severely condemns all exploitation of the needy and underprivileged. Probably no message does so more pointedly than when James declares in his Epistle that those who live in wanton pleasure while dealing fraudulently with workers have "condemned and killed the just" (5:6). James here applies to the exploited worker the same term, *dikaios,* that Peter in Acts 3:14 employs when designating Jesus as "the Holy One and the Just." The crime of killing the just (defrauding the worker) is given added severity by the term *phoneō,* which, in the Gospels, Jesus used in reciting the divine commandment against murder (Mark 10:19) and also when he identified the Pharisees as sons of them who "killed the prophets" (Matt. 23:31).

The widespread plight of the impoverished has been routinely worsened by the additional sporadic horror of famine, flood, earthquake, and epidemic diseases. Christian voluntary agencies have long responded compassionately to such disasters. Many historians concede that the humanitarian movements of the West, although now often humanistic, had their original motivation in evangelical religion. World Vision alone, reaching out to the hurt and suffering of people in ninety nations, has channeled considerably more than $1 billion to famine and relief efforts. The Foreign Mission Board of the Southern Baptist Convention applies all monies received for famine relief to its designated purpose; none goes into administrative or overhead costs. These responses anticipated by decades such recent secular ventures as Live Aid, which feature rock stars and film talent. Not only has the secular response been tardy, but its ad hoc nature created massive distribution problems due to its lack of on-site facilities for implementation except through previously established agencies.

Compassionate response to the destitute is nonetheless to be encouraged universally. Concern for the needy is not solely a Christian duty but devolves upon every human being. Not all world religions share this concern, and Christianity assuredly has a distinctive motivation for compassion in its emphasis that all human beings bear the *imago Dei,* that Christ died for sinners, and that love of neighbor is a cardinal commandment. By contrast, Hindus have resented efforts to improve the lot of the

Harijans as an attack on Indian religion, heritage, and culture, since one's status in this life is considered fixed and inescapable until reincarnation. The fact is that the largest pockets of human poverty exist in India, Bangladesh, Pakistan, and Indonesia where Hinduism, Buddhism, and Islam prevail.

Since the Communist revolution, voluntary programs for addressing human need have been increasingly attacked by a Marxist social analysis that emphasizes justice rather than compassion, insists that redistribution of wealth is an ethical requirement, and charges those who defend a market economy with perpetuating unjust structures that socialism would destroy. It is noteworthy, however, that after the Chernobyl nuclear disaster, Soviet state-approved rock stars launched a program to assist radiation victims in a political context in which the welfare state presumably eliminates the need for such voluntary alternatives.

Given the continuing poverty of many of the 350 million Roman Catholics in Latin America, priests in the late 1960s called for an option that distanced the Catholic church from its traditional alliance with the wealthy aristocracy and instead favored the poor. Judeo-Christian emphasis on the dignity and worth of human life increasingly stirred conscience over the existence side by side of enormous wealth and luxury and of abject hunger and poverty. Activist priests, nuns, and laity increasingly fused Catholicism and Marxism in a theology of revolution, or more moderately, a theology of liberation, which is now promoted also in Africa and Asia. In Brazil two in three of the Catholic bishops today champion liberation theology.

Perhaps the greatest modern challenge to the evangelical concept of social justice, liberation theology deserves our special attention. It is important to understand from the outset that the basic gulf between the two schools of thought concerns the authoritative basis on which each system is founded. Instead of building on the Bible as inspired revelation, liberation theology begins with praxis and considers doctrine to be a second step. It considers action in the social arena to be the true beginning point for a theology and regards all other efforts at theologizing as ahistorical and therefore aligned with capitalist and reactionary forces. Marxism, moreover, provides the scientific grid for constructing this praxis-oriented theology. It is not surprising that liberation theology grew in Catholic soil, where the principle of *sola scriptura* has never been accepted. Also, insomuch as liberation theology has pronounced metaphysical theological concerns to be a tool of capitalistic oppression, traditional evangelism has no role, and theological universalism is assumed to be correct.[1] What matters is the creation of the new socialist society, even if that goal must be achieved by violence. Socialism has become the eschatological hope and a parable of the kingdom of God.[2] Liberation theologians fail to see that the term *liberation* neither exclusively nor adequately expresses the biblical concept of salvation, and they fail to grasp the full biblical picture of the new man in Christ.

The wide appeal of liberation theology, even among many who would identify themselves as evangelicals, only underscores the need for a comprehensive, scriptural vision of social justice. This vision may indeed criticize traditional Christian formulas and interpretations of the church's role in society. Nevertheless, a truly biblical approach will be more durable, give better results, and will include spiritual regeneration in its agenda. Such a theology will not be, like the false faith attacked by the apostle James, divorced from practice and useful only to demons.

Meanwhile, pockets of human discontent continue to serve as fertile ground for ideological exploitation. It is easy to substitute one type of exploitation for another, while amid distress, hope is fueled by illusory promises and expectations. Fascism, nazism, and communism have all dangled a utopia of sorts, only to multiply human suffering and disillusionment. Champions of revolution and liberation theology now often project their option as if no credible alternative exists. Yet, socialism has nowhere achieved the glittering goals it promised, not even where totalitarian leaders hold absolute state power to enforce it. As the tide of emigration of refugees attests, multitudes of Third World inhabitants would prefer to flee to the capitalist West. Socialism has scant hope of succeeding where government planning cannot be universally imposed, and state absolutism soon extends its powers beyond the arena of economic policy. The political bu-

---

1. Gustavo Gutierrez, *A Theology of Liberation* (New York: Orbis, 1973), 150.

2. William R. Coats, *God in Public: Political Theology Beyond Niebuhr* (Grand Rapids: Eerdmans, 1974), 178.

reaucracies lack omnicompetence to manipulate financial policy successfully. More than that, a citizenry deprived of economic incentives lacks the altruism that welfare statism assumes. Both Soviet-sphere and Chinese-sphere communism now make widening concessions to private profit in order to encourage maximal production.

Seldom acknowledged is the spectacular economic achievement of the market system. Capitalist economics provides incentives that lift a vast multitude from the lowest economic level of society to a self-sufficient middle class. In contrast with ailing neighbor states in the Third World, Singapore, Hong Kong, Taiwan, and South Korea exhibit remarkably virile capitalist economies. The hard fact is that socialism has a plan for the redistribution of wealth but lacks capacity to produce the wealth it would redistribute; capitalism can produce wealth, provides multitudes of jobs, and offers participation to any who would share the risks and rewards of free enterprise. The Marxist countries deplore Western culture as morally retrogressive and imperialistic, undermine its existing freedoms, steal its technocracy, and seduce the poor abroad with promises of capitalist-like abundance.

What, then, is a preferable approach to the staggering problem of human impoverishment, and what are its presuppositions?

Insofar as they fall outside the bounds of critical need, the first response is to emphasize to the impoverished the importance of self-responsibility and self-reliance, rather than of dependence on society and on government for survival. Even emergency survival aid is but interim opportunity to shape a more self-reliant future; it is not a prelude to perpetual care.

The next reponse is in terms of the nuclear and extended family. The critical importance of the family as the primary social unit must not be undermined by an emphasis on societal care that neglects familial responsibility. Third World parents who multiply offspring to guarantee old-age assistance are hardly to be commended for worsening the population problem, or to be rewarded with unlimited social support benefits.

Next, the state's special duty to its citizens, paralleling the duty of citizens to the state, is to be reinforced. A state concerned for justice will have a written constitution that assures respect for legal equality across consecutive regimes and will acknowledge transcendent justice to which all such constitutions are answerable. Without constitutional guarantees of human rights, political revolution serves no higher end than self-interested violence. The Marxist revolution in Ethiopia, for example, has become a context in which Communist authorities practice political starvation and divert humanitarian relief from needy citizens to Communist military units. A pluralistic society that recognizes the legitimacy of dissent and protest is incompatible with the Communist emphasis on ideological hatred of whatever retards the Red Revolution. The biblical mandate to respect human dignity is equally binding upon right-wing and left-wing governments. Political persecution, torture, and wrongful imprisonment and execution receive the judgment of God, whether they be practiced in the name of communism or of anticommunism.

Yet, it is not a service to other nations to force upon them democratic processes for which they are unready or which are considered unwelcome. What is imperative is the right of political self-determination, one that includes the possiblity of self-correction. The American Revolution did not remove power from the people and transfer it to an absolute state or sovereign; it preserved the political power of the people, including the right of conscience to appeal to the will of God and against the will of the ruler. The French Revolution of 1789 rebelled against all authority and thus had no safeguard against lawless violence. The Russian Revolution of 1917, like the French Revolution, sought the demolition of established structures and could offer no alternative but totalitarian rule on the absence of transcendent absolutes.

What then of the critical need for universal social transformation? Nothing in either the Old Testament or in the New Testament applauds the existing human social situation: Man and society are desperately flawed, lost in sin, and doomed. Everywhere the pages of Scripture echo the call to repentance and warning of dire judgment. There is here no indifference to the social predicament of mankind; indeed, a devastating judgment of the nations is divinely pledged. The human condition has widened since biblical times through population expansion. The material contrasts distressing to the impoverished have become more evident because the mass media portray luxurious lifestyles alongside abject hunger.

The biblical view is concerned for the whole self and for the whole of society; it protests not only against exploitation but against neglect of the poor. Its view of wholeness (in salvation) deals with the entire human condition, with human beings as psychosomatic beings, and it seeks their reconciliation and restoration to God and to each other. No thesis of theology has been so much emphasized in this generation as the fact that biblical redemption has a view to the whole man and to society as a whole, and that God is concerned about human impoverishment at every level. Against the privatization of religion, biblical theism not only embraces salvation of the soul and individual moral renewal but also calls for service of God in the world and confrontation of social injustice in the name of the holy Creator and Lord.

Yet, nowhere does Scripture consider private property unethical, although it regards property as a divine stewardship. Nowhere does it consider wealth immoral, although it views it as a providential opportunity to minister to others and warns rich and poor alike that security is found in God alone. Nowhere does it champion equalization of wealth as a mark of virtue, although in certain circumstances some believers practiced it among themselves. In short, Scripture attests the morality of private property and of material reward.

Although Jesus practiced charity to the poor (John 13:29) and the Christian movement has singularly exemplified it, the Bible is concerned for the poor not only in the context of voluntary charity but of law and justice as well. The distinction is important, since *agapē* confers what is not legally due another, while justice deals with a legal due. The Mosaic code stipulated certain rights for the poor, including access to gleanings and to spontaneous sabbatical-year growth. No interest was to be charged by Hebrews on loans to the poor, nor was a profit to be added when food was sold to them. The Old Testament law built into Hebrew politico-economic structures a safety net that enabled the poor to escape perpetual indebtedness.

But while such regulations guaranteed personal liberty and a livelihood, courts were not to be partial to the poor (Exod. 23:3). Poverty may be self-inflicted (Prov. 6:6), and sometimes even the poor may oppress the poor (Prov. 28:3).

While concern for the poor was a conspicuous element of God's covenant with Israel, that concern also reflected creational morality. Even Sodom was condemned because it neglected the poor and needy (Ezek. 16:49). The godly person recognizes and promotes the rights of the poor, and the righteous king defends those rights (Prov. 29:7; 31:9) and judges the cause of the poor with justice (Ps. 72:2).

The New Testament even more vigorously than the Old affirms God's concern for the poor and introduces Jesus as inaugurating the eschatological year of Jubilee. It focuses on poverty in both a spiritual and a material sense, and it predicates comprehensive deliverance on the forgiveness of sins. Jesus begins the reversal of poverty and human participation in the kingdom, which is promised to his disciples, although complete reversal of the plight of the poor awaits the future. When Jesus said, "The truth shall make you free" (John 8:32), he spoke of the scriptural Word, of evangelical orthodoxy. To point to Marxism as biblical rescue of the poor is to defraud them. Only from spiritual redemption will arise the values, attitudes, programs, and conduct that adequately alters individual and social conscience and behavior.

The human history of tyranny, brutality, and slavery stand in evident contrast with the call to redemptive transformation. The new society that the Bible envisages is not fallen mankind living under restructured economic conditions. Unjust structures are, indeed, in need of change, but to expect utopian improvement is futile without a moral alteration of the character of humans who pervert the principles of justice. The Scriptures do not expect utopia by the structural reorganization of an unregenerate humanity, however much society may be forcibly conformed to speculative idealism and theoretical altruism. Implementation of preferred structures by a totalitarian hierarchy cannot replace individual enthusiasm, all the less so since rulers not only lack the omnicompetence to dictate creatively the ideal content of social justice but also seek special privileges for themselves.

It is not Marx the theoretician but Jesus the Redeemer who is the bearer of authentic redemption. It is not Marx's example but Christ's that is definitive for the evangelical view. In his sinless life and his resurrection-victory over death, Jesus thwarted and put to rout powers of evil and injustice that would have destroyed him. On the basis of his salvific power, he summons humans to a new community. Marxism repudiates the priority of God in human affairs and the need for a revelatory identification of justice, including the legitimacy of property rights and of reward; it denies the evil in fallen human nature that requires spiritual regeneration; it supplants the moral categories of sin and death by economic analysis of class conflict and material redistribution.

The new society as biblically charted is the body of regenerate believers over which the crucified and risen Christ rules as Head. As he challenged sin and injustice, so too his followers, as a new society, are to exemplify that confrontation and to extend his victory over the forces of iniquity, confident that Christ himself at the eschatological summit will finally and forcibly destroy the evil powers. The church is on the one hand a distinctive *ekklēsia* (called out of the world), yet on the other hand a *diaspora* (scattered worldwide as salt and light).

The confrontation of injustice, in New Testament context, is to be waged on two frontiers, church and state. The church's proclamation of God's Word, evangelization of the masses, and example of moral concern is indispensable. But no less important is the universal role of civil government, which in the New Testament era is no longer theocractic but assumes diverse forms, and which deals with outward conformity to law but not with motivation and metaphysical legitimation. The state is to promote justice (not to creatively define it). Civil government, no less than the church, is divinely willed, and each instrumentality has its distinctive mission. Civil government is to require conformity to law, under threat of penalties; the church proclaims forgiveness of sins and new life in Christ as an indispensable yet voluntary option. The state is not to decide between theological alternatives, or to evangelize, or to impose penalties for spiritual lethargy. The church is not to seek to legislate sectarian beliefs and practices. Yet, both church and state have a necessary commitment to justice, the former on the ground of a biblical revelation and mandate, the latter on the ground also of creational, constitutional, and civil law. The Christian carries within himself this dual commitment to church and civil government, knowing the latter no less than the former to be theistically grounded. But Christian or not, all human beings are to live by the law of the land, assured that God wills civil government to preserve justice and restrain anarchy, and that the legal code itself is therefore answerable to the transcendent will and law of God.

The evangelical stance is that the sinful perversion of divinely created structures must be vigorously confronted and challenged. The protest of Old Testament prophets against social wickedness at personal risk to themselves, the insistent demand of Jesus for moral and spiritual integrity in all relationships of life, placed on the defensive the world structures and entrenched attitudes and practices of the time. The Hebrew prophets warned unjust rulers against the imminent judgment of God and declared also that barbarous enemy nations would overrun and besiege them if rulers and people did not change course. Yet, at no time—not even in the so-called holy wars of Israel—did the people of God consider their task to be that of overthrowing pagan empires in order to inaugurate a just society. The vision of universal justice and peace was a messianic program that distinguished a present interim voluntarism from a future coercive climax.

Yet the evangelical tendency to contract the Christian message to personal evangelism, to identify sin primarily in terms of personal immorality, and to assume that multipled conversions would moralize the social order led to a failure to confront the world order with a demand for justice and to elaborate a full-orbed doctrine of society exhibiting God's purpose in the public arena and the crucial role of the Christians in it. That role includes a vocational service in the world. It requires public witness to the standards by which Christ, the coming King, will judge the nations and to which he expects them even now to conform (in short, the divine commands that detail what love of God and neighbor implies) as well as public exhibition as a member of the new society of what Christ's lordship involves in the life of the redeemed. It demands identification with the oppressed and exploited and the impoverished together with bold protest against practices, policies, and structures that discriminate against and disadvantage the needy. It elaborates the nature and predicament of man and society to overcome false notions of fate and destiny. It exhorts confident trust in the providence of God who will himself implement final judgment upon the powers of wickedness and promotes compassionate voluntary programs to assist the indigent toward self-support and encourage them in turn to instruct others. It sensitizes neighbor responsibility worldwide, while it encourages assistance programs in which all nations participate on a proportionate basis whenever voluntarism fails to cope with survival needs.

But the aspirations of the poor are cruelly accelerated where ideologies arise to promise immanent utopia, as in the case of atheistic Marxism and of Shiite Islam, and of so-called Christian revolution of liberation theology. These ideologies have in common the promise of an immanent, just society that elevates the poor and dispossessed, and a fundamental commitment to violence if necessary to achieve it.

The oldest of these ideologies is Shiite Islam (championed by ten percent of the Koranic world), which has engaged in thirteen centuries of holy war with the goal of promoting a global Islamic revolution through which a universal government of Allah will achieve governance by Muslim theologians and clergy in command of the armed forces. The present leader of this ideological revolution, Khomeini, has in the current war against Iraq sacrificed two hundred thousand Iranian lives. These were mostly the young, the poor, and the desperate who could be readily radicalized and enticed to terrorism and violence by dangling before them the promise of heavenly reward for religious martyrdom. Khomeini opposes the system of government that prevails in all non-Shiite states—that of Iraq because it exalts nationalism over religion, that of Israel because it assertedly exists on Islamic territory and is considered an agent of America, that of America because of corrupt Western values that the Shah tolerated in Iran. Shiites readily resort to terrorism to promote their "society of the just." Violence is prized all the more because two martyrs devoted to an Allah-legitimated revolution and armed with a few bombs can, in a barrier-crashing vehicle, confront a modern superpower's presence in Lebanon and gain worldwide exposure on the mass media. Terrorism is declared the means of liberation, the first phase of holy war that presently equates the United States and Israel with Satan and anticipates a pro-Islamic revolution that levels all opposition.

Communist revolution is deliberately atheistic, aiming to deprive human beings of the consolation of religion amid injustice and to remove the prospect of supernatural reward for patient endurance of affliction and to remove future judgment for violence. It turns violence into a revolution-promoting virtue and suspends all conceptions of right and of justice of state absolutism. What the Shiites legitimate by appealing to Allah, Communists legitimate by appealing to the Party and to Marxist social analysis. Such Marxist analysis does not, in fact, fit the history of Near Eastern Islamic states, and many Western critics insist that Marxists impose a prejudicial conception of class conflict upon other states also.

The theology of revolution has its origins in Latin American near-feudal countries, where a vast gulf has for centuries divided rich and poor, and where even many Catholic social critics now accept the Marxist indictment of capitalism and profess to offer biblical legitimation for a socialist alternative. The main difference between revolution theology and liberation theology is that the former affirms that God actively promotes historical justice through revolutionary violence, whereas liberation theology approves violence only as an activity of final desperation. In Roman Catholic and Protestant ecumenical circles today, many frontier theologians are so addicted to liberation theology that those who challenge it are viewed as indifferent to human rights and to socio-economic justice, and are held to be distinterested in a realistic resolution of the problem of poverty and hunger. No theologian is considered worthy of that professional designation unless he is engaged in revolutionary struggle for liberation of the poor, and theology is considered ipso facto false or irrelevant if it is not devoted to socialist reform of economic structures.

The debatable assumptions here are numerous. Among them are the following:

1. The divinely mandated task of Christianity is to enforce a particular politico-economic policy upon the nations.
2. Socialism is a biblically legitimated economic view.
3. Marxism offers an objective analysis of society.
4. The world predicament can be rectified preeschatologically in terms of universal justice.
5. God's covenant should be translated into a program of contemporary political and economic idealism.
6. Univeral redistribution of wealth will overcome the economic crisis.
7. The role of the church as an exemplary new society gifted with a new mind and will is less significant than the alteration of social structures.
8. Jesus Christ enlisted the apostles in a direct challenge to earthly political powers and promoted a revolutionary alternative to the Roman Empire.

If a cadre of contemporary activist theologians or radical post-Anabaptist mercenaries insists upon falling back upon violence as necessary to bring about instant justice, that is ideologically their prerogative in a free prerevolutionary society. If they act on this delusion, they should be prepared to pay the consequences in a postrevolutionary society that entrenches law and order bureaucratically or precludes further corrective revolution. But if they encourage the already disenchanted masses to think that clerical violence, or mass violence clerically encouraged, will assuredly better their lot, or may not in fact worsen it, they will add disillusionment to disenchantment and unwittingly turn hope into grief.

The evangelical alternative is predicated on the following counter-assumptions that its adherents insist accord with the Judeo-Christian Scriptures:

1. Only Christ at his second coming will by decisive power inaugurate the permanent and universal rule of justice and peace.
2. Justice is nonetheless biblically revealed as obligatory on all human beings and nations.
3. God desires its inscription on the hearts and in the practices of society as a whole and wills civil government as an instrument of justice and order.
4. The depth of sin is so radical and its range so extensive that apart from redemptive regeneration personal and corporate selfishness frustrate the possibility of social utopia.
5. The regenerate church as a new society is to exemplify in mind and will the standards by which Christ will judge humanity and the nations.
6. Jesus Christ has, in his resurrection, already personally demonstrated his power over all the forces of evil and injustice that would have destroyed him.
7. As Head of the regenerate body of believers, Christ wishes the church to engage vigorously in the protest against world injustice, to identify biblical alternatives, and to proclaim the forgiveness of sins and exemplify the new moral life and energy bestowed by the Holy Spirit in personal and public relations.

8. As Christ became poor for us, godly people are voluntarily to exemplify the compassion that devolves upon everyone in respect to the weak and indigent neighbor, beginning with one's own household and the household of faith and reaching also to the family of mankind.

9. Christians should promote, support, and engage in just government that avoids discrimination against and penalization of the poor.

10. The churches should project work programs aimed at self-support and encourage the voluntary extension of such effort by those who succeed.

11. Instead of escalating the legitimate demand for survival needs into an illegitimate expectation of sharing others' earnings and an aspiration for material affluence, or the satisfaction of wants rather than of needs, the church should stress that only God truly enriches life and is its security, and exemplify apostolic contentment with life's sufficiencies.

12. A market society offers greater opportunity for economic reward for diligent workers who share its risks.

13. As the wealthy have greater opportunity and responsibility by the stewardship of providentially bestowed possessions to share in the extension of the gospel and in the alleviation of material need, so the economically less favored have opportunity and responsibility for trust in God's providential care and the patient expectation of the true messianic utopia.

A proposal to restructure society on Christian principles is advanced by North American evangelicals who assume that the new society must currently exhibit a uniform religio-political nature. Led by R. J. Rushdoony, the Christian Reconstruction movement calls for the complete refashioning of society in accord with scriptural Law.[3] The proposal, projected as a Calvinist social model, has theocratic overtones. The approach not only presupposes a postmillennial eschatology—that is, that Christians can usher in a world utopia before the return of Jesus Christ—

---

3. R. J. Rushdoony, *Institutes of Biblical Law* (Phillipsburg, N.J.: Presbyterian and Reformed, 1973).

but it implies also that Christians should and can establish a universal theocratic political order. This development can hardly escape open conflict in the political arena over rival metaphysical ultimates proclaimed by Jews, Christians, Muslims, Hindus, Confucians, atheistic Communists, and others—a conflict, moreover, in which professing Christians will be divided into champions of theonomous-orthodoxy, liberation-Marxism, and those who insist that in the present pluralistic context, the state does not have the prerogative of imposing religious imperatives on society.

The question remains whether before the eschatological end time, one single political program is to be imposed upon humanity in the name of Christian social conscience. Christians are indeed obliged to conform their beliefs and actions to biblical revelation. They are to proclaim and to live those convictions boldly and to involve themselves in the public arena. It glosses the depth dimension of sin and its consequences to dangle the prospect of utopia before a deliberately unregenerate society and to prize social concern above that of the holistic concerns of Moses and Isaiah. The alleviation of poverty is a noble concern, highly desirable, even if in fallen human history it is not a universal prospect. Yet, it is extravagant optimism not to wonder whether a redistribution of wealth, instead of ennobling life permanently for some, may not unwittingly impoverish it for all. Only when the whole biblical mandate is obeyed will the concerns for justification before God, social justice, and material need all be met. Any attempt to address these concerns by looking to another authority for guidance will produce a distorted, false, and ineffective gospel.